The New India

PROGRESS THROUGH DEMOCRACY

THE MACMILLAN COMPANY
NEW YORK • CHICAGO
DALLAS • ATLANTA • SAN FRANCISCO
LONDON • MANILA
BRETT-MACMILLAN LTD.
TORONTO

"I do not want my house to be walled in on all sides and my windows to be stuffed. I want the cultures of all lands to be blown about my house as freely as possible."

M. K. GANDHI

The
New India

PROGRESS THROUGH DEMOCRACY

Planning Commission, Government of India

THE MACMILLAN COMPANY
New York • Toronto • London • Manila
1958

We are concerned with the shaping of the future of India. It is therefore with a sense of the burden of history upon me, upon us, upon this House, that I face this problem. It is also with a great sense of humility because, however great, however competent we may consider ourselves, we are small in relation to this mighty theme, that is, the building up of India, taking this country and its millions of people forward.

—PRIME MINISTER NEHRU,
in laying India's Second Five
Year Plan before Parliament,
May 23, 1956.

This book has been prepared by the following Study Group set up by The Planning Commission: Douglas Ensminger, Representative in India, The Ford Foundation; Tarlok Singh, Joint Secretary, Planning Commission; J. J. Anjaria, Chief, Economic Division, Planning Commission, and Chief Economic Advisor, Ministry of Finance; E. P. Moon, Advisor, Planning Commission; D. K. Malhotra, Deputy Secretary (Plan Coordination), Planning Commission; Jean Joyce, Executive Associate, The Ford Foundation, India.

Introduction

India's aspirations are set out in its Constitution, which aims at securing for all its citizens

Justice, social, economic and political;
Liberty of thought, expression, belief, faith and worship;
Equality of status and of opportunity; and [promoting] among them all Fraternity assuring the dignity of the individual and the unity of the nation.

The methods adopted by India and the institutions it seeks to establish for achieving economic and social development are part of its ideal of a free and democratic society which aims at rapid and continuous economic progress with the largest possible measure of social justice.

India's First Five Year Plan, which ended in March 1956, prepared the way for a greater national effort. The Plan evoked widespread enthusiasm, opened to large sections of the people the opportunity of service in the common cause of eliminating poverty and raising standards of living, and strengthened the national economy.

The Second Five Year Plan, which commenced in April 1956, is a natural sequel to the First Plan. It carries forward the community development and other programs initiated in the First Plan and also seeks to lay the foundations for large-scale industrial development.

Since the Parliament of India gave its approval to the Second Five Year Plan, the need has been felt for a publication which would set out for readers abroad the underlying approach and main features of India's economic and social programs. This volume is an attempt to meet this need. It has been prepared at the request of the Planning Commission by a special study group. The Planning Commission welcomes *The New India: Progress Through Democracy* as an objective presentation of the principles and aims of the Second Five Year Plan and the programs of development embodied in it.

The study group consisted of Dr. Douglas Ensminger and Miss Jean Joyce of The Ford Foundation, and of four members of the staff of the Planning Commission, Messrs. Tarlok Singh, J. J. Anjaria, E. P. Moon, and D. K. Malhotra. The task of preparing the first draft of the manuscript was entrusted to Miss Jean Joyce. The manuscript had the benefit of being reviewed by Professor Edward Mason, Dean of the Graduate School of Public Administration, Harvard University, and by Dr. Eugene Staley, Senior International Economist of the Stanford Research Institute. On behalf of the Planning Commission, I wish to express our appreciation of the service rendered by Miss Joyce, who devoted a great deal of labor to the preparation of the book.

The Planning Commission has sponsored the publication of this study in the hope that it may bring India and its aims and problems closer to the people of other countries. We in India have profited from their experience. Their efforts and ours are part of a common goal—the building up of a world community founded upon peace, freedom, and democracy, in which mass poverty, disease, and ignorance are eliminated and the people of every land develop according to their own genius.

V. T. KRISHNAMACHARI
Deputy Chairman
Planning Commission, India

New Delhi, December 15, 1957

Contents

The Development Programs

SECTION I. AGRICULTURE AND RURAL DEVELOPMENT

ix

The New India:
Progress Through Democracy

India's Second Five Year Plan is designed to lift the Indian economy and the Indian people forward, and speed the rebirth of India as a modern nation.

The Plan's immediate aims are economic and social—to raise living standards, to increase national income, production and employment, to provide a richer and fuller life, to break further through the barrier of poverty which has held the Indian people and the Indian economy stagnant in a swiftly developing world. In doing so, it seeks to translate into practical action the aspirations and ideals of the millions of the country, and give to each an opportunity for service in the nation's growth.

But the Plan's significance, perhaps, lies as much in its method as in its aims.

Each nation, as it shapes its future, draws upon its own national traditions and beliefs. In its struggle for independence, India placed means above ends to win freedom without violence. So today India endeavors to follow Gandhian methods of peaceful change, and to win economic and social freedom, like political freedom, without hate, violence or injustice.

India hopes to avoid the class conflicts, the social waste, the oppressive concentration of public or private power and wealth, which have often accompanied rapid industrialization and economic advance. It has keyed its economic planning to the principle of social justice, so that all groups may benefit and grow in opportunity as the economy progresses. India proposes to carry forward not one or another group or class, but all its 384 million people.

India seeks, moreover, to bring about its rapid transformation from a backward to a developed nation by democratic means.

In its plans to bring schools, medical care and new knowledge to India's villages, to create new steel mills, to build roads, ports and ships, to harness the rivers, to irrigate millions of acres and bring light and power to thousands of villages and small industries, India will take each step forward with the consent, the consultation, the participation of the people.

India recognizes that in doing so it has embarked on an experiment in democratic planning which is perhaps larger and more complex than any in the modern world. Some have called it a fateful experiment. But India sees its task not merely as one of increasing national production and national wealth, but of bringing the values of freedom into harmony with the values of economic progress. It believes that the quality and success of its democratic planning, of its economic growth, depend on the degree to which the individual citizen is able to grow through participation, through the spreading of opportunity and through the strengthening of democratic processes and institutions.

India is aware that it must find its own solution to the problem of democratic planning for intensive economic growth. It will welcome and draw upon the ideas, the experience, the counsel and help of other nations; yet its final pattern and methods must inevitably be its own. It will be neither dogmatic nor doctrinaire. It has determined, within its two guideposts of social justice and peaceful democratic means, to remain flexible and pragmatic in its economic methods. India must strike its own national balance between liberty and progress, central control and private initiative, national planning and local authority. Progress so planned and won is surer and more lasting. It will more surely conserve the strength of the Indian people, uncompromised by methods foreign to their traditions.

To accomplish its great task, India feels that it must have not only internal peace, with a minimum of social tensions and class conflicts, but external peace. Its hope is not to develop a self-sufficient economic machine, but a nation which, in a comity of nations, can play a role of interdependence, mutual trade, friendship and assistance.

Seen in perspective, the beginning of a Five Year Plan and the ending of a Plan are vital dates in a nation's history. If not today, they will become so, because they represent each major step forward, each measure of a nation's growth. Planning and progress are, however, a continuing process, a continuing march. The five years of the Second Plan are only a period fixed for convenience in planning. India must think in terms of even longer periods—a third, a fourth and other future Five Year Plans. This is but the Second. At its end, even if all its goals and hopes are won, India will not have come to the end of its journey. There is no end of a journey, where a nation is marching.

Yet for India the next few years are the crucial years. India's social stability, its future as a democracy, its freedom as a nation depend upon the speed with which, in the next five and ten years, it pushes the pace of its social and economic growth.

"If in the course of these five years," India's Prime Minister has said, "we achieve what we have laid down in our second Five Year Plan, it will be a great victory—one of the greatest that India has won. And not only will it be a victory but a prelude to other victories. . . . We will have crossed that dangerous barrier which separates an underdeveloped country from a developing country, and once we have done that, it will be easier and faster going."

But as India marches ahead, it hopes it may contribute more than pulling itself and its own people forward. To the degree that India progresses, under democracy, India hopes it may contribute to peace —the peace of Asia, and perhaps of the world.

What is on trial in India's Second Plan and all its future plans is, in the last analysis, whether democracy can solve the problems of mass poverty. It is a trial perhaps never before made in such an atmosphere of urgency.

In some nations there are those who say that the democratic process cannot solve these problems, or cannot solve them fast enough. India believes that it can do both; its Second Plan is testament to that belief.

In meeting this great challenge to democracy, India will owe much to the good faith of other nations, who share its belief in the democratic principles of human dignity and individual freedom. But it must, in the main and in the end, draw for its strength, for constant refreshment of its faith and spirit, on its own heritage, on the skills, the vitality, the wisdom of its own people.

Above all, India will draw on the precepts of the great master who led the nation to Independence, and pointed the way to social and economic freedom.

From Mahatma Gandhi's principles of non-violence, of social justice, of adhering to right means to achieve right ends, of setting the individual as the one supreme consideration, India takes confidence and courage that a new way—a way of peace—may be found to lift its own, and perhaps other of the world's hundreds of millions of poor and oppressed, out of the darkness of poverty into the light of opportunity and freedom.

CHAPTER I

The Underdeveloped Nation:
Problems and Assets

1. THE PROBLEMS: INDIA AT THE DAWN OF
INDEPENDENCE, 1947

India's First Five Year Plan, which ended in May 1956, made the
first breach in the barrier of poverty which had so long held back
India's economy and people. But it was what the Prime Minister
called but a "preparatory venture," a first attack on India's problems as an underdeveloped nation.

Many of these problems are familiar, as those common in nearly
all underdeveloped countries. But some of them were unique to
India, one of the oldest and most densely populated countries of
the world. It may be helpful to look again at where India stood on
the day it won its Independence, August 15, 1947.

On that day the Indian people, united and uplifted by their non-
violent struggle under Mahatma Gandhi, faced their future of freedom with high hopes and exaltation.

5

Then as they, and their leaders, began to study how the new Government could bring the nation forward into the modern world, and give political freedom meaning in terms of higher living standards and more opportunities for the Indian people, the problems ahead seemed staggering, and to some almost impossible of solution.

The most overwhelming of India's problems was mass poverty.

Other nations at various periods in their history have had the problem of poverty, but in India poverty affected not thousands or even tens of thousands of people. It affected, and engulfed, tens of millions.

Perhaps the size of the problem can best be seen by giving some brief comparisons.

India at that time had a population of about two and a half times as large as that of the United States, about 347 million people. Out of all these, only a fraction, perhaps 5 per cent or so, had a living standard which could be regarded as satisfactory even in Indian conditions.

At the top extreme were the few rich: some of the big landlords, a handful of successful families of trade or industry, the princes who had long ruled over large or small territories. The gulf between these few rich and the millions of poor was as great perhaps as in any nation in modern times.

In the 5 per cent, yet fairly well below the few of great wealth, was a growing middle class—men in Government service, professional workers, lawyers, doctors, engineers and other professional men, small shopkeepers and businessmen, teachers and others. Yet even for these, and even in the cities, an income of $60 a month was the privilege of relatively few. A schoolteacher earned $20 to $30 a month, a young engineer perhaps $80 to $100.

Below this favored 5 per cent, these privileged few, extended the vast sea of poverty. It included more than 300 million people.

India's poverty of that time was outside the experience and, for many, beyond the imagination of the West. Even among Asian nations, the poorest in the world, India stood nearly at the bottom, in any comparative scale of prosperity.

It is perhaps impossible to describe what such poverty meant in terms of human beings and human lives. Certainly the most that could be said for the living standards of millions in India was that they were a testimony to the human capacity for survival.

Many, faced with food scarcity and never-distant threat of famine, endured what Gandhi called "an eternal compulsory fast." Mud huts in thousands of mired and wretched villages matched the slums of India's cities, which rivaled or even exceeded the worst known in the West in the most depressed periods of Western history.

Preventable diseases like malaria, smallpox, cholera and others cause half of all deaths. Infant and maternal death rates were among the worst in Asia. One statistic may be enough. In 1946 life expectancy for a new-born Indian child was thirty-two years.

To ease or relieve the poverty, or provide opportunities to rise above it, there were few public and social services. In 1947 less than one child in three of primary school age was in school and only one adult in seven could read and write. In the village areas there was one doctor to 25,000 people, one hospital to 50,000.

Only one city in four had a safe drinking-water supply or sewage-disposal system. Not half of even the larger towns had electricity. Only a scattering of India's 560,000 villages were serviced by all-weather roads or by any form of public transportation.

Indeed, although millions in the cities fared as badly, most impoverished of all were the village people, who formed then, as they do today, the vast majority of India's population. India is a predominantly rural nation, and contains perhaps more than a fifth of the world's rural people. In their tens of thousands of impoverished and backward villages, Gandhi found them "slowly sinking into lifelessness," with "chronic starvation and slow death" resulting in "a process of dehumanization."

At the bottom of the rural social and economic ladder were those without land or status—the landless laborers, who made up perhaps a third of all India's rural people, some 48 millions; or more, for example, than the entire population of France. For them, an average family's earnings were as low as $100 a year. Many of these were Harijans, those once called the untouchables, who, in the villages as in the cities, were always the most impoverished.

Even farther than the village people from any opportunity for advancement were India's tribal peoples, numbering some 18 million, who in their primitive, if colorful, societies felt the worst of India's poverty.

For poverty, even among the poor, was unequally shared. With its great inequalities of income, India also had inequality of class, status and opportunity. The few "educated" lived, as the poet Tagore commented, in the upper part of a house divided, and the vast illiterate millions lived below, with no stair between. India's social structure was perhaps the most deeply stratified of any country in the world. Gandhi's vigorous leadership had set up great currents of change, but for many, old and outworn attitudes still prevailed toward rank, caste, social status, education. For the low caste, the untouchables, the have-nots, few doors of opportunity were open.

Another of India's overwhelming problems, and in part the cause of poverty, was unemployment, of a kind and extent perhaps rarely experienced elsewhere, except possibly in the depths of the world depression in the early 1930's. India's joint family system, under which shelter and food are shared with a wide group of relatives and dependents, conceals and lessens the hardship of unemployment, particularly in the villages, yet the problem in terms of social and economic waste and potential discontent was one of the most serious in India.

Underemployment—sometimes as little as a few days' work a week —was also high in both city and village. Gandhi called the enforced idleness, for nearly six months of the year, of the overwhelming majority of the population India's "problem of problems"—"a tremendous tragedy" for which an original solution must be found. Among the landless farm laborers, perhaps one-fourth—or even a third —were surplus to the needs of agriculture. Even young men and women college graduates could find no jobs for which their training had fitted them—and the problem of the "educated unemployed," which all underdeveloped countries have to some degree, was particularly acute in India.

What were the reasons for India's poverty, its heavy unemployment—problems which, as Gandhi said, few nations in history had ever faced on such a scale?

The key lay in the fact that India had, for the past twenty to thirty years, made so little progress that, in the face of a rising population, it was economically almost at a standstill. While other nations over that period were going ahead producing more—in Japan, national production more than doubled, for instance—there were almost no gains whatever in the amount of food and other goods and services produced in India. In some ways India's economy had actually gone backward. Income per person had gone down; production from farms and industries had barely risen at all.

Economic stagnation is a characteristic of underdeveloped "pre-industrial" countries. It is not fully understood just why economies stagnate in this way; the causes are many and complex. But for India some of them are clear.

Some causes were social in origin: the low level of education, the technical ignorance and backwardness of the majority of the people, lack of business enterprise, the restrictions of caste. Some were economic—such as the lack of capital to invest in new industries and enterprises. This shortage is a common difficulty of underdeveloped countries.

In some cases both factors were intertwined. This was certainly the case with India's backward agriculture which, in a vicious cycle, brought poverty and still more backwardness to India's millions of rural people. Even though three-fourths of the entire population worked on the land, Indian yields per acre were the lowest in the world and the lowest in Asia—about one-third of those of Japan or China. What's more, over the previous twenty to thirty years, even the amount produced per person had been going down.

Lack of knowledge of improved seeds and farm methods, lack of farm credit, of farm extension services, dependence on fickle rainfall—in India there are only one or two monsoon or rainy seasons a year—were some of the reasons. Without help, the average farmer living on the bare edge of survival had not the means to risk new and, to him, untried improvements.

An antiquated feudal land system destroyed for many farmers even the incentive to produce more. Under this system small farm owners as well as the many sharecroppers and tenants had to pay oppressive rents, in many cases 50 per cent or more of their crops, to various types of landlords. Many, if not most, of these landlords did not cultivate the land themselves, or take any of the risks of farming, or invest in improvements.

Food shortages were made worse by the partition in 1947 of undivided India into Pakistan and India, and by the separation of Burma. The lands embraced by Pakistan contained one-half the irrigated fields and the richest food-producing areas of undivided India. Burma, a big rice producer, had traditionally supplied undivided India. Altogether, lands yielding an average of over 2 million tons of food a year were withdrawn from India upon Independence. Food rationing and price controls, begun in India as elsewhere during the war, had to be continued, as well as heavy imports of food to be paid for with India's scarce foreign exchange.

In a nation with millions of village poor, there were few markets for the goods produced by city workers and industries. Indian industry, indeed, was virtually stagnant. It produced, to be sure, the tenth largest industrial output of countries of the world, and second largest in Asia (after Japan), and in the previous thirty years it had grown considerably. But it was on the whole undeveloped, and was certainly not growing rapidly enough to provide either sufficient employment or a rising standard of living for a growing population.

For example, the Indian iron and steel industry, one of India's most active and enterprising, was producing only half of the country's very limited needs, in spite of plentiful raw materials. Most of the major industries were operating far below capacity. As an interesting comparison, during this period Japanese industry was already contributing a third of total national production.

One very serious result was that industry was not creating enough new jobs to relieve unemployment. In the fifty years from the beginning of the century, a period when in every other developed country more and more people were finding jobs off the farms,[1] there was in India very little increase in the number of jobs in industry or in other non-agricultural occupations. By 1947 manufacturing industries employed barely 2.4 million workers.

In part this stagnation of industry was due to the shortage of capital common in underdeveloped countries. In part too it was due to the fact that, as is also characteristic of "pre-industrial" countries, little of the money that was available was invested in basic industry. With a few notable exceptions, the wealth of the fractionally small class of the rich was usually put into land, into conspicuous spending and leisure, into speculative and high-profit-making enterprises, into manufacture of consumer goods, rather than into basic industries.

Small industries as well as large were stagnant. The village craftsmen had been dealt a hard blow by factory-made goods, foreign and Indian. While some continued to make a meager living at their hand looms and potter's wheels, some craftsmen had to become agricultural laborers, and others had gone to the cities in hope of finding factory jobs.

The poor crops, the inertia of industry meant a poor nation as well as a poor people. India's total national income for all of 1947 was considerably less than that earned in one month in the United States at that time, and about equal to that of Canada, a country with about one twenty-fifth as many people.

Some of India's economic problems had been accentuated by the war. India had not, it is true, like its next-door neighbor Burma, had its ports destroyed or its villages ravished. Yet the war had been accompanied by destructive inflation and shortages.

Railway and other services deteriorated because of overstrain, and because of lack of money and time for maintenance. Shortages of cloth and housing, as well as of food, had pushed the workers' cost

---

[1] In the United States farm population shifted from 37 per cent of the total working population in 1900 to 12 per cent in 1955.

of living up to three to four times the pre-war level. Home building had come virtually to a standstill. In the cities congestion and over-crowding brought more and more acute social and economic problems.

The twenty to thirty years of economic stagnation, topped by the dislocations of war, were for India especially severe because its population was growing so swiftly. India's *rate* of increase in population is lower than that of Japan, or the United States or Canada, and far lower than that of South American countries. But even at this lower rate, India's already vast population was increasing by 5 million new souls a year. Moreover, the rate of increase had been going up for the previous quarter-century, as improved health services, however inadequate, were lowering the number of deaths from epidemics and disease.

Merely to keep up with its yearly increase, to maintain even its poor levels of living, India had constantly to go forward. To stand still was to go back. In thirty years—by 1977—it was estimated the population would be half a billion.

As population rose, demand and pressure for land had become more and more intense. As we have seen, in the preceding fifty years no new jobs were being created off the farms. Agriculture had to absorb the entire half-century's gain in population. The proportion of people working at agriculture was continually rising, and population density in some areas was among the highest in the world.[1]

Pressure on the land was also showing itself in more and more un-employment in the villages, in the breakup of family farms into smaller and smaller fragments, in waves of migration to the already overcrowded cities.

Poverty, unemployment, a stagnant agriculture and industry, great inequalities of income and opportunity, a mounting population—these then were some of the problems facing the new Indian Government and the newly independent Indian people in August 1947.

Added to them was the immediate expectation of the people that

[1] West Bengal has 806 persons per square mile; Travancore Cochin (now Kerala) has 1,015 persons per square mile.

Independence itself would solve India's problems, that the poverty and backwardness so long linked with colonialism would almost automatically disappear along with colonial rule.

Added further were the sudden shock and tragedy of Partition, when undivided India was cut asunder to form the two nations India and Pakistan. It was like the dismemberment of a living body: industries were cut off from their raw materials; the pattern of agriculture was disrupted; railways and civil services were severed; nearly 8 million refugees, leaving homes and lands behind, streamed into new India.

2. THE ASSETS

Yet against its staggering problems, the new Government could balance assets that made possible India's rebirth.

Among these were important physical assets—for although India in 1947 was poor, it had considerable *potential* wealth, resources which, if rightly used and developed, could create for the first time more income and opportunity for the Indian people.

India, for instance, ranked among the more favored nations of the world in total natural resources. There were extensive known reserves, among the highest grade in the world, of iron, manganese, bauxite; there were considerable coal, titanium, mica, and atomic materials such as thorium ores. Early surveys had shown the possibility of oil in the eastern states, principally Assam. India's legendary rivers offered a potential for hydroelectric power perhaps among the highest in the world.

Industry, though small, had at least made its beginning, and was served by an extensive railway system, the largest in Asia—a legacy of British rule. The already industrialized area, for example, of the Bengal-Bihar-Orissa triangle, was considered to have in railway facilities, power and natural resources one of the richest concentrations of resources for development in all Asia.

Another promising asset was the increase that could be expected in farm production. Given improved seeds, fertilizers and better methods of cultivation, and the education of farmers in how to use them, enormous increases over the extremely low yields were possible.

India also had a vast reservoir of manpower—of people to do the work of rebuilding the nation. Made use of with imagination and boldness, this vast work force could indeed be not a problem but a resource, and become one of India's most valuable means of producing new capital and wealth.

India could also draw upon one of the most valuable assets available today to a developing country—the technical and scientific knowledge of the advanced nations. Some economists believe that such technical knowledge could be for India, as for many underdeveloped countries, a resource which was the economic equivalent to the untapped continent available to the United States 150 years ago.

There were other assets, social and political in nature.

Surely one of these is the character and concepts of the Indian people themselves. In applying itself to a great new national endeavor, India could draw upon cultural and spiritual resources which had throughout its checkered history welded India into cultural, if not physical, unity, and which had again and again over the centuries been able to enrich human thought, philosophy and religion.

On his visit to the United States in late 1956, the Prime Minister described this background against which India seeks rebirth as a modern democratic nation:

India is supposed to be given to contemplation . . . and something of that contemplative spirit still remains. . . . But, at the same time the new India of today has also developed a certain dynamism and a passionate desire to raise the standards of her people. But, with that desire is blended the wish to adhere to the moral and spiritual aspects of life.

India is a country steeped in history and tradition, with a civilization nearly as old as recorded time, and a culture nourished on its own soil and blended happily with those of other peoples and of other lands. This year, we celebrated in India and in many other countries, the 2500th anniversary of a very great son of India, the Buddha, who gave us a message of peace and compassion. . . . During these millennia of history, India has experienced both good and ill. . . . But she has remembered the message of peace and tolerance. . . . In our own time, this message was proclaimed by our great leader and master, Mahatma Gandhi, who led us to freedom by peaceful and yet effective action on a mass scale.

Such traditions have permeated the life and thought of the humblest villager, and bred in him a deep patience, wisdom and tolerance, and encouraged India to count upon its people as one of its great assets for dynamic growth by peaceful democratic means.

Surely too the Gandhian heritage was in itself another of the great assets for India's resurgence as a democratic nation. To Gandhi's leadership and to his principles, independent India owed its unity of new purpose, its common agreement that the new government must, and by peaceful democratic means, dedicate itself to the advancement of the Indian people.

The fact that a new Government was born of non-violence, with peaceful transfer of authority and friendship on both sides, is one of the richest legacies which the Father of the Nation left to new India. The British withdrew from India in a manner honorable to both sides and worthy of their own rich tradition of freedom, leaving a fund of goodwill and eagerness on the part of India to forgive and forget and to remember only the best of the past. Despite wounds caused by Partition, most Indians felt that they had forged new bonds of unity between rich and poor, between north and south, east and west, and that they now had the means and the opportunity to grow into a great modern nation.

With such a background the new Government was able to transfer to the problems of development not only the strong administrative structure of the former Government but the full resources and energies of the Indian people. Highly trained and organized, India's civil service, the "old steel frame" of British India, as well as other administrative services in the States, were absorbed at once to the service of free India. So too was the judiciary and police system which had established both a mechanism and respect for law and order over the entire country. The new Government commanded the loyalty of an army which, both by training and tradition, was committed to subserve a unified nation. Under Gandhi, the non-violent freedom movement itself had produced many leaders who had won national trust and respect. That they took positions in the new Government gave the confidence and sense of national unity so important in countries newly independent.

Backed by the strong nationalist sentiment, the new Indian Government was able to bring together 552 separate princely States,[1] effectively and with little disturbance, into a single nation with a sense of unity unique in all India's history. It was also able to withstand the bloody crisis accompanying Partition, and to set about, with speed and public confidence, the gigantic tasks of economic and social reconstruction.

Such were the assets that made development possible, as India's overwhelming problems made it imperative.

As India's leaders looked beyond the immediate needs of unifying the States, and settling the refugees from Pakistan, they began to plan how the development of the nation and its people might be achieved on the basis of India's own traditions as well as on the technological advances of the Western world.

Their first decision was that India must shape a Constitution that would assure political and religious freedom through a secular democratic government. This Constitution, which drew upon the great liberal traditions of Western political thought as well as India's own heritage, was adopted in January 1950. It asserts, in its opening paragraphs, that its aims are to secure for all citizens:

JUSTICE, social, economic and political;
LIBERTY of thought, expression, belief, faith and worship;
EQUALITY of status and of opportunity; and to promote among them all
FRATERNITY assuring the dignity of the individual and the unity of the
  Nation.

The Government's second decision was to hold a popular election, so that before its people and the world the new Government might be based on the will and consent of the governed.

---

[1] The princes and maharajas retained their titles, but gave up control of the States. They were given, for their lifetimes, a generous privy purse from the public funds.

The first election, believed to be the largest free election ever held, took place in the winter of 1951–1952. One hundred and six million voters participated, or over 60 per cent of all those eligible, including men and women from the most remote villages.

India's third decision was that it must plan for national development in a direct attack upon poverty. This decision, too, took strength from India's new Constitution, which placed upon the State the obligation to "strive to promote the welfare of the people," and work toward securing social and economic as well as political justice.

Development was indeed a matter of greatest urgency. India could not risk the haphazard development, the costly mistakes of a nation with a hundred years to grow, or of a nation of great wealth. The high expectations and great needs of the Indian people meant that India's stability, its future as a democracy, even its freedom as a nation depended on swift advance out of stagnation to growth and opportunity.

3. THE FIRST FIVE YEAR PLAN: DEVELOPMENT BEGINS

The First Five Year Plan, begun in 1951, was the Government's first concentrated effort to develop the nation and its people. Organizing all the country's energies and resources, the Plan had three overriding aims. The first was to start building up, by democratic means, a new pattern of society which would create, through higher living standards, through increased employment, production and a larger measure of social justice, a richer and fuller life for the people.

Side by side with this, it was hoped to develop agriculture and both large and small industry so that all parts of the economy and of the people might have the maximum benefit. It was also hoped to get a firm start on important long-range programs of development—on big irrigation and power projects, on conserving natural resources, and on building up the necessary organization of administration and training, and even the enabling legislation, to form the basis for later and more rapid growth.

The most immediate need was to relieve the serious food shortage and the rising inflation. Little progress could be made in the country as a whole, in industry or elsewhere, unless food became more plentiful, and unless the great mass of backward and impoverished rural people were awakened to new farming methods, to a new outlook, to a new vitality.

The Plan's agricultural effort emphasized new irrigation, land reclamation, a national extension service and rural development program. Considerably helped by favorable rains, it was on the whole eminently successful. Foodgrain production alone went up nearly a fourth, or by 11 million tons, and agricultural production as a whole by 19 per cent.

Through irrigation and land reclamation, the Plan increased the area under crops by 26 million new acres. Important land reforms were initiated. Almost 80 million people—nearly one-fourth of rural India—were put under a dynamic rural development and extension program. This rural program indeed, which brought for the first time the means and knowledge for self-help to a vast, illiterate rural population, must be counted as one of the First Plan's greatest achievements. It became, perhaps more than anything else, the symbol of the resurgent spirit of India.

While the Plan's gains in social services were modest in view of the great needs, 6 million more children went to primary schools; high school and college education began to be adapted to the needs for a democratic developing nation; a start was made on organizing health services.

What had been planned for large industry was chiefly to stimulate factories to use their capacity to the full. With the new public confidence in the nation's future, investment in industry increased; and industrial production rose steadily, until by the end of the Plan period in 1955–1956 it was 38 per cent over 1951 and almost two-thirds higher than in 1947. New factories, public and private, built the pattern of a new and more diversified industry. A good start was made in organizing a system of stimulating and assisting small industries; in modernizing the run-down railways; in improving and extending roads, in enlarging ports and shipping.

Income went up along with production. Although the most the Plan had hoped for was an increase of 11 per cent in national income, the actual increase was 18 per cent. Even with a growing population, this meant an increase of almost 11 per cent in income per person.

With rising production and careful financial planning, inflationary pressures went down and prices became more stable, in spite of a somewhat strong upward trend just at the end of the Plan period.

To finance the Plan, the Government and private enterprise each expended just under Rs. 2,000 crores [1] ($4 billion each, or together a total of $8 billion) on development programs.

To meet its share of these expenditures, the Indian Government relied almost entirely upon its own resources. The Indian people contributed voluntarily in small savings Rs. 237 crores ($474 million). In rural development areas, villagers stimulated to new enthusiasm and means of self-help, gave freely of labor, land, savings and materials to build schools, roads, health centers and other village improvements. In some areas their contribution has exceeded that of the Government, and for the nation as a whole equaled Rs. 24 crores ($48 million).

Foreign assistance from the United States (including the Wheat Loan), from the Colombo Plan and other sources made up the "vital balance" of 10 to 12 per cent of the Government's costs of developing the nation and its people.

The Need for Faster Development

The First Plan's gains were encouraging and substantial, significant among those of other underdeveloped Asian nations over the same period. But, aside from reaching and sometimes exceeding many of its targets and considerably strengthening the Indian economy, the Plan—and with it the Government's entire effort, in and out of the Plan—did something more. It mobilized the energies and spirit of the people and brought a new sense of hope and confidence in

[1] The rupee, equivalent to about 21 U.S. cents, is the basic unit of Indian currency. A crore of rupees (Rs. 1 crore) equals roughly $2 million.

India's ability to solve some of its own problems. For the first time, too, new and ever larger groups of the Indian people were able to participate in a national effort for their own advancement.

Yet the pace of development was still too slow, and many urgent problems were yet unsolved. No real gains were made on unemployment, which appeared to be increasing. Investment in industry, in development programs of all kinds that would create new wealth, jobs and opportunities, was still small or uneven, although considerably higher than before the Plan. Income and living standards, although higher, still left India a nation of impoverished people.

CHAPTER II

The Difficult and Tremendous Journey

To India, then, the First Five Year Plan was only a preparation, a first start toward growth. The real beginning in the colossal task of rebuilding the nation—"that difficult and tremendous journey"—is the Second Five Year Plan.

In preparing it, India was forced to take a long look ahead, to set up goals for ten and twenty years from now, and analyze carefully what would determine how far and how fast it could advance toward them.

There are of course many human and social factors that will determine how India grows, and how quickly. There are political factors as well. All these are supremely important in any developing nation.

But it will be useful to discuss first the more specifically economic factors which determine a nation's growth. It will thus be possible to see in economic perspective India's chances for development as a

21

modern nation able to bring increasing living standards and opportunities to its millions of people.

Looking ahead, India's planners concluded that, in economic terms, there were four basic factors which are the key to India's growth over the next five years, the next ten, the next twenty. The Second Plan and every future Plan would have to make attack on all of them.

The first factor is how quickly India can produce more—more of everything: of goods, services, machines, and above all food. Without increased production India can only distribute poverty, and as its population grows, incomes and living standards will go down. By producing more crops, more goods, however, India can produce higher incomes, more employment, higher living standards, and at the same time have capital to invest in schools, health, factories, irrigation and power, and the like.

In the five years of the Second Plan, India proposes to push the 1956 production level up by one-fourth more; to double it in fifteen years (that is, by the end of the Fourth Plan, 1970–1971); and raise it by 2½ times in twenty years. To reach this goal, however, India must adopt new and better methods of production.

To use the Prime Minister's phrase, India is industrially at the "cow-dung stage." [1] The jump to the age of atomic energy is a long one. Millions are employed in cottage and small industries which largely depend on outmoded techniques. Millions of village farmers are illiterate and backward. To most of them, modern methods, machinery and other tools are unfamiliar or even unknown.

A democracy, however, cannot force adoption of new technologically advanced methods at human and social cost. Each farmer must be taught, not forced, to use improved farm methods, fertilizers, and so on. The introduction of new machinery must be so paced that it will not throw men out of work without hope of new jobs when unemployment is already dangerously high. Each craftsman must be trained to understand and use new methods and tools. Clearly for India the pacing of technological advance is as crucial as the advance

[1] In India cow dung is burned for fuel.

BHAKRA-NANGAL: This river-valley development project, India's largest, by 1961 will irrigate 3,600,000 acres of farm land and supply over a half-million kw. of electricity for Punjab and Rajasthan. The Nangal hydel-canal headworks, shown here, opened in 1954 and is now watering 1,200,000 acres.

POWER ON THE FARM: The Bhakra-Nangal system supplies power for this Punjabi farmer to pump well water for field irrigation. His old Persian wheel (right), once turned by bullocks, may also be power-driven.

FUEL FOR INDUSTRY:
The Burmah Shell Refinery at Bombay. Exploration and development of India's promising oil resources have a high priority in India's Second Plan. Experienced foreign oil companies are taking a valuable part in India's oil development through technical assistance and financing.

TELEPHONE ASSEMBLY:
India's rising demand for phone service is being met by increased production of instruments at the Indian Telephone Industries Factory at Bangalore. In the ten years ending in 1960–1961, India will have nearly tripled the number of instruments in service across India.

itself. It must involve some compromises not faced by countries which do not have great pressure of population, nor by countries with high employment or with a century or more to grow, nor by countries which are not committed to democratic methods, social justice and peaceful non-violent change.

Yet, the speed with which India can bring about adoption of new and more productive methods is the most important single factor in development, not only in the next five years but over the next quarter-century.

The second key to India's future development is the rate of growth of population. Any effort to raise income and living standards per capita, to relieve unemployment and pressure on the land, and to provide education, health and other essential services is constantly faced with the problem that by the end of the Second Five Year Plan period alone (1961) there will be a minimum of 25 million more people to provide for; and by 1976 probably 100 million more or 500 million in all.

These are admittedly conservative estimates. India must run fast merely to stand still. An essential condition for actual progress in incomes and levels of living per person is an effective curb in population growth.

The third economic key to India's development is the rate of investment, or the proportion of the nation's total income, public and private, plowed back into building the railways, steel mills, ports, power plants, and so on, on which modern industrial society is based, and which are essential to increasing the nation's future productive capacity.

Any going economy takes a part of its national wealth for these purposes both voluntarily, as individuals personally invest in new business or factories, and through taxes to the Government for public services and facilities.

In advanced or rapidly developing countries, the savings for investment are at least 10 to 15 per cent of national income, and usually considerably more,[1] and are saved over and above a high or relatively

[1] In 1955 in the United States it was 11.6 per cent, in Japan 22.3 per cent.

high standard of living. On the other hand, underdeveloped nations, which produce little and thus have little surplus wealth, consume almost all they are able to produce, and the rate of investment is usually low—around 5 per cent of total income. This was the rate in India at the start of the First Five Year Plan. By the end of the Plan, it exceeded 7 per cent.

A rapid shift from the rate of 5 per cent to 12 per cent or more has been said, by some economists, to constitute an "industrial revolution."

In any case, what is clear is that development cannot take place rapidly unless a larger and larger portion of national income is put into industries, power and irrigation projects, and the like. One way to do this in underdeveloped countries, which produce little surplus wealth, is deliberately to hold down living standards and consumption of goods so that funds may be gathered to invest in development.

It might be possible for a nation following non-democratic methods to compel its people or sections of them to accept a very low or static living standard, and thus gather funds for development by heavy taxes, forced "savings" and sale of a large share of the crops.

Democratic underdeveloped countries, however, cannot build factories, power plants, and so on, at human and social cost, but must keep living standards rising, at the same time as they draw off funds for investment. This is certainly true in India, as perhaps in many newly independent nations, where the winning of political freedom was accompanied by a "revolution of rising expectations" among the people for better living standards.

The crucial test of democracy, therefore, is whether, in an underdeveloped country, it can achieve a rate of investment and of economic progress comparable to totalitarian nations. India believes that democracy can meet this test. It believes that if the people are permitted to understand and share in the nation's problems, if they are brought into partnership with their Government in planning and carrying out development, a free people is capable of making the enormous contribution—in energy, skills, savings and even sacrifice—necessary to carry themselves and their nation forward.

It is by such methods that India hopes to mobilize its people and resources, in its vast national endeavor. By doing so, it expects to succeed by the end of the Second Plan in securing a rate of investment of 11 per cent, as compared to 7.3 per cent in 1955–1956. At

How India Compares in INCOME

NATIONAL INCOME, Average 1952-54
(in billions of dollars)

U.S.A.	$$$$$ $$$$$ $$$$$ $$$$$ $$$$$ $$$$$	299.0
U.K.	$$$$	39.5
France	$$$!	31.7
W. Germany	$$!	25.0
India	$$!	22.3
Japan	$$!	16.5
Brazil	$!	12.8
Pakistan	!	5.6
Philippines	!	3.2
Egypt	!	2.7

$ = 10 billion dollars

PER CAPITA INCOME, Average 1952-54
(in dollars)

U.S.A.	$$$$$ $$$$$ $$$$$ $$$$	1,870
U.K.	$$$$$ $$$	780
France	$$$$$ $$!	740
W. Germany	$$$$$!	510
Brazil	$$!	230
Japan	$$	190
Philippines	$!	150
Egypt	$!	120
Pakistan	$	70
India	!	60

$ = 100 dollars

Source: U.N. Statistical Paper E–4, 1957

the end of twenty years, India hopes the rate will be 17 per cent, which the Planning Commission considers a high but not unattainable figure.

The ten years of the Second and Third Five Year Plans, however, are the most crucial in determining India's future. To give the Indian economy now a big enough push so that it can go ahead expanding and producing more almost under its own power, the step-up in investment in the Second and Third Plan periods must be relatively larger than will be required later. It is the effort to cross this "threshold," or what some economists call this "take-off point" in economic development, that, at a time when living standards and the saving potential are already low, requires some measure of foreign capital and assistance.

The fourth and final key, again in purely economic terms, to India's development over the next twenty years, is how much it will get in production in return for every rupee spent. With India's limited funds, every rupee must yield the highest possible return in more goods, services and production.

Put another way, India must achieve the best possible use of all its resources—its land, its labor, its capital, its industries, machinery and equipment, old as well as new—to get the highest possible yield in production.

Much can be done without new expenditures—as, for instance, by more efficient use of land, by organizing and using surplus labor more effectively, by efficient administration of various development programs.

Where funds must be invested, as in new plants or machinery or irrigation projects, India must make the greatest efforts, in planning and organization, to get the highest production out of every rupee invested. New machinery must not be held idle because of bottlenecks in transport or raw materials or lack of trained workmen. Improved seed and fertilizers must be made available at the right time and place in the sowing season, and farmers educated to use them, so that fields newly irrigated by costly dams and canals can give their highest yields.

In deciding how to invest its limited funds to get the most production for each rupee spent, India has special problems and questions. How much of its funds should be put into projects which need little capital but use large numbers of workmen? What is the relative production per rupee between the two? How many yards of cotton cloth, for instance, will India get per rupee spent on modern textile machinery using little labor, as compared with the yards produced by hundreds of thousands of hand weavers using improved looms that cost relatively little?

These are important questions where, as in India, capital is scarce and must be used sparingly, and where capital in the form of foreign exchange (dollars, pounds sterling, and so on) is very scarce indeed. Modern machinery not only requires scarce capital but, since it must be bought abroad, also requires scarce foreign exchange.

Moreover, in India there is a vast population with high unemployment, and highly mechanized industry needs relatively little labor. Recent rough calculations for India indicate, for instance, that more than tripling steel production, as presently planned, will require not triple the present number of workers, but only about twice as many more.

The Second Plan clearly recognizes that even the high rise expected in national production and income will not solve unemployment, although it will create a very substantial number of new jobs.

It is generally accepted among economists that in India and other countries with high unemployment, some projects should be specifically chosen to use large amounts of labor. For each rupee invested production may be less, the same or even higher, depending on the kind of project. In any case, providing employment is an important objective in itself and a social, indeed a political, necessity.

For India, the problem is seen in particular clarity where small and hand industries, employing many, must compete with large mechanized industries employing few. The most notable and difficult case is in cotton textiles where complete mechanization of the industry would destroy the employment of the hundreds of thousands of hand weavers.

In investing its limited funds, therefore, and planning its future development with a view to higher employment as well as higher incomes, India has to work out an acceptable balance between those which use large amounts of capital and those using large amounts of labor, choosing as nearly as it can those which give the best returns not only in production but in employment.

Another problem on which India must make a start in the Second Plan is to get some relief from pressure on the land, cutting down the now excessive proportion of people engaged in agriculture. All developed countries have a far lower proportion of the working population engaged in agriculture than does India. In general, the proportion in agriculture and in industry is one of the clearest indications of economic growth, or lack of it.

What India hopes to do over the long term is at least to keep to a minimum any increase in workers in agriculture, so that the present proportion of 70 per cent may be cut down gradually, possibly to 60 per cent or so over the next twenty or thirty years. The traditional hand industries and trade and services are already oversupplied with labor. While it is, as we have seen, both desirable and necessary in the transition period to increase employment somewhat in these fields, in the long run the big need is to create employment in large- and small-scale industry, in construction, housing, transport and communication. National investment over the Second and later Plans must, therefore, be channeled more and more to these industries.

Looking twenty years ahead at all these problems affecting its development, India made some estimates of the future pattern of its growth, and set up some targets it hopes to reach.

Briefly, in economic terms, India's goal in twenty years is a nation where national income is two and a half times as high as in 1956, and where per capita incomes have doubled. Stated another way, what India hopes to get well under way in the next five years, certainly in ten, is its industrial and agricultural revolution, creating a more abundant economy which produces and consumes more of its own and the world's goods, and which has developed its own momentum to go constantly forward.

Stated in more precise figures, India's pattern of growth is foreseen as follows:

TWENTY YEARS OF GROWTH: 1956-76

	AT THE END OF					% IN-CREASE 1956 TO 1976
	1ST PLAN 1955-6	2ND PLAN 1960-1	3RD PLAN 1965-6	4TH PLAN 1970-1	5TH PLAN 1975-6	
National Income (Rs. crores)	10,800	13,480	17,260	21,680	27,270	152.5
Total Net Investment (Rs. crores) (total for entire Plan period)	3,100	6,200	9,900	14,800	20,700	576.7
Rate of Investment (as % of national income)	7.3	10.7	13.7	16.0	17.0	132.9
Population (millions)	384	408	434	465	500	30.2
Capital-output Ratio (over the Plan period)	1.8:1	2.3:1	2.6:1	3.4:1	3.7:1	—
Per Capita Income (Rs.)	281	331	396	466	546	93.9

(All at 1952–53 prices)

CHAPTER III

Revolution with Social Justice

Certainly economic factors alone will not determine India's rate and manner of development over the next five or the next twenty years. As the dynamic ferment of change sets in, social unity and political stability are paramount necessities.

And so too is India's ability to provide the incentives, the social and political climate, the sense of national purpose that can arouse progressively greater participation of all the Indian people in the work of development—drawing their effort, their faith to the service of the nation.

Social and political stability, public support and participation depend almost directly on how well India is able to bring the benefits of economic development to all classes of people.

India's study of industrial revolutions, current and past, shows that they have usually been accompanied at least at the beginning—that is, the stage where India now is—by enormous human misery, social upheaval and class conflict; by the weakening, or even the elimination, of whole groups in society—of cottage craftsmen, or of landlords, or of peasants, or of middle-class entrepreneurs; by the growth of industrial slums and poverty; by concentration in the hands of the few of excessive wealth and power; by the further depression of those groups which at the outset were already most weak and disadvantaged.

As India views it, such evils could result from industrial revolution only because political democracy was not then completely effective. Workers, farmers, economically or politically oppressed groups were not fully represented in parliaments and governments, and were thus not protected against injustice or assured a fair share of industrial progress. It was only as governments became more fully representative that they saw to it that larger and larger numbers of people won equality of economic opportunity and social justice, fair labor laws and social security, and shared in the benefits of national development.

In India political democracy has come first. The only course possible for India as a democratic government is to see that the benefits of industrialization, as it progresses, are shared with the many as well as with the few, and that political freedom brings increased economic freedom for all groups in society.

Economic and social democracy cannot be in India merely the end products of industrial revolution; they must accompany it, keep pace with it and, what is even more important, by releasing the initiative and energies of the people, be the very instruments to bring it about.

Even in its early stage of incomplete industrialization, India has not escaped some of the evils of the haphazard growth of industry, of slums in the more and more overcrowded cities, the economic depression of some groups and classes of society who lost their integrated part in the old village communities. India is aware of these evils, and that so far it has not avoided them.

As India stands on the threshold of its industrial revolution, therefore, it is determined to choose a new pattern to bring about great economic change without conflict, political or economic oppression or destructive social upheavals. It proposes, by peaceful democratic means, to carry forward, not one group, but all groups—villagers, farmers, small businessmen, large industrialists, low caste and high— so that not one but all may advance in living standards, in opportunity and human dignity.

To do this, while developing with the speed and on the scale that India proposes is, as it has been called, a fateful experiment.

India takes its approach and its courage for this experiment from its long heritage of philosophic and religious belief in the dignity of man, which found its most recent expression in the teachings of Mahatma Gandhi, the Father of the Indian Nation.

The great legacies of Mahatma Gandhi are on the one hand the conviction that economic and social freedom must be the goal of new India, and on the other a body of principles through which India's economic, like its political, revolution should be brought about.

India feels indeed that its present economic revolution is a continuation of its earlier political struggle. For Gandhi, India's freedom struggle itself was inseparable from the struggle for social and economic equality for the people. "The two things, social re-ordering and the fight for political Swaraj [self-rule], must go hand in hand; there can be no question of precedence." Swaraj, he taught, must not be the substitution of one government for another, but "the poor man's Swaraj," with full economic freedom for the "starving toiling millions."

He saw economic advancement as a political as well as social necessity:

Economic equality is the master key to non-violent independence. . . . A non-violent system of government is clearly an impossibility so long as the wide gulf between the rich and the hungry millions persists. The contrast between the palaces of New Delhi and the miserable hovels of the poor laboring classes cannot last one day in a free India in which the poor will enjoy the same [political] power as the richest in the land. A violent and bloody revolution is a certainty one day unless there is a voluntary abdication of riches and the power that riches give and sharing them for the common good.

Identifying himself with India's poor, he turned the thoughts of the nation to the needs of rural millions for whom life was "an eternal compulsory fast," who "live because they cannot die at will." He warned that if the village perishes, India will perish too, and urged the rich, the city people to go to the villages to come in "living touch" with the poor by "working for them in their midst, sharing their sorrows, understanding their difficulties, anticipating their wants."

Whether the British remain or not, it is our duty always to wipe out unemployment, to bridge the gulf between rich and poor, to banish communal strife, to exorcise the demon of untouchability. . . . If crores [tens of millions] of people do not take a living interest in this nation-building work, freedom must remain a dream and unattainable either by violence or non-violence.

To the big landlords, the princes, the other rich, he urged anew the ancient Hindu principle of trusteeship, in which wealth is considered held in trust to share with and serve the interests of the poor.

Gandhi urged that the social re-ordering, the more equitable distribution of wealth, should come by non-violent means. For to him "means are everything; as the means to the end." Democracy itself, where there will be equal freedom for all, can only be the outcome of non-violence. "The spirit of democracy cannot be imposed. It has to come from within."

A new social order cannot be forced; that would be a remedy worse than the disease. I am an impatient reformer. I am all for thorough-going, radical social re-ordering, but it must be an organic growth, not a violent superimposition. . . .

What is needed is not extinction of landlords and capitalists but a transformation of the existing relationship between them and the masses into something healthier and purer. . . . In India a class war is not only not inevitable but it is avoidable if we have understood the message of non-violence. . . .

Let us not be obsessed with catchwords and seductive slogans imported from the West. Have we not our own distinct Eastern tradition? Are we not capable of finding our own solution to the question of capital and labor? . . . It is surely wrong to presume that Western socialism or communism is the last word on the question of mass poverty.

There are other Gandhian concepts that have today strong influence on the thought and planning of India's continuing revolution. One of these is a distrust of concentration of power and wealth in the hands either of the State or of individuals. This distrust was Gandhi's basic objection to industrialization. Gandhi felt similarly the need for decentralization of authority; and urged the strengthening of the villages, so that they might become strong centers of local government—"perfect democracy based on individual freedom" —which could resist and offset a concentration of power by State or industry.

Gandhi also had a strong faith in cooperative action, as a way for the poor to pool their efforts and slender resources for producing and marketing goods. Gandhi felt that if cooperation were based on strict non-violence, it could "change the face of the land and banish poverty."

It is with these Gandhian beliefs and principles that India approaches the struggle for economic freedom today. It is this Gandhian heritage that has created the egalitarian social climate, the national social conscience which has made it possible to launch a war against poverty, to plan for national development in terms of social justice, with the widespread support of all classes of the people, and without the violent opposition of the privileged few.

Gandhi's basic principle, social justice, was made the principle of State policy by the Indian Constitution, and India has set social justice as both the means and the goal of its development and entire planning effort.

A society in which social justice is secured, India calls today a "socialist pattern of society." This phrase, used in the Second Plan, is considered a translation into more concretized terms of the concepts of social justice.

"What do we mean when we say 'socialist pattern' of life?", asked the Prime Minister in laying the Second Plan before Parliament. "Surely we mean a society in which there is social cohesion without classes, equality of opportunity and the possibility for everyone to have a good life." [1]

The Second Plan puts it precisely: "The accent of the socialist pattern is on the attainment of positive goals; the raising of living standards; the enlargements of opportunities for all, the promotion of enterprise among the disadvantaged classes and the creation of a sense of partnership among all sections of the community. These positive goals provide the criteria for basic decisions." [2]

Gandhi's other basic principle—that economic advance must be accomplished by democratic non-violent means and peaceful change —is fundamental to all India's planning.

We have already seen that India's first act as an independent nation was to base its Government on a liberal Constitution and on free democratic elections.

In planning its development, the democratic means which India as a parliamentary democracy has chosen are three: democratic persuasion to bring about participation and cooperation of all; democratic planning—involving all groups, from the village to the national Government—at all levels; and the use and strengthening of democratic institutions to administer and speed development.

Perhaps the clearest statement of what India means by "democratic persuasion" has been made by the Prime Minister:

I believe in our capacity in India . . . in winning over people rather than fighting them . . . We can bring about social changes and developments, under pressure of events, by the pressure of democracy and also by the friendly democratic approach, rather than the approach of trying to eliminate each other and the stronger party winning.[3]

We realize, of course, that the interests of various groups in the country clash, that there are class conflicts [as] the interests of a landowner are not the same as the interests of his tenant. . . . We do not ignore

[1] May 24, 1956.
[2] Second Five Year Plan, p. 24.
[3] Prime Minister to the National Development Council, Jan. 20, 1956.

it . . . to ignore it would be to ignore reality. But, nevertheless, we do not encourage class conflicts, as some people do, but try to resolve them, to lessen them.

If vested interests come in the way they have to be removed; but, in doing so, we shall pursue the friendly cooperative way, because we mean ill to no one and because we realize that ultimately the good of the individual or the group can only come fully when the whole nation and our 360 million people advance.

Therefore, the test is always the good of the masses of our people. This combination of firm adherence to principle and objective, and yet a friendly approach even to those who differ and whose interests clash with that objective is the way Gandhiji taught us. It is in keeping with the genius of India.[1]

This choice of democratic persuasion as a means of development has led India to create and strengthen organizations which can reach to and consist of the people themselves, to stimulate widespread democratic planning of and participation in development activities. A democratic system has been set up (it is described in Chapter V) for making each Plan a plan to represent the needs and aspirations of the people.

District and village governments are being strengthened both for planning and for administering programs. For the enormous task of raising village living standards and agricultural production, a national extension service and a rural development program were launched whose basic approach is democratic persuasion of the people to adopt improved methods and participate in self-help.

Thus, adherence to the principle of democracy for economic growth is itself forcing formation of democratic institutions and an extensive democratic substructure to the Central Government.

India is very conscious that *time* will be one of the most important influences on the *way* it develops as a democracy. To give economic content to democratic political institutions, the *speed* with which changes are brought about is as important as their substance.

For India, as for other Asian nations, time is short. It cannot afford a slow rate of progress. Its problems are urgent not in the sense

[1] Prime Minister to State Congress Committee Presidents, March 9, 1955.

that they can be quickly solved but because they are deep-seated, and need constant and prolonged attention.

But even with the pressure for rapid development, for rapid improvement of the living standards of its people, India feels that *continuity* of effort and continuous and sustained growth based on a balanced scheme of priorities is essential. It has determined to avoid the error of proposing or seeking quick and spectacular achievements which would be followed by depressions, severe jerks, breaks and social reversals.

India knows, however, that continuity of action turns largely on the working of the political system, so that the crucial test of the democratic approach in India, as no doubt in other countries of southern Asia, lies in its ability to sustain over many years, with the general support of the people, adequate development effort and stable policies for economic and social change.

It feels, therefore, that its job is not merely to increase national production, or achieve social change, but to so develop the institutions of democracy that political change can be harmonized with continuity of constructive effort, and that the foundations are laid on which the nation as a whole, and every part of it, can raise a strong, enduring structure.

For sustained continuous growth, peace is essential, as are peaceful friendly relations not only with other Asian nations, but with the comity of nations. India does not seek development in isolation; it does not wish to build up an all-sufficient economy either for peaceful or for military purposes. India feels, moreover, that its own progress will in some measure benefit from the development of other countries roundabout India.

Given India's stage of underdevelopment, its need to study and draw upon the techniques and experience of advanced countries, its need to exchange both goods and services, it must seek, and it wishes to seek, development as part of a peaceful and interdependent world economy.

Remaining at peace with its neighbors and the world, India hopes that it will be possible to devote the nation's full efforts and resources to strengthening its economy, to setting in motion the forces of orderly continuous growth, and to meeting, as a democratic government, the rising demands of its people for social and economic advancement. By doing so, as it progresses under democracy, India hopes it may, at the same time, contribute to peace—the peace of Asia and perhaps of the world.

It is with these considerations, these social concepts and these high hopes that India has approached her Second Five Year Plan. The foundations for many of them were already there as India became an independent nation. Over the First Plan, these concepts grew, evolved and were, to a degree, crystallized by the increasing experience and confidence, the firmer sense of direction that emerged as the First Plan progressed.

They are the product, therefore, of Indian experience, and of the interaction of economic and social forces already aroused by development upon the cultural patterns and traditions of the Indian people. Whatever they may owe to the thought and experience of other nations, the final product is, as it must be in all nations which respect and find strength in their own heritage, uniquely its own.

CHAPTER IV

The Eight Basic Decisions

India calls the Second Plan its "grand strategy in the war against poverty." It has even been described as the most concentrated effort ever made by a parliamentary democracy to achieve economic development while advancing human freedom.

The Plan has specifically four objectives. The size and importance of the Plan come from its attempt to achieve them all, all at the same time.

The four objectives to be achieved by 1961 are:

1. *A sizable (25 per cent) increase in national income* to raise the still depressed living standards;
2. *Rapid industrialization,* especially the development of basic industries;
3. *A large expansion in employment opportunities;* and
4. *Reduction in inequalities* in income and wealth, and an increasing measure of economic and social justice for all groups.

Behind these objectives lie eight significant decisions. They are based on India's assessment of the economic factors that will determine India's growth over the years and on the social principles which must guide all India's development. These eight decisions are at the heart not only of India's approach to the Second Five Year Plan and to its planning in general, but of India's view of the whole course of its future development.

1. *The Second Plan must be big—big enough and powerful enough to begin to lift the Indian economy across the "threshold" to a developed nation.*

The Plan is double the size of the First, measured by the proposed expenditures of the Government alone. Private enterprise by itself is expected to spend considerably more than was spent in the First Plan by Government for all purposes.

The Plan has set itself high—very high—targets for gains in production in food, in industry, for advance in incomes, in social services.

India feels that a massive plan with high targets is not a matter of choice but of necessity. The First Five Year Plan, while its gains were considerable, showed that modest effort cannot push the country forward far and fast enough. India must make a new effort— bolder, more far-reaching—to mobilize to the utmost its people, its resources and its energies.

It feels it cannot attempt less, under the intensive pressures of time, of a rapidly multiplying population, of rising popular demands, or under the external political pressures for swift development.

India will, at all times, keep its planning flexible, sensitive to new needs, to new problems of financing or administration, to new data and findings, to important social and economic changes. Conscious that this Second Plan is but one of a series of future Plans, India will constantly keep it attuned to the needs of long-term planning, and ever ready to adjust to new assessments of India's future growth.

Looking ahead, it is clear that the next few years are the crucial years. India must, in these years, make the supreme effort to cross the "threshold" between an underdeveloped and a developed nation and give the economy the momentum to carry itself forward. And India must in these years show that democracy can organize itself to make this effort, can successfully attack the problems of mass poverty and bring a backward nation and its people up to new levels of income and opportunity.

Economic development in its early stages, and before the new plants begin production, will admittedly put a severe strain on the Indian economy. India has faced the fact that the Second Plan would demand efforts beyond efforts to mobilize the resources—the financial resources, the manpower, the skills, the administrative competence necessary to carry out the vast and complex programs of the Plan.

Yet India believes it is more important to organize to make these efforts and to meet this strain than to compromise the core of the Plan or to cut down its essential targets.

At this crucial period of its growth, India feels that the Plan must reach not to the lower but to the upper limit of India's possibilities.

Here, a bold Plan in itself has essential advantages. Its very boldness can be a direct inducement to a larger effort, to more effective administrative measures, and can capture the imagination, enthusiasm and participation of the people not only to give their best efforts but to accept inconvenience or even sacrifice. India is well aware that governments and their people do not—in some cases cannot—act as readily to solve problems which are not urgent, as they do and can under pressure of necessity in a great and challenging national endeavor.

Can so massive and bold a plan succeed? The Prime Minister believes that "in the final analysis any effort is an act of faith. [For us] that act of faith fundamentally is in the capacity of the Indian people. All I can say is that I have faith in the capacity of our people." [1]

If in the course of these five years, we achieve what we have laid down in our Second Five Year Plan, it will be a great victory—one of the greatest that India has won. And not only will it be a victory but a

[1] Prime Minister to Parliament, Sept. 7, 1956.

prelude to other victories, because then we will have established our feet soundly and we can march then without relying too much on others. We will have crossed that dangerous barrier which separates an underdeveloped country from a developing country, and once we have done that, it will be easier and faster going.[1]

2. India will develop first and above all its agriculture and its rural people.

India is now, and in the foreseeable future will remain, a predominantly agricultural nation.

The Indian Government feels that in a nation where nearly three-fourths of the population work or depend on agriculture, the advance of the rural people is more clearly than any other the testing point of democratic development.

The more so, since in a nation of poverty India's rural people are those most impoverished. To bring water to parched Indian fields, schools and health clinics to some 300 million villagers, light and power to rural homes and industries, new knowledge and new means of self-advancement—it is such tasks as these that will demonstrate the new Government's capacity to achieve progress for and with the Indian people.

As India develops its industries, some shift from agriculture to industry and trade is planned and will take place. Yet for many decades, even generations, rural people, rural society will characterize Indian culture and economy.

What India hopes to evolve, certainly over the immediate future, as part of its whole effort of rural development, is a vital rural society which produces most of its own food and a valuable share of its other needs, and which, at the same time, offers its people richer opportunities for a more satisfying social, economic and cultural rural life.

To some degree such a rural society takes inspiration from Mahatma Gandhi's ideal of village democracy and the development of

[1] Prime Minister to All-India Congress Committee, Indore, Jan. 4, 1957.

village people, but in new India it is conceived also as the essential economic and social foundation for a rural nation making the difficult and tremendous journey of development.

Perhaps India's greatest challenge is how rapidly and how well it can advance its millions of backward impoverished rural people, and, at the same time, secure by democratic means a sharp, steady rise in agricultural production.

Increased agricultural production is an urgent necessity. To support industrialization requires agricultural surpluses which can, on the one hand, pay for investment at home and for purchase of equipment abroad, and, on the other hand, feed the nation's people in village and city.

India's choice indeed is either to increase farm production or face certain failure in carrying out the Plan in full. In the final analysis, agricultural production will determine India's capacity to meet the demands and needs of national development. As Gandhi said prophetically in 1916, India's salvation lies in the villages, with the Indian farmer.

The advancement of the rural people and the sharp stepping up of farm production have proved in other nations under rapid development the crucial test of social policy and of social and political stability.

The Indian Government has observed with particular interest the experience in eastern Europe. Speaking in late 1956 to the National Development Council, the Prime Minister pointed to the significance to India of this experience:

Recently we have known those developments which have taken place for some time in eastern Europe—Poland, Hungary, etc. . . . At the back of these political developments and conflicts there has been tremendous strain on their economy. . . . By and large it was the lessening of agricultural production that . . . affected them. They were anxious to promote industrial growth and they had to do it. . . . They did it even at the cost of agriculture, even at the cost of many other necessary articles. . . . Their economy suffered very greatly, and more particularly agriculture suffered. They actually did not even have enthusiasm for agriculture because their attention was drawn into other things, and also too rapid changes in the political set-up affected their agricultural structure. . . . In the world context the significance of these events has been tremendous, and for the future we must draw the lesson from it.[1]

The Indian Government feels that, whatever the pressures for rapid results, its own solution to assuring a substantial rise in farm production must have as its aim, above all, the welfare of the rural people. India's constant purpose is so to provide the rural people with the incentives and the means of self-help and self-government that they move constantly forward, planning and working for their own development, contributing their strength, production and democratic vitality to a nation in swift economic and social transition.

3. *India will develop its industries—but with a careful balancing of large and small industry, of the heavy industries basic to economic growth, and the traditional small and hand industries essential to employment and social stability.*

The decision to develop India's industries in a basic and balanced manner dates from well before the Second Plan. It rests on the fact, accepted in every advanced country, that high levels of production are the source of wealth, of rising incomes, of higher employment and living standards.

A rough scheme for free India's industrial development was drawn up as early as 1946. Although the critical food shortage made it necessary for the First Plan to put highest priority upon agricultural production, the Government's aggressive stimulation of industry, in an effort to expand unemployment and encourage more activity among Indian enterprises, is one of the notable characteristics of the latter part of the First Plan. It is now considered that the First Plan should have included even more vigorous development of heavy industries, principally steel.

The Second Plan puts a major emphasis on the heavy and basic industries, particularly steel production and fabrication of steel into producer goods. Expenditures by the Government alone on large and

[1] The Prime Minister to the National Development Council, Dec. 8, 1956.

medium industry (and on the facilities for industry—mineral development, transport, communications, and power) will exceed what was
spent by the Government in the First Plan for all purposes.

Not only from the point of view of financial resources but of the
effect on the economy, the programs for these industries are the
Plan's hard core. The dynamism of the Plan, its ability to give the
Indian economy the powerful push forward across the threshold of
development, lies in its emphasis on these industries.

India believes, moreover, that its own stability, both internally and
as a free, independent nation, depends on the degree to which it develops industries to produce for the nation and its people. Reviewing
the final draft of the Second Plan with the National Development
Council, the Prime Minister emphasized: "Without the growth of

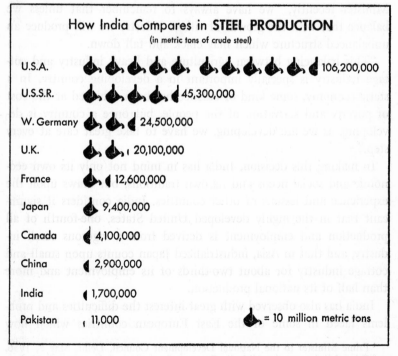

How India Compares in **STEEL PRODUCTION**
(in metric tons of crude steel)

U.S.A.	106,200,000
U.S.S.R.	45,300,000
W. Germany	24,500,000
U.K.	20,100,000
France	12,600,000
Japan	9,400,000
Canada	4,100,000
China	2,900,000
India	1,700,000
Pakistan	11,000

= 10 million metric tons

Source: U.N. Statistical Yearbook, 1956

industries, there can be no real progress from the point of view of wealth formation and employment, and even from the point of view of our country being able to maintain her freedom." [1]

India's goal is not industrial self-sufficiency. Industrialization is expected to bring about an expanding economy, producing and buying more and more of the world's goods in a constantly growing foreign trade.

At the same time as India speeds the growth of heavy industry, it is keenly aware of the need to balance its industrial development. It has made a clear decision that it will not force heavy industries at the expense of other parts of its economy, not only of its agriculture but of its small-scale and village industries.

"While we believe that the industrial progress of India will depend and must depend on the growth of heavy industry," said the Prime Minister recently, "we have always to remember that unless we balance that with the growth of village industry we will produce an unbalanced structure which may crack and fall down.

"This balancing between agriculture and heavy industry and cottage industry is specially important in a developing country. In a static economy, some kind of balance has been achieved at the cost of poverty and starvation of the people, but once a country is developing, as we are developing, we have to take great care at every step." [2]

In making this decision, India has in mind not only its own economic and social needs and its own traditions, but draws upon the experience and lessons of other countries. India considers it significant that in the highly developed United States, one-fourth of all production and employment is derived from a vigorous small industry, and that in Asia, industrialized Japan counts upon small and cottage industry for about two-thirds of its employment and more than half of its national production.

India has also observed with great interest the difficulties and problems faced in some of the East European countries which now

[1] Prime Minister to the National Development Council, Delhi, May 2, 1956.
[2] Prime Minister to the All-India Congress Committee, Indore, Jan. 4, 1957.

themselves recognize that their overstress on heavy industry has unbalanced their economies, and been a key factor in internal stresses and conflicts.

"It is an extraordinary thing," said the Prime Minister, "how the wheel has turned a full circle. From this complete emphasis in these [East European] countries on heavy industry, they suddenly found that while heavy industry is necessary and important, they must have other bases for their economy—otherwise, difficulties arise—and they have come back to what we have been saying in our own way all these many years, i.e., the development of village industry and handicrafts. That is a lesson for us." [1]

The balanced industrial structure that India hopes to evolve is of three parts or layers: the heavy basic industries which are the necessary underpinning for any developed economy; a vigorous small-scale industry, advancing in modern techniques, complementing and in part supplying large industry; and a progressive rural industry producing largely for the villages and sustaining rural employment and social cohesion.

Small-scale and hand industries now form a large and important part of India's economy and of its social and cultural life. They contribute 10 per cent of India's total production, most of it in consumer goods, and an amount equal in value to the production of India's medium- and large-scale industries. They employ 11.5 million persons, or 29 per cent of all people employed outside agriculture.

The so-called "small-scale" industries, partly mechanized and usually located in or near the cities, are among the important growing points of the Indian economy, comparable to the small business of the West. In India, as in far more advanced economies, they are, and can with development become even more, important training grounds for large industry, and constitute a strong sector of free vigorous enterprise providing opportunity, income and a productive role for an expanding middle class.

The majority of hand industries are in village areas, and are, and with development will become even more so, a major source of non-

[1] Prime Minister to the All-India Congress Committee, Indore, Jan. 4, 1957.

agricultural income and employment outside the cities. For many of the village artisans they represent, moreover, a traditional way of life, and provide them with a socially and economically integrated role in village society.

What India proposes is to stimulate both these types of industries, so that they too, as the steel plants and other heavy industries come up, may grow in strength, efficiency and production. A concerted, nation-wide system of industrial extension services and technical assistance is proposed by the Second Plan which will encourage and help both village and small-scale industries to adopt modern tools and methods. This is of course essential to small business if it is to compete. But it is equally essential to hand industries as well, to step up both production and quality.

With the development programs proposed over the Plan, the small and hand industries are expected to provide not only their present large share of employment, but half a million new full-time jobs in addition, and considerable part-time employment. Their production is expected to rise by as much as 30 per cent, and to contribute a substantial share of the consumer goods required to meet the *increase* expected in demand as incomes and employment rise.

The development of these industries, and especially of the village industries, can mean a more decentralized as well as a more balanced industrial economy. It can slow down the flood of migration to the cities which today, as in Gandhi's time, is "draining the lifeblood of the villages" and creating ever more serious problems of city congestion, unemployment and social unrest.

To many who recall Mahatma Gandhi's encouragement of hand spinning, India's decision to foster hand industries is of some historic as well as economic interest.

Observing how modern textile mills had thrown thousands of rural hand weavers out of work, Gandhi had the insight to understand the dangers of industrialization and rapid introduction of labor-saving machinery in India's rural economy with its high unemployment. "I would welcome every improvement in the cottage machine, but I know that it is criminal to displace hand labor . . .

unless one is at the same time ready to give millions of farmers some other occupation in their homes." For him, the encouragement of village crafts, which he symbolized by hand spinning, was a way of giving the millions of village poor some means of employment, larger income, a gain in self-respect, a valued and productive part in village life.

Thus today, even as Gandhi foresaw, the fostering of small and hand industries is a necessary part of balanced industrial development, an essential aspect of balanced social, as of economic, growth, not only in this period of India's transition to a modern nation but, it may well be, for a long time into India's future.

4. *India will increase living standards and consumption at the same time that it builds its industries.*

Any nation, democratic or otherwise, which seeks rapidly to expand its economy must, as we have seen, consume considerably less than it produces, and put the amount saved into power plants, industries, railways, and other development. Some nations appear to have gone too far in this direction in order to achieve spectacular growth. They have drained off so large a portion of their income for industrial development that the people's living standards were forced down, for years together, at great human and social cost.

India has no wish to force its development at such cost, nor as a democratic nation could it do so. To India, where living standards are already appallingly low, the very purpose of development and planning is to raise incomes and increase demand and living standards. Or, to cite again the Prime Minister, "Our industrialization has a predominantly social aim—to meet the pressure of wants of the great majority of our own people." [1]

India considers development itself as a process of creating new and more demands and of finding ways, by fuller use of resources, to meet them. The chief justification for building heavy goods industries at all is that it will make possible later an expanded and more efficient flow of consumer goods.

[1] Prime Minister to the Canadian Parliament in 1949.

For India, then, there is no question of reducing consumption. The only question is how fast it can increase.

The delicate choice for a democratic underdeveloped nation is what proportion of its resources to put into consumer industries, as against heavy industries, railways, and the like, during this critical period when resources are limited. Arriving at the right balance is extremely difficult. Some measure of sacrifice is inevitable if the rate of investment in the economy is to be increased.

The compromise India hopes to achieve is to keep living standards and consumption moving up, but to regulate the *rate* of increase, if necessary restricting or holding down consumption for short periods.

In statistical terms, what the Second Plan proposes is a rise in production of consumer goods of about 21 per cent as against a 25 per cent increase in national income, with the difference plowed into national development projects. The Second Plan emphasizes that if foreign and domestic resources are not available in the amount expected in the Plan, it will be necessary to restrict consumption more than this.

The nub of the problem is, of course, increasing all production rapidly, so that it is high enough to raise living standards on the one hand and at the same time have sufficient income left to invest in development.

5. *India will take advantage of every possible way of growth consistent with democracy to develop the nation and its people.*

No ready-made solutions, no tried and true rules exist for developing a vast impoverished backward nation, under pressure, by democratic means.

The methods by which the United States developed its richly endowed, sparsely settled continent by free enterprise, during a century or more; the ways by which Britain and the nations of Europe carried through industrial revolution and arrived, in the twentieth century, at various modifications of socialism; the growth of Japan to a modern nation—none of these experiences apply directly or in detail to Indian conditions, although they provide, of course, many lessons and examples of the problems of development.

Similarly, the methods of growth adopted in the U.S.S.R. and Eastern Europe—although some of their problems were similar to India's—have only a limited interest for India's social and democratic development.

India, therefore, must seek and find many of its own economic answers, its own ways to solve by democratic means its vast and urgent problems of development. For India this is a great challenge. It must find its own answers to the problems of capital and labor, of developing a vast backward rural population; and, a matter of particular importance, it must find its own solutions to the relative role of the State and private enterprise in economic development. In the light of the modern history of developing nations, it is India's approaches to this latter point which have evoked considerable interest in the West and elsewhere.

There is without question in India a strong egalitarian sentiment, a belief, not unfamiliar in advanced democratic nations of the West, that a nation's industries, its industrialists, its businessmen, as all parts of its economy, have a social, indeed moral, obligation to benefit society as a whole and create more equal opportunities for all. In India this attitude in large part arose and became widespread because of India's early unhappy association with exploitative colonial industry; and because, with notable exceptions, capitalism in India, as in all pre-industrialized societies, for a long time had not progressed enough to provide the wages, the goods, or social and economic benefits and relationships which characterize the most enlightened mid-twentieth-century capitalism in the West.

For India, where there is so vast a gulf between the few rich and the millions of poor, this experience resulted in distrust of large concentrations of wealth and economic power in the hands of the few. As we have seen, Gandhi named this distrust as one of his major reasons for opposing industrialization. For those few modern industries he felt essential, he advocated ownership or management as a trusteeship held in the interest of the people, so that industry might operate "under the most attractive and ideal conditions, not for profit but for the benefit of humanity."

These attitudes found some expression in the Indian Constitution which provides that the State, in striving for social, economic and political justice, "shall direct its policy to securing that the ownership and control of the material resources of the community are so distributed as best to subserve the common good"; and that "the operation of the economic system does not result in the concentration of wealth and the means of production to the common detriment."

India is convinced, however, that it cannot root its policies in rigid socialist dogmas or other doctrinaire theories, or apply foreign ideological approaches which were adopted by other nations in very different conditions. India must remain flexible and pragmatic in its economic structure, hold itself open to experiment, reshape its policies from time to time in the light of experience and the test of practical conditions.

Replying to doctrinaire socialists who urged nationalization of all Indian industries, the Prime Minister put the matter succinctly: "The whole philosophy lying behind this Plan is to take advantage of every possible way of growth, and not, by doing something which fits into some doctrinaire theory, imagine we have grown because we have satisfied some textbook maxim of a hundred years ago." [1]

We are no longer playing about with words and phrases and with ideological approaches. Naturally, there is always some basic ideological approach to a problem, but the academic approach is not enough for us, because we deal with actual problems and try to seek some solution, partly of course by the ideological approach, but more so by considering the actual problems that we have and the experience that we have gained.[2]

With this pragmatic approach, India has made the basic decision to choose a "mixed economy" using all three ways of economic de-

[1] Prime Minister to Parliament, May 23, 1956.
[2] Prime Minister to the National Development Council, May 2, 1956.

velopment which, in democratic nations, have proved effective: (1) public enterprise, (2) private enterprise, and (3) in fields especially suited to it, "middle-way" cooperative enterprise.

The Indian Government will assume predominant and direct responsibility for setting up new heavy and machine-making industries which are essential to an industrialized economy, and for development and expansion of the public utilities, power and transport facilities needed to serve basic industries. The dynamism of the Plan, its ability to push the economy forward, lies, as we have seen, in getting these industries into rapid production.

Setting up steel plants and other heavy industries will involve not only large investment, but enormous administrative and organizational problems. For example, not hundreds but thousands of skilled workmen, industrial engineers and technicians have to be trained abroad, not in the future but immediately. In some cases, for new steel and manufacturing plants, whole new cities and transport facilities must be built.

Surplus private capital for such heavy investment is not available, nor is Indian industry sufficiently developed to have surplus technical and managerial staff to organize and to administer so vast and rapid an expansion program.

It is inconceivable, for instance, and without precedent even in the most rich and advanced nations, that steel capacity could be tripled in five years, as the Second Plan proposes, by private manufacturers alone.

The Government sees parallels in its action to the experience of Sweden, France and the United Kingdom, where various basic industries are owned and managed by the State. The Government, moreover, feels that the urgency of development has put the nation on "a war footing" similar to those periods of national emergency in which other democratic nations have given their Governments special powers.

At the same time as public enterprise is developed, India has taken the major decision that it will place a continued heavy reliance on private enterprise in major industry and throughout the economy. This decision contrasts, of course, with that of doctrinaire socialists, or of totalitarian countries.

Private enterprise now produces and will be expected to produce over the Second Plan period the major portion, about 90 per cent, of India's national output, at the same time as Government increases its investment in basic industry. The Indian Government is keenly aware that the increased production proposed over the Second Plan period depends on the development and intensive activity of private enterprise, and that the Plan as a whole can go through only if there is simultaneous and balanced development by both public and private industry.

It is India's view that private enterprise must have as much freedom as possible to develop, providing always that its development is consistent with the targets and objectives of the Plan. The deliberate policy of the Government is to stimulate private enterprise and channel it into constructive nation-building industries, and open more and more opportunities for development by private capital, both Indian and foreign. The Government has already been of considerable assistance to key private industries in securing domestic and foreign capital for expansion, and negotiating for technical assistance from foreign firms and governments to help Indian industries modernize and expand.

Big industry is of course only one area where the Government relies on private enterprise. The Government is deliberately stepping up its program for strengthening small industry which is nearly all privately owned and run; and intensifying its development program for agriculture, which is wholly in private hands.

The broad relationship which India conceives between public and private industry was set forth in the important Industrial Policy Resolution,[1] issued in April 1956, just before submission of the Second Plan to Parliament. In general, the Government feels that at the present stage of India's development the field for industrialization is so vast—and "occupied by nobody"—that both the private sector and

[1] See Section on Industrial Development, and Appendix.

FERTILIZERS INCREASE CROP YIELDS: An Indian farm extension agent (right) points out the finer size and quality of sugar cane which has been fertilized with ammonium sulphate, compared to the cane grown without fertilizer. The farmer who made the experiment is at the left; in the center is an American agricultural extension adviser, in India under the United States Technical Assistance program.

FERTILIZER PRODUCTION EXPANDS: The Government fertilizer plant at Sindri. Active extension work among farmers more than doubled the use of fertilizers in the five years of India's First Plan. Most of the increased demand was met by the Sindri plant. Over the Second Plan, Sindri will be expanded and three new plants built to meet a demand expected to increase over six-fold.

AUTOMOBILE ASSEMBLY: Indian and foreign manufacturers collaborate in India's infant automobile industry. The industry expects to double production by 1961, and use more domestic-made parts. Above: Hindustan Motors, Ltd., in Calcutta.

WORLD'S LARGEST EARTH DAM, at Hirakud in Orissa, was completed in January 1957. Part of a vast multipurpose power, irrigation and flood-control system, Hirakud serves the potentially great industrial area in Eastern India.

public sector can and should advance to the task together. They should function "in unison," as "parts of a single mechanism."

Government planning for India's future over the next five, ten and twenty years has also given Indian industry new confidence and assurance of the nation's future needs and markets, and of supplies of raw materials and transport. This assurance in India's expanding future has proved perhaps the most important single stimulus to private capital to seek long-term investment in nation-building industry. The considerable enlargement by Government of basic utilities and enterprises in the Second Plan is indeed, in the view of the Indian and foreign economists, necessary to the vigorous growth of private enterprise.

India is aware that a forced rate of economic development, and especially rapid industrialization, raise, for India, the problem of concentration of economic power, of decision making and authority in the hands of both private industry and the State. India's traditional distrust of centralized power, so strongly expressed by Gandhi, has been reinforced by watching the consequences of concentrated State power in totalitarian nations.

"The whole problem of modern civilization is that all this industrialization leads to a concentration of power," the Prime Minister told the National Development Council. "How to reconcile this inevitable concentration of power, this inevitable centralization, with individual freedom, is the problem of modern civilization. . . . But I do think India, situated as she is, has a chance of developing, on her own lines, a relatively high standard of living without getting into all the difficulties and dangers which this mad race for economic or other power has brought about." [1]

India hopes to offset overcentralized administrative power by deliberately broadening the democratic base of planning and by strengthening village and District government, as discussed in following chapters.

India has also proposed to stimulate development of a third sector

[1] Prime Minister's address to the Standing Committee, National Development Council, Jan. 7, 1956.

to balance the power of public and private enterprise. India hopes to find, as has Sweden, this "middle way" through a cooperative sector.

Looking at the vast numbers of small and cottage industries, and of small landholders, that are in no way to come under State control, India feels that these groups must develop the strength to act as a countervailing power, to the State on the one hand and to large private industry on the other. Since these small farmers and artisans do not individually have strength or capital, India feels that for them to join in economic and social cooperative societies is essential as a way to help the little man hold his own and gain strength and opportunity.

India believes that, particularly in the rural areas, cooperative action like village self-government is a valuable means of achieving social cohesion in a period of rapid social change. A system of cooperative community organization, which touches on all aspects of village life, helps the weaker groups, which develops services and benefits for the community as a whole, is, India feels, essential to sustain India's rural millions, and to bring them the benefits and experience of democracy.

What is visualized is democratic voluntarily organized cooperatives to embrace much of agriculture, rural trade and village and small industries, and even eventually medium industries as well, for production, marketing and supply; cooperative land management by local village councils, and cooperative farms; and cooperative endeavor by village people to plan and carry on local development activities.

India recognizes that its hopes of such extensive cooperative action can be fulfilled only with skilled organization, education and leadership. To use the energies and skills of the rural unemployed and landless laborers, to make agriculture efficient in spite of tiny fragmented farms, to pool efforts and capital of millions of small farmers and craftsmen—these pressing needs give India the stimulus to seek new imaginative solutions for organizing voluntary democratic cooperative action.

India is aware that it remains to be seen how a mixed economy with the balance strongly tilted in favor of Government and co-operative enterprise will function. Can it, taking all aspects together, provide a high enough rate of capital formation, and call forth the degree of effort associated with a system based on profit? Can it ensure a large enough increase in national production to eliminate the specter of poverty and unemployment?

It knows that before these questions can be answered, more experience in organizing public enterprises and in working with co-operatives is needed, and that all its proposals must submit to "the test of practical achievement."

In the final analysis what is clear is that India today is in an ideological ferment in which all methods of growth *consistent with the democratic process* are being examined, and as far as possible applied experimentally. India sees no conflict between its devotion to democracy, and the achievement of its objectives of economic development. As long as welfare and prosperity are sought through freedom, social institutions and forms of economic organization will be, in the main, responsive to the needs of the community and will preserve the permanent values.

6. *India will seek the development of all groups and classes among its people, and of all regions of the nation, so that there may be a growing equality of income and opportunity.*

The rise in national income expected over the Second Plan poses for India, as for any country, the question of who benefits by the rise. In the past, in many countries, economic development has been accompanied by increasing inequalities in income, wealth and opportunity. A relatively small class of the people—businessmen, industrialists, large property holders—has tended to benefit first and benefit most as the economy developed, while to other groups, advancement, opportunity and employment came only indirectly and far more slowly. Sometimes, as well, a few regions in each country, favored by natural resources, harbors and transport, have advanced rapidly, while others have lagged behind.

In India, as we have seen, the gap dividing the privileged and the underprivileged is already great, as it is between various groups and between regions.

India has determined that the Second Plan as a whole, and its specific programs, will seek not only to close the vast gulf which has long separated India's privileged and underprivileged, but to avoid, so far as may be, any growth of new inequalities.

India has made this decision in its belief that, for social justice, all groups must share in the benefits of progress. It also does so in the knowledge that where large depressed groups or regions exist in any economy, and where the economy is deprived of their potential incomes and markets, of their initiative, skills and energies, the nation as a whole fails to that degree to advance, and may, as well, develop destructive conflicts and tensions.

India recognizes that it is beyond India's resources today, and probably for some time to come, to provide the universal free education, the social security, the unemployment and old-age insurance, the adequate nation-wide medical services that in the last twenty to thirty years have assured an ever growing measure of social justice in many of the advanced countries of the West.

Yet as India plans its development, the objective constantly before it is, as expressed in these words of the Prime Minister:

> Whatever we desire, it is for the 384 million people of the country and not for any small group or individuals. It does not mean that everyone will get everything, but absolutely equal opportunities should be given to all the 384 million people. This cannot be achieved suddenly by magic or law; it will take time. But, nevertheless, we must move in that direction and must move fast. We can lay down targets. Everyone in the country should have the primary things of life—food, clothing, housing, education, sanitation, medical health, employment and work. Our thinking should always be in terms of the masses of our people.[1]

As it raises national income as a whole, the Plan will deliberately take steps to assure that incomes and standards of living are at the

[1] Prime Minister to the Federation of Indian Chambers of Commerce, March 5, 1955, New Delhi.

same time raised for those now at the bottom of the social and economic ladder.

It is for this reason that India over the Plan years will develop the small-scale and village industries which can spread the gains in employment and income; that it will develop India's long-depressed rural people; that it will press ahead with land reforms permitting more small farmers to own or have secure rights to their own farms; that it will foster the growth of cooperatives, and encourage the growth of strong, representative labor unions.

India will also continue to extend education to more and more children; it will expand health care and housing, with especial concern for the underprivileged in city and village. For tribal peoples, for Harijans and others in the so-called "scheduled castes," for the landless laborers—groups long neglected and often oppressed for reasons of caste or status—the Plan has special programs, to assure their advancement as groups, in addition to the benefits and improved social services they may receive from the Plan as a whole.

India is also concerned that the proposed increase in consumer goods should benefit the lowest as well as the higher income groups. A very large proportion of the additional consumer goods produced will, therefore, be those most used and needed by low-income groups —principally food and cloth, which take from 60 to 70 per cent of the average Indian family's earnings.

While there will continue to be some in India of great wealth, India believes that artificial limits on income would affect incentives to invest and to produce more. It feels that the chief function of a growing economy is to produce *more* wealth for all, rather than to distribute poverty. India will, as other modern democratic countries do, rely upon progressive income taxes, and, most recently, on new taxes on wealth and expenditures, to lessen the vast gulf between rich and poor and to see that all may share fairly in the cost, as in the benefits, of development.

The Plan will also try to reduce the inequalities between region and region in India, so that all parts of the country may begin together the journey to development, with long-backward areas, like long-backward groups, sharing in the nation's progress. For a time, regions already advanced will, to be sure, go ahead faster, since their already developed natural resources, and facilities of transport and power, make possible quickest returns in production and employment. But, for example, the new Bhilai steel plant rising among the primitive villages of Madhya Pradesh, the Hirakud River Valley project in the tribal forests of Orissa, the new irrigation canals to the Rajasthan desert, the rural development program spreading across the nation—these and similar Plan programs will begin to bring not one region but all India's 384 million people forward.

7. *India will at every step of its progress associate the people in the villages and districts with planning and development, so that their initiative, energies and cooperation are awakened and assured, and may serve as the constructive and creative instrument of development itself.*

The initiative, skills, the democratic vitality and aspirations of the Indian people are the nation's greatest resource, its greatest potential strength. To develop this vast resource is India's highest challenge and obligation.

The tremendous task of carrying 384 million people forward cannot succeed—cannot even be done—unless it has the wholehearted cooperation of the people themselves, and unless they themselves help to achieve their own aspirations.

India believes that if the people are awakened, if they are helped to develop their own leaders, to form the village and District councils, the voluntary democratic organizations through which they can work, they can be a tremendous force, the means itself, for securing their own advancement.

Some countries under development have chosen another path, putting their stress on building organizations that would fit into a scheme of centralized planning, a centralized State apparatus, whose primary purpose is to fulfill given physical targets and provide surpluses needed by the economy. India has been interested to observe that these countries are now making some changes in their centralized systems as they have confronted social conditions and gained fresh experience.

India believes that its people should be free to shape their own way of life and livelihood, to dispose as they will of their own crops or of the goods they produce, and be freely able to take advantage of each new opportunity for growth. As the nation moves forward, the essential thing, India feels, is to make freedom secure and broad-based, to bring the people into close association with their Government and especially with the working out of its national plans for development.

In framing the Plan itself, in carrying out the development programs in every State, District and village, and above all, perhaps, in the development of the rural people, India relies upon, and will strengthen the initiative and energies and leadership of its people.

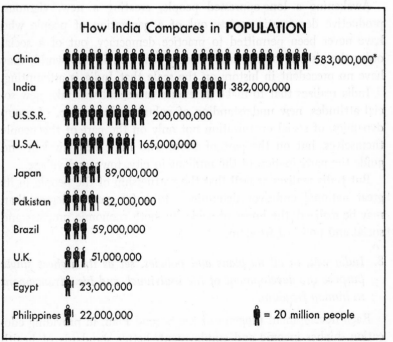

How India Compares in POPULATION

China	583,000,000*
India	382,000,000
U.S.S.R.	200,000,000
U.S.A.	165,000,000
Japan	89,000,000
Pakistan	82,000,000
Brazil	59,000,000
U.K.	51,000,000
Egypt	23,000,000
Philippines	22,000,000

= 20 million people

Source: U.N. Statistical Yearbook, 1956

* For 1953.

As the newly appointed State Development Commissioners met for the first time in 1952, the Prime Minister expressed this view which underlies all India's efforts:

Obviously it is necessary to plan, to direct, to organize and to coordinate, but it is even more necessary to create conditions where spontaneous growth from below is possible and can take place.

It is not good enough often to sit in our offices and decide everything according to what we consider is the good of the people. I think the people themselves should be given the opportunity to think about it and thus they will affect our thinking as we affect their thinking. In this way, something much more integrated and living is produced, something in which there is a sense of intimate partnership—intimate partnership not in the doing of the job, but in the making of the job, in the thinking of the job.

Awakening a long-oppressed people, creating a new, vigorous, productive democratic society out of a generation of people who have never been permitted to practice democracy, out of a social order that is one of the most deeply stratified in the world, may have no precedent in history on the scale that India is attempting.

India realizes that to make its efforts successful will take new social attitudes, new understanding of voluntary leadership, of group dynamics, of social organization not only on the part of the people themselves, but on the part of those who must help awaken and guide the participation of the millions in city, town and village.

But India realizes as well that the partnership of the people in its great national endeavor determines, to a far greater degree than may be realized, the hopes of achieving both economic progress and social and political freedom.

8. *India will, in all its plans and policies, set as its highest single purpose the development of the individual, and his advancement in human freedom.*

Each development program of the Second Plan, in providing education, higher income and employment, better standards of health and housing, in improving rural life and the means of self-help, in strengthening self-government, has as its final focus the welfare and growth of the individual, the enrichment of the human spirit.

The Prime Minister has put India's purpose in the following words:

It is not enough for us merely to produce the material goods of the world. We want to produce the material goods of the world and to have a high standard of living, but not at the expense of the spirit of man, not at the expense of his creative energy, not at the expense of all those fine things of life which have ennobled man throughout the ages.

We have definitely accepted the democratic process . . . because we think that in the final analysis it promotes the growth of human beings and of society; because, as we have said in the preamble to our Constitution, we attach great value to individual freedom; because in the final analysis we want the creative and adventurous spirit of man to grow.[1]

Mahatma Gandhi believed that "the individual is the one supreme consideration." In all its planning, its means of development no less than its ends, India intends that this consideration will remain supreme.

Together these eight decisions form the underpinning of the Second Plan's aims, principles and methods, and of the planning for India's future. They are India's own decisions. They represent in some instances a marriage of imported knowledge with domestic necessity; others rise wholly from the Indian conditions and traditions.

Whatever their source, their character is shaped by India's needs, and the test of Indian principles. If some are pragmatic, or compromises unfamiliar to the West, India feels that for a nation in revolution, solutions as well as problems conform to no orthodox pattern. The only consistency lies in principles and objectives: to bring the Indian people forward to greater social and economic opportunities, and to secure social justice by peaceful democratic means.

[1] The Prime Minister to the All-India Congress, Indore, Jan. 4, 1957.

CHAPTER V

How India Plans

To India, planning is the strategy of forcing the pace of development. For those who have a long distance to cover there is no choice.

WHY PLANNING IS NECESSARY

Very wealthy countries, and countries already highly developed, have not felt it necessary to plan for future development except in a period of crisis, such as war. It is widely believed, however, that for nations with underdeveloped and stagnant economies, government planning is essential.

Action to awaken a stagnant economy involves a complex of steps —among them, developing natural resources, improving and expanding technical training and creating a body of trained manpower; building up organizations and institutions to serve as tools of development, such as a banking system and credit facilities to provide capital for farm and industry; land reforms; encouraging investment and risk-taking in productive enterprises; awakening a backward rural society.

None of these things can be done, unless they *are* done, by positive action. Simply *permitting* these things to happen cannot be expected to produce them in any short period, although it may over a long period, as in the one hundred years or more taken by most Western countries to develop. Industries, banks, universities, the farming community, which have long been static, cannot be expected suddenly to come to life, to adopt new methods and reforms (many of them costly and difficult to learn) rapidly and on a large enough scale.

A Government must have and use the power to plan the basic programs and reforms necessary, to stimulate and influence economic activity directly. The Government's administrative competence, its funds, its leadership, its coordination of all factors that make for growth, are the key to any major development effort. Growth is not likely to take place in spite of government, or under a poor or restrictive government.

Planning is not new to India. For nearly two decades before Independence, a series of plans, under the British Government, the Indian Congress Party and other sponsors, attempted to work out some solutions to India's overwhelming problems. Drawing up an India program for the six-year Colombo Plan was one of the first tasks of India's Planning Commission in 1950. The First and Second Plans are in part built upon these earlier plans.

For India, indeed, planning has long been considered a necessary function of government. As India sees the planning and development problems of other new countries, it feels fortunate that it had so much early preparation for planning, that the people so widely accept it, and that there is a continuity of approach, commonly understood and agreed upon by the people and their leaders in government, to planning needs and methods.

THE PLANNING COMMISSION

India set up its Planning Commission only a few weeks after it adopted its Constitution as an independent republic, in January 1950. This Commission in 1952 produced the final draft of the First Five Year Plan and in 1956 the Second Plan.

The Planning Commission was given, for guidance, the Directive Principles of the Indian Constitution—to promote the welfare of the people by securing social, economic and political justice. To win these objectives, the Commission's task is to assess the nation's resources, draw up a plan to use them with proper priorities and allocation, determine the conditions, machinery and adjustments needed to make the plan succeed; appraise the progress of the plan from time to time and make any recommendations necessary to facilitate it.

The Planning Commission's chairman is the Prime Minister of India. Among its seven members are three Cabinet Ministers, including the Finance Minister and the Minister for Planning, three other full-time members, and a Deputy Chairman. There are few other countries in which the Prime Minister himself chairs the planning body, and where members include Ministers with key responsibilities in the national Government. The Planning Commission's close links with the Finance Ministry [1] and with the Cabinet Secretariat have been of the greatest importance in assessing the financial requirements of the Plan.

The Commission's technical and economic staff, of about 250, is divided into sections dealing with each major part of national development—agriculture, health, industry, education, scientific and technical manpower, land reform, international trade and development, and others. These sections work closely with the relevant Ministries at the Center and in the States to review needs, programs and progress.

In drafting the national Plan, the Planning Commission acts primarily to establish national priorities, to balance the needs of dif-

[1] In India the Finance Ministry has a budgeting as well as a treasury function.

ferent parts of the economy, to recommend the size and broad directions of the activities to be taken up in each field, and to reconcile
the claims of the various Ministries in the Central and State Governments, the consumer needs of the people and the investment
needs of the economy, the needs of today and the needs of the
future. In doing so, it is the Commission's job to seek as much
guidance as possible from other agencies of government, from private
enterprise, and from informed persons outside government, so that
basic decisions and policies, and the final Plan itself, represent the
nation's best collective judgment and wisdom.

In estimating the nation's resources, the Planning Commission's
function, perhaps more than that of any other persons or agencies of
the Indian Government, is to foresee not merely the country's physical resources—so much coal or transport or steel—but also to estimate
how far the people themselves can progress and contribute, so that
the final Plan may reach not to the least but to the highest capacities
of a people joining in a great national endeavor.

Specific development programs for inclusion in the Plan come
largely from the States and Central Governments, not the Planning
Commission; although the Commission, with its view of the nation's
over-all needs, may suggest and help develop programs of national importance that should be adopted. All major new programs and policies
evolved by the Central and State Ministries, beyond those already in
the agreed-upon Plan, are generally discussed with the Planning Commission.

Unlike many other countries, India must carry out its planning
with and through a federal system in which the States are important
units in their own right. In planning both methods and aims, the
State structure is respected. State plans account for nearly half the
national planning budget; and it is these State plans and programs
which most directly and immediately affect the millions of people in
tens of thousands of villages.

Once formulated, the draft Plan is submitted to the National
Development Council, composed of the Chief Ministers of all States,
plus members of the Planning Commission, and the Prime Minister

as Chairman. The Council, which is taking an ever more significant role in national planning, was formed in 1952 specifically to review the working of the Plan, to consider important questions of national, social and economic policy, and to strengthen and mobilize the effort and resources of the nation in support of the Plan. Both the draft Plan and the final Plan are subject to review and change by the Council.

In the course of shaping the Plan, the Commission consults representatives of different groups in Parliament. At important stages, proposals are considered by the Cabinet, as by the National Development Council. Once the final Plan is approved by the Cabinet and Council, it is signed by the Planning Commission, and presented to Parliament. When approved by Parliament it becomes an operating document for both the Central Government and the States.

The Planning Commission functions are advisory. Administration of all programs is in the hands of the States and the Central Government. The Planning Commission has, however, advisers on program administration who tour the States, and continually assess progress and recommend any special action required to move the programs ahead. It also conducts information activities, to acquaint the people with the Plan and to stimulate public participation.

DRAFTING THE SECOND FIVE YEAR PLAN

At every stage the Planning Commission and the Central and State Governments deliberately and constantly seek to involve the Indian people in the planning of their own advancement.

The manner in which the Second Five Year Plan was prepared and presented illustrates methods of planning in a democracy.

Early in 1954 the Planning Commission asked the States to arrange that Districts and villages prepare plans for the Second Plan period (1956–61), especially in relation to local agricultural production, rural industries and cooperation. In general, this was done at the village level by councils of village leaders meeting with their project officers or District officials to decide the village's need of schools, culverts, minor irrigation works; at the District level, by District officials deciding on needed roads, bridges, District hospitals.

These plans formed some basis for the draft plans presented by State Governments to the Planning Commission. Though the total contribution to the national Plan may have been limited, the very process was an opportunity, perhaps unique on such a scale, for "grass-roots" participation in national planning.

During the same period the Planning Commission was drawing upon the analyses, proposals and experience not only of the various Central Ministries, but of the Central Statistical Organization (a Government body set up in 1951) and of the Indian Statistical Institute (a private independent organization); upon preliminary plans of the States and the Central Ministries; and upon the views of a considerable group of independent economists and technical experts, both Indian and foreign.

As a result of these mutual consultations, a rough outline of the framework of the Plan, as issued in March 1955, and a set of "working papers" were prepared. Their stated purpose was not to present a set of targets but the broad order of magnitudes involved—and thereby to start the process which would end in the formulation of the Plan.

The public was asked to study and comment upon these papers, and they were submitted to the panel of economists, outside the Government, for criticism. The Prime Minister, in submitting them to the National Development Council for review, said he attached "the greatest importance from now onwards to the public being associated with the Plan. This, I think, is the essence of what we call the people's Plan."

The press, members of political parties, business groups, individual economists, discussion forums, and simply private individuals responded in full to this invitation, and the volume of public interest and free comment on the proposed Plan has few parallels elsewhere.

Specific plans from the States, setting forth State needs, proposals and probable resources, came to the Planning Commission in July of 1955 and until October were discussed, coordinated and reconciled with national proposals, objectives and resources, in day-to-day consultations between State and Central Government officers and their counterparts in the Planning Commission. Discussions also took place between the Planning Commission and the Chief Ministers of the various States, with their colleagues.

The Plans of the several Central Ministries were similarly presented and discussed. These State and Central Ministry proposals are in general well prepared and presented. Since some of them called for two to three times more resources than were actually available, one of the chief tasks of the Planning Commission was to negotiate an acceptable balance, keeping national priorities and resources in view.

In early 1956 a draft memorandum was considered by the National Development Council, and finally a draft outline embodying the result of all these discussions and negotiations was made public. A fresh round of comment was invited from economists, Indian and foreign, from political parties, the press and the public, from a committee of Parliament members, a considerable number of foreign analysts, and finally from a full meeting of the National Development Council in late January.

The final Plan, approved by the Council in early May, was laid before Parliament on May 15. Parliamentary discussion on the Plan lasted over a period of several weeks and ended in the then expected ratification. Affirming "the common determination of the nation," Parliament called upon "all citizens of India to work wholeheartedly for the full and timely realization of the Plan's targets and aims."

While this process of democratic planning is unique in history, its result has been precisely what India hoped—that the Plan now accepted and in motion is not one imposed by a Central Government, but a matter of widest public participation and over-all agreement.

ANNUAL AND PERSPECTIVE PLANNING

The Planning Commission does not consider planning as a once-for-all exercise every five years. The Second Plan is to be kept flexible, and regarded as a broad framework for a series of annual Plans.

Under its First Plan, India did not prepare as such separate yearly

Plans. Annual Plans now, however, will make possible more rapid adjustments to economic and financial trends, to increases (or decreases) in agriculture and industrial production, to inflationary pressures or to food and other shortages, or shortage of foreign exchange, to new research and statistics that throw new light on old problems, to new technological developments. Continuing and healthy assessment of progress will help reveal what new means or incentives or leadership may be necessary to overcome weak or lagging spots in the total program.

To its annual and five-year planning periods, India is now adding "perspective planning." In a country just beginning development, especially heavy-industry development, planning must be keyed to goals over a ten- to twenty-year period. Heavy capital investment bears fruit only later on. Big irrigation and power projects or new steel plants require up to four years or more to come into full production.

The Commission must plan ahead for demands for certain goods and services that might arise as development proceeds—for steel, fertilizer and cement, or transport, natural resources, consumer goods. The Commission is now doing perspective planning for the next fifteen to twenty years for irrigation, for heavy industry, for transport, for manpower needs, for the potential production and demand of agriculture.

Regional planning is just beginning. Surveys have been launched to see how the now unequally developed regions of India may be brought into fairer balance, and integrated development within regions achieved.

STRENGTHENING PLANNING MACHINERY

Over India's First Five Year Plan, the nation and the people grew considerably in their understanding of the problems and needs of planning, far more aware of how it affects their lives and future, and of how they can contribute to it. State Governments and Ministries have developed greater skill in the techniques of planning, and are now far better organized to plan with assurance and accuracy.

As confidence has grown, the Planning Commission has, at the same time, given considerable thought to the fact that inevitably planning places power in the hands of the planners, of those who make the decisions which are the essence of planning. It realizes that if costly mistakes are to be avoided and the democratic process strengthened, planning machinery needs both direction and appropriate checks and balances, a steady improvement of research and information on which objective decisions may be based, a constant weighting of economic decisions with human and social judgment, and a constant broadening of the democratic base of planning.

The Commission is, therefore, strengthening planning machinery at all levels. The Commission itself is taking steps to see that development of all parts of the economy, particularly the growth of industry, transport and power taken together, and the growth of industry and agriculture, can be coordinated harmoniously. Priorities and allocation of resources, including raw materials, power, foreign exchange and manpower, are under constant review. The divisions on perspective and regional planning and on scientific and technical manpower were added in the fall of 1956, as were new units for international trade and development, and statistics and surveys.

Planning units were set up in most States during the First Plan period. These units plan largely through coordination with the various State Departments—Agriculture, Irrigation and Power, Industries, Education, Health, and so on.

Over the Second Plan, the planning job in the States will become larger and more and more complex. It will include measuring State needs for manpower and training, finances, raw materials, transport; gathering data on employment and prices, on small savings campaigns, on land reforms, and the like. The Planning Commission, therefore, has urged that State planning units be expanded and strengthened, and closer ties worked out with their State's economic and statistical staffs. It has also urged that the units more frequently consult with non-official State leaders such as the State's representatives in Parliament and others. This would parallel on the State level what the Planning Commission is now doing in the Central Government, in working frequently with especially designated consultative committees of Parliament members, as with other public and non-official leaders.

Under a new system, effective January 1957, Planning Commission advisers work with the States on yearly planning of development programs, and discuss State needs in relation to national needs before rather than after each State draws up its annual budget.

At the District and village level the Commission has, as we have seen, urged much greater emphasis on District planning, and on planning by village panchayats and development councils, with the active inclusion of local non-official leaders.

Planning for and with the private sector has been one of the difficult and weak spots revealed by the experience of the First Five Year Plan. When formulating the First Plan all that the Government attempted to do in regard to private industry was to make an estimate of what each industry was likely to do or could be expected to do.

As a means for planning for the private sector, it was decided that Development Councils be set up for individual industries, composed of people representing the interests of industry, labor, technicians, and so on. These Councils were to take responsibility for the planning and development of each industry and for keeping in close touch with progress in their industries. The Councils have not taken the shape contemplated. The Commission believes that more effective ways and means to plan with the private sector must be found.

RESEARCH AND EVALUATION

Over the Second Plan, a strong effort is being made to get more basic economic research done, and to collect statistical data necessary to give essential economic underpinning and conviction to some of the Plan's underlying assumptions, and to assess progress more sharply.

India has advanced greatly in economic and social research since the First Plan was drafted, and research and analytical data are now playing an increasing part in framing policies. The Planning Commission through its Research Programmes Committee, established in 1953, now finances and oversees an extensive body of research in private universities; more of the Ministries are adding research personnel; the Indian Statistical Institute and the Central Statistical Organization are doing extensive studies. A National Council of Applied Economic Research was formed as a private association early in the Second Plan period with encouragement of Government and private industry, to work both on Government and on private contracts.

The National Income Unit in the Central Statistical Organization, and the National Sample Survey, both set up at the beginning of the First Plan, have become significant fact-finding agencies, the first on income only, the second in a wide group of studies on employment, consumption, crop survey, manufacturing industries, and others. Another important research agency is the Agricultural Credit Department of the Reserve Bank. Noteworthy special studies on agricultural labor, on rural credit, on taxation, have been completed, adding significantly to India's more precise knowledge of these important economic and social problems.

Statistical work is also being strengthened in the States; State Statistical Bureaus work with the Central Statistical Organization to give a firmer basis for State planning.

Nevertheless, in many areas basic facts and studies are lacking, and economic studies play a relatively small role in determining investment priorities.

To build up India's now relatively short supply of trained economic personnel, special programs in economic and social research have been begun by five leading universities [1] and in the Indian Statistical Institute.

Within the Planning Commission the progress of the Plan is kept under continual assessment. The progress of rural development in particular is reviewed by a Programme Evaluation Organization, set up at the beginning of the rural development effort. The Evaluation Organization, which has field units, publishes periodic reports on the rural programs, as well as special analyses and studies of particular rural problems.

[1] The Universities of Delhi, Bombay, Utkal (Orissa), Punjab and Madras; also the Gokhale Institute of Economics and Politics, Poona.

On all phases of the Plan, the Indian Government also welcomes and encourages assessment by independent economists and other specialists, Indian and foreign, to a degree which may exist in few countries. Planning in India may indeed be most notably characterized by its constant effort to assess and re-assess, to shape and re-shape, to seek and take advantage of every useful democratic method which can bring rapid economic and social advancement to the Indian people.

INDIA'S SECOND FIVE YEAR PLAN:

◆ ADVANCE OF AGRICULTURE AND RURAL PEOPLE

All of rural India—325 million villagers—covered by the rural development program.

A 28 per cent rise in agricultural production, with a 25 per cent increase in foodgrains production alone.

21 million more acres put under irrigation.

Every cultivated acre supplied with fertilizers and improved seed.

Continued progress on land reform, and more opportunities for landless laborers.

◆ RAPID DEVELOPMENT OF INDUSTRY, POWER, TRANSPORT

A 64 per cent increase in (net) industrial production.

Intensive development of basic industries with a 150 per cent increase in capital goods production alone.

Three new steel plants, with over 230 per cent increase in steel production, including doubled private steel production.

Intensive development of village and small-scale industries, to increase their production by 30 per cent.

A 100 per cent increase in electric power production; and 58 per cent increase in coal production.

Modernization and improvement of railways to carry at least 35 per cent more freight and 15 per cent more passenger traffic.

Expanding transport, with 19,000 more miles of surfaced roads, and enlarged ports, harbors and shipping.

◆ FULLER EMPLOYMENT

10 million more jobs and employment opportunities.

An intensified manpower program to prepare and secure trained personnel for development.

Special programs for training and absorbing the educated unemployed.

TARGETS FOR INDIA'S GROWTH, 1956–1961

♦ HIGHER LIVING STANDARDS

An 18 per cent rise in income per person, or a rise from $56 a year (1956) to $66 (1961).

A 21 per cent increase in consumer goods, to include:

A 16 per cent increase in cloth available per person, or a rise from 16 yds. a year to 18 1/2 yds.

An adequate and more balanced diet, including not only cereals, but more milk, eggs, vegetables and fruits.

Primary school for nearly 8 million (23 per cent) more children.

Nearly 2 million (25 per cent) more homes.

12,500 (11 per cent) more doctors, and 3,000 more rural health clinics.

♦ MORE INCOME FOR NATIONAL DEVELOPMENT

Increased national production and income will make it possible to save larger amounts for investment in national development, at the same time that living standards rise.

At the end of the Second Plan, 11 per cent of national income, as against about 7 per cent at the end of the First Plan, is expected to be invested.

♦ WHAT THE PLAN WILL COST

Rs. 4,800 crores, or double the amount for the First Plan, will be spent by the States and the Central Government to achieve these goals.

Rs. 2,400 crores in addition is expected to be invested over the Second Plan by private enterprise in industry, agriculture and other development.

CHAPTER VI

The Second Five Year Plan
in Outline

The Second Five Year Plan, adopted by India's Parliament in September 1956, represents, then, the combined programs and projects, the mutual hopes and plans of the Indian people.

The actual Plan itself may be described and summarized in one of several ways. It may be presented as a group of the specific targets and objectives which India has set for itself over the five-year period. This gives, perhaps, the best bird's-eye view of the Plan as a whole, and its scope and purpose. A summary of these targets is given at the beginning of this chapter.

The Plan may also be presented as a summary of the major development activities and programs to be undertaken over the five-year period.

Later in this chapter there is given such a condensed summary of these major programs, together with the Government expenditures for each.[1]

The major development programs of the Second Plan are, as the summary shows: agricultural and rural development, irrigation and power, industry and mining, transport and communications, and what India calls social services—education, health, housing, labor, welfare of tribal people and the untouchables, and so on.

It is important to note that the Plan does not include the cost of maintaining regular Government programs, services and activities. Nor does it include even the cost of maintaining the special develop-- ment projects and programs begun in the First Plan and earlier, such as education, health, irrigation works, and the like, which have now become regular parts of India's services to its people.

The Plan represents only the *added* effort, the *new* development programs, the *new* stimulation that India proposes to push the nation and the economy forward.

Comparison of the Second Plan with the First shows the tremendous step-up in virtually every type of development activity, and some shift in emphasis between different types of programs. The biggest jumps are in rural development, in industry, large and small, and in transport.

The size of each program and its relative emphasis in the Plan reflect directly the basic decisions which India has taken as guides to all its planning: the advancement of India's rural people, the development of basic heavy industry, and of village and small industry, the lifting of living standards of the people through increased consumer goods and social services.

The doubled size of the Plan as a whole reflects, of course, India's basic decision to plan big and boldly, to give the utmost effort, the most powerful stimulus to India's growth.

Exactly what each development program includes, and its detailed

---

[1] Expenditures planned for the various development programs necessarily represent only those to be made by the State and Central Governments. Exactly what private enterprise may spend cannot, naturally, be detailed with the same certainty over five years as can budgeted Government expenditures. Expected private investment in various programs is given on p. 131.

targets, are given in later sections. The highlights of each program are as follows:

Agriculture and Rural Development

The Plan's two most significant programs are: first, to extend to all of village India (325 million people) a rural development program with a national agricultural extension service and system of self-help; second, to get the sharp 28 per cent increase in agricultural production absolutely essential to make the Plan as a whole succeed.

The two are very closely linked. The rural development program will, as it spreads over India, be used as the main instrument to raise agricultural production, as well as to create a vital, productive and democratic rural society.

To increase farm yields and incomes, the Second Plan will greatly expand irrigation, increase production and use of fertilizers and of imported seeds. Land reforms will be pressed further so that there are more equal land distribution and more incentives to produce. Co-operatives will be encouraged vigorously for farm marketing, credit and supply.

India hopes also for more diversified crops so that Indian diets will have more protective foods—more vegetables, fruits, dairy products, fish, meat and eggs. Programs for animal husbandry, fisheries, and so on have been stepped up markedly.

By all these means India hopes to step up farm incomes by 17 per cent by the end of the Plan, and double agricultural production in the next ten years.

Irrigation and Power

Twenty-one million more acres—nearly half as much as in all India's pre-Independence history—will be put under irrigation. Nine millions of these acres will be irrigated by new wells and other minor irrigation works, most of which will be built by villagers. The other 12 million acres will be watered by 195 new irrigation projects, concentrated on medium rather than large-scale projects, to be launched over the Second Plan.

Electric power production will be doubled. All towns of 10,000 population or over will be electrified, and 85 per cent of all towns of 5,000 to 10,000 population. About half of all power and irrigation expenditures will be used to carry on or complete large projects begun under the First Plan.

Industry and Mining

To build the industry basic to a modern economy, India will set up three new modern steel plants, and build the townships and train the workers and managers for them. Private steel manufacturers will be helped to double production, and steel output as a whole will be more than tripled. Three new fertilizer plants will be built, and steel foundries, and many heavy engineering and electrical equipment plants. Production of basic machinery and other capital goods is expected to increase by 150 per cent. Government expenditures for industry will be over four times higher than during the First Plan. Private enterprise will also invest heavily in basic industries. Industrial production [1] as a whole will go up by 64 per cent, and targets for many industries are double, and more than double, the production of the First Plan.

To provide raw materials for industry, mineral development is enormously stepped up, with a target of 58 per cent more production —or 22 million tons more of coal alone. A vigorous new program on mineral development will be put under way, principally on coal and lignite production and mineral surveys.

At the same time an intensive program to develop village and small industries will include a national industrial extension service network for small manufacturers and craftsmen, technical assistance, credit supply and marketing services. Government alone will spend four times more on small and village industry development than over the First Plan, and production from all small enterprises will go up by 30 per cent.

[1] Net.

DEVELOPMENT PROGRAMS OF THE SECOND FIVE YEAR PLAN

Showing Plan Budget Provisions, and Comparisons with First Plan [1]

	FIRST PLAN		SECOND PLAN		% INCREASE SECOND PLAN OVER FIRST PLAN
	Amount Rs. Crores	% of Total	Amount Rs. Crores	% of Total	
I AGRICULTURE AND RURAL DEVELOPMENT	357	15.1	568	11.8	59.1
Agriculture	241	10.2	341	7.1	41.5
Agricultural Programs	197	8.3	170	3.5	
Animal Husbandry	22	1.0	56	1.1	
Forests	10	0.4	47	1.0	
Fisheries	4	0.2	12	0.3	
Cooperation	7	0.3	47	1.0	
Miscellaneous	1	..	9	0.2	
National Extension and Community Projects	90	3.8	200	4.1	122.2
Other Programs	26	1.1	27	0.6	3.7
Village Panchayats	11	0.5	12	0.3	
Local Development Works	15	0.6	15	0.3	
II IRRIGATION AND POWER	661	28.1	913	19.0	38.1
Irrigation	384	16.3	381	7.9	
Power	260	11.1	427	8.9	
Flood Control, Investigations, etc.	17	0.7	105	2.2	
III INDUSTRY AND MINING	179	7.6	890	18.5	397.2
Large and Medium Industry	148	6.3	617	12.9	
Mineral Development	1	..	73	1.5	
Village and Small Industry	30	1.3	200	4.1	

IV TRANSPORT AND COMMUNICATIONS	557	23.6	1385	28.9	148.7
Transport	497	21.0	1309	27.3	163.4
Railways	268	11.4	900	18.8	
Roads	130	5.5	246	5.1	
Road Transport	12	0.5	17	0.4	
Ports and Harbor	34	1.4	45	0.9	
Shipping	26	1.1	48	1.0	
Inland Water Transport	..	..	3	0.1	
Civil Air Transport	24	1.0	43	0.9	
Other Transport	3	0.1	7	0.1	
Communications	60	2.6	76	1.6	26.7
Posts and Telegraphs	50	2.2	63	1.3	
Other Communications	5	0.2	4	0.1	
Broadcasting	5	0.2	9	0.2	
V SOCIAL SERVICES	533	22.6	945	19.7	77.3
Education	164	7.0	307	6.4	
Health	140	5.9	274	5.7	
Housing	49	2.1	120	2.5	
Welfare of Backward Classes	32	1.3	91	1.9	
Social Welfare	5	0.2	29	0.6	
Labor and Labor Welfare	7	0.3	29	0.6	
Rehabilitation of Displaced Persons	136	5.8	90	1.9	
Programs for Educated Unemployed	..	..	5	0.1	..
VI MISCELLANEOUS	69	3.0	99	2.1	43.5
TOTAL	2,356	100.0	4,800	100.0	103.7

83

¹ Figures given are for original First Plan allocations. During the First Plan period some adjustments were made in some programs. These are noted in later pages where specific programs are described.

Transport and Communications

To expand railways, roads, ports and harbors to carry the great increase in freight and passenger traffic expected in a fast-growing economy is one of the biggest tasks of the Second Plan. Railway expansion is particularly urgent. The amount of railway freight traffic that will need to be carried is expected by 1961 to be 50 per cent higher than in 1956, and even with the considerable expansion planned, the railways may be able to carry only 35 per cent more. Ports will be enlarged and shipping increased to help carry the increasing traffic. A network of motorable roads will also be expanded and 19,000 more miles of surfaced road will be built. A greatly expanded program for unsurfaced roads will work toward the goal of a road reaching every village in well developed agricultural areas.

In communications, the Government will greatly increase radio, telegraph and telephone facilities, with the aim of putting post-office and telegraph service within every five miles of every village.

Social Services

Education, health, housing and other social services will be expanded along with agriculture, industry and transport. All social services, taken together, will get nearly twice as much funds for development as under the First Plan.

Primary schools will bring 8 million more children (6 to 11 years) to school, and increase at about the same rate as over the First Plan. Secondary schools are to be improved in quality; there will be stress on multipurpose education rather than college preparation only. Colleges and universities will rapidly enlarge facilities for technical education, medicine, engineering, sciences—that is, the training of young men and women for the work of national development.

Special effort will be made to bring education to groups long underprivileged. Three million fellowships and scholarships for primary and secondary education, for example, are being made available to untouchables, or Harijans. Rural higher institutes are being set up to bring the benefits of higher education to the village people in terms of village needs and life.

In health, the top-priority programs include extending clinics and health services to rural areas, with particular stress on maternal and child care; improving water supplies and sanitation; making a wider and stronger attack on preventable diseases like malaria; and carrying rapidly forward a population control program.

Housing, social welfare, labor and other social service programs are to be expanded; all are described more fully in later chapters.

It is important to summarize what the Plan hopes to accomplish not only in specific programs and targets, but in some of its broadest objectives: in national production and income, in employment, in living standards, in the amount of savings that can be drawn off into investment in national development.

What the Second Plan Hopes to Accomplish in Production

A 25 per cent increase in total national output [1] is one of the four top objectives of the Second Plan. The comparable rise over the First Plan was about 18 per cent.[2] The production of more goods and services is the key to India's rise from poverty—to the creation of more wealth for all to share.

To achieve a total increase of 25 per cent, the Second Plan will push up production in every part of the economy. As we have seen, it expects a 64 per cent increase in net output by large industry, 30 per cent increase by small industry and enterprises. It expects farm production to go up by 28 per cent—an enormous increase from a once stagnant agriculture. Altogether by the end of the Plan, India's total national production will have gone up by about 40 per cent in the ten years since the start of the First Plan.

The following chart shows the production expected in each major section of the economy, and the proportionate change in each.

[1] Net.

[2] The First Plan's actual target was only 11%, as compared to the Second Plan target of 25%. The early target was substantially exceeded, the actual First Plan increase in output being about 18%.

RISING PRODUCTION: Ten Years of Growth, 1950-51—1960-61
(Net output in Rs. Crores, 1952–1953 prices)

Per Cent of Total

Agriculture

4,450	48.8
5,230 Up 18%	48.4
6,170 Up 18%	45.8

Commerce, Transport, Communications

1,650	18.1
1,875 Up 14%	17.4
2,300 Up 23%	17.1

Professions and Services, Government Administration, etc.

1,420	15.6
1,700 Up 20%	15.7
2,100 Up 23%	15.6

Large and Medium Industry

590	6.5
840 Up 43%	7.8
1,380 Up 64%	10.2

Small Industry and Enterprises

740	8.1
840 Up 14%	7.8
1,085 Up 30%	8.0

Construction

180	2.0
220–Up 22%	2.0
295–Up 34%	2.2

Mining

80	0.9
95–Up 19%	0.9
150–Up 58%	1.1

Total

9,110	
10,800–Up 18%	
13,480 Up 25%	

 1950-51   1955-56   1960-61

The chart makes clear that not only will production as a whole go up, but that over the Second Plan industry will contribute a distinctly larger share than ever before to India's total production, and agriculture proportionately less. In other words, the Second Plan will bring India a little further along in its journey from a predominantly agricultural nation.

What the Second Plan Hopes to Accomplish in Higher Incomes and Living Standards

As production goes up, a 25 per cent rise in national income is expected to result.

It is out of this sizable rise that India expects to be able to raise income per person, lift living standards, and at the same time increase the amount of funds available for investment in national development.

Generally speaking—in terms of the nation as a whole, not of any single group—the 25 per cent rise in national income will make possible an increase in consumer goods and services of about 21 per cent. The comparable increase in consumption over the First Plan was 16 per cent.

Higher living standards, expressed as consumer goods, will include 18½ yards of cloth per person as against 16 yards in 1956. It will include more food, and, if agriculture is more diversified as well as more productive, a more nutritionally balanced diet of pulses (legumes), milk, fats, fruits, vegetables and sugar as well as food grains.

Higher living standards will also come from the increase in health and education, housing and other social services.

We have already seen, however, that if foreign exchange is not available in the amount needed to help finance the Plan, India cannot raise living standards and production of consumer goods by 21 per cent. It must cut down the rate of increase in order to get adequate funds for development.

While national income and national living standards are rising, India's population will, of course, also be increasing.

The planned rise in income is, however, sufficiently large so that even for a larger number of people there will be more *per person*.

Income available *per person* will go up 18 per cent, or from Rs. 281 ($56) in 1955–1956 to Rs. 331 ($66). This compares with an increase in income available per person of 11 per cent over the First Plan.

Similarly, the *per person* increase in consumption will be about 13.3 per cent, as the larger number of people share in the increased output of consumer goods. This compares with about an 8 per cent rise over the First Plan.

What the Second Plan Hopes to Accomplish in Investment

Out of the 25 per cent higher income over the Second Plan, India expects a larger share than ever before to be available for investment in India's development, over and above the amount needed to raise income and living standards.

Out of the 25 per cent rise in income, 21 per cent is taken off for increased consumption, and the balance goes into investment in new industries, into irrigation and power development, into schools, roads, railways—the bones and sinews of economic and social growth.

By the last year of the Second Plan, 1960–1961, India hopes that 11 per cent of India's total income will be invested in national development. This includes investment both by government and by private enterprise, and compares with a rate of about 7 per cent at the end of the First Plan.

How much Government and private enterprise will invest in the Second Plan as a whole, and how much in industry, in agriculture, and so on, is shown in the chapter on financing the Plan. In total, Government investment will be 2½ times higher than in the First Plan, private investment 50 per cent higher. The ratio of total Government to total private investment will be roughly 3:2; this compares with an about equal investment by Government and private enterprise over the First Plan.

What the Second Plan Hopes to Accomplish in Employment

The Second Plan expects that its programs—for expansion of industry, transport, agriculture, and so on—will create 10 million new full-time jobs and employment opportunities. This compares with about 4.5 million jobs created by India's growth and development over the First Plan.

Sizable as this number of 10 million new jobs is, it will still be only just enough to absorb the new people who will be seeking work—the young men and women who will, over the Second Plan, come of the age to need employment.[1] It will not reduce the size of India's present high unemployment backlog—another indication of how very fast India has to run even to stand still.

Any basic solution to India's deep-seated problem of unemployment can only be expected over a long period. The most that can be hoped for in the next five years is that the Second Plan will prevent any worsening of unemployment, while India develops some basic industries and small and rural industries, and begins other large development works which will eventually step up all employment.

For the large number of people who now have only part-time work, the Second Plan expects that irrigation projects, small and cottage industries, and agricultural development will give the now underemployed some increase in work and income.

A very considerable share of the increase in employment under the Plan is expected to come from the expansion in private enterprises, with self-employment in cottage, small and medium industries playing an important part. The fact that village and small-scale industry is expected to provide half a million new jobs makes clear a major reason for the effort to develop these industries.

What the Plan Will Cost

The Second Plan will, as we have seen, cost the Indian Government a total of Rs. 4,800 crores ($9.6 billion), which is about 2½ times the

---

[1] Yearly population increases in India are now about 4.5 to 5 million a year. About 2 million people a year reach the age to need employment.

figure for the First Plan. Of this, the State Governments will put in about half, the Central Government about half.

In addition to this Rs. 4,800 crores of Government funds, about Rs. 2,400 crores is expected to be invested by private enterprise.

The Second Plan is big, and its cost high in relation to India's resources, but it is small still in relation to India's needs. For example, even though health programs will get double as much as under the First Plan, the amount is only a third as much as is needed to provide a reasonable standard of maternal and child care, malaria control, pure water supply, and medical services in rural areas.

As another example, the Education Ministry estimates that Rs. 1,000 crores would be needed to fulfill the Indian Constitution's requirement for universal primary school education—or more than a fifth of total expenditure planned by the Government for all purposes.

Expenditure on the Plan will not, of course, constitute total Government expenditures. National defense, general Government administration, basic postal services, the carrying on of development programs begun in the First Plan or earlier are not included. The Plan represents only a little over half of India's total Government expenditures.

The Indian Government in its Second Plan has set itself high and bold targets. It recognizes that to achieve them successfully will require the highest degree of organization, of administrative and managerial competence, and efforts beyond efforts from Government, from private enterprise and the Indian people.

The Government recognizes too that if India achieves every target of the Second Five Year Plan by 1960–1961, it will still be a very poor country, with average incomes far below those of Japan today, to say nothing of Europe and the United States.

But by pressing ahead to win its targets, India will by 1961 have made its first real breach in the barrier of poverty, its first real beginning on the difficult and tremendous journey to development.

CHAPTER VII

Employment and Manpower in India's Development

India's greatest potential resource is its 384 million people; its greatest challenge is to put their energies and skills to work rebuilding the nation and fulfilling their own aspirations.

At present, India is faced with a seeming paradox. On the one hand there is acute and chronic unemployment; on the other there is a severe shortage of trained men and women—of doctors, skilled workers, artisans, teachers, scientists, engineers, nurses.

For the Second Plan, then, the immediate question is one of creating employment. The broader question is how, at the same time, to recruit, to train, and to use the kind and number of people needed at every level now and in the future for the vast and complex task of development.

Put briefly, India's manpower problem is one of quantity, quality and organization.

EMPLOYMENT

Creating new employment is one of the key objectives of the Second Plan. Heavy unemployment and underemployment in the cities and the villages are easily among India's most serious human and social problems.

For India and other undeveloped countries with vast rural populations, densely pressed on the land, the task of creating new employment is of great complexity. Certainly there is no easy solution; above all there is no quick solution.

As we have seen, for India anything approaching full employment can only be achieved over a period of time, after intensive development yields new industries, new opportunities for jobs in construction, in transport and communications, in rural development programs, in health, education and other services.

While India must always keep in sight the country's future needs, and train men and women for the kinds of jobs that will develop as India progresses, its employment policies, certainly over the Second Plan, and no doubt over the immediate future Plans as well, must be keyed to the needs of the transition period. As such, they must inevitably involve solutions and even compromises not familiar in the West.

These solutions require new imaginative approaches to employment, the constant view that India's vast pool of manpower is not a problem but a resource. It calls for solutions, not alone in statistical terms of how much financial investment will produce how many jobs but above all in human and social terms, of how the creative energies and skills of the Indian people may be released and guided to the work of the nation.

Here the answers lie as much if not more in social as in economic factors—in the confidence and enthusiasm of the people, in the human and social skills of every development officer, administrator, and village extension worker, in the growth of local leadership and of effective forms of social organization; as well as in providing technical help, funds, stimulus for specific development activities large and small, individual and cooperative.

As India works toward these ends, it must at the same time, during this transition period, assess its specific employment needs and how it may solve them.

These needs are three. First, jobs must be made available for those who each year will come of age to seek work. Second, India must develop job opportunities for those who are now unemployed, both in the cities and in rural areas. Finally, opportunities for additional work must be created for those who are *under*employed, that is, those who have employment for only part of the time they wish and need to work.

A special problem, felt chiefly in the cities, is that of the educated unemployed.

It will be useful to get some picture of the size and character of each of these problems, in so far as facts are available.

While there is no India-wide survey giving precise figures, India's total labor force—the number of people at work and needing work—is now estimated to be at least 154 millions. Over the Second Five Year Plan, at least 10 million more people, or 2 million a year, will come of the age to need and look for employment. This is believed to be a conservative estimate.

Unemployment figures are at best only estimates, but it is believed that about 5.3 millions have no employment. This is the most conservative figure. The number who are *under*employed is known to be very much larger.

Of the 5.3 million of unemployed, about half (2.5 million) are in the cities, although cities represent but a sixth of the total population. On the average about one in ten of the city working population is unemployed.[1] The number of persons *under*employed (those who work a quarter or less of the time they are willing to work) is three or four times the number of wholly unemployed. Unemployment and

---

[1] In Calcutta, where refugees continue to flood in from East Pakistan, it may be as high as one in five.

underemployment taken together affect at least one out of five in the cities' labor force.

These high figures reflect the ceaseless tide of migration from the villages. Nearly half of the city unemployed are villagers seeking city jobs for the first time.

How high unemployment is in the villages is not known precisely, but it is certainly very high. Estimates put rural unemployment at 2.8 millions. Among agricultural laborers unemployment is as high as 16 per cent.

Rural *under*employment is widespread. Agricultural laborers *average* 82 days without work per year; some, in southern and western India, average over 110 days—or about a third of a year—without work. The International Labor Office estimates that "disguised unemployment" (persons seemingly at work but whose production is marginal) in rural areas runs as high as 15.5 million persons. Stated another way, one-fourth to one-third of all of India's agricultural workers are believed to be "surplus" to the needs of farming under present farming methods and conditions.

Taking the conservative figures for the 10 million who will seek work over the next five years and the number of now unemployed in city and village, the Planning Commission estimates that 15.3 million new full-time jobs would have to be created over the Second Plan to wipe out unemployment. The total amount of work needed by the *under*employed cannot be clearly estimated, but is obviously very considerable.

It is not of course possible or even necessary at this stage in India's development to wipe out unemployment completely. Nor is any highly developed country even at the peak of "full employment" without some unemployment.

Over the Second Plan India expects so to plan its development programs and so to direct and encourage investment that 10 million new full-time jobs will be created, and considerable part-time employment.

In this effort India will be guided by three general principles:

1. The Second Plan will bring about some small shift into non-

agricultural occupations from the present excessive dependence on agriculture.

2. It will give emphasis and inducement to development programs and techniques which use a maximum amount of labor, assuring at the same time that basic mechanized industries vital to the country's swift growth are being established, and that more productive techniques are adopted as rapidly as possible.

3. It will provide, in its rural and industrial programs and elsewhere, the means and stimulus to self-help, and to the creative participation and initiative of the people themselves, in both individual and cooperative work, for developing their farms, their homes, their villages and their enterprises.

The solution to the problem of rural unemployment and underemployment lies in the long run in a shift from excessive dependence on agriculture toward jobs outside agriculture. The Second Plan hopes, as we have seen, to start this shift as it channels and encourages investment to non-agricultural development projects. While village industries are one essential source of employment in this transition period, in the long run jobs must be created in large and small-scale industry, in construction, transport and communications, and services.

Since India is, however, and will remain in the foreseeable future a predominantly agricultural economy, the problem of rural employment will continue to be one of the highest importance. Mahatma Gandhi called it in 1926 India's "problem of problems." Today as well, the productive use of a vast unemployed and partially employed force of rural workers undoubtedly constitutes one of India's sharpest social and political challenges.

India has already had some valuable experience with using large groups of rural laborers, in voluntary but paid employment, under the direction of private voluntary agencies, in large construction projects such as building an embankment to retain the destructive Kosi River, and work on the Yamuna River bund.

While such means can be more fully explored and used, the solution lies also in some reorganization of agricultural production. India's efforts and proposals toward agrarian reorganization, suited to its own conditions and its choice of democratic means, are discussed in a later chapter.

Under its present programs for agricultural development, the Second Plan expects to create 1.6 million to 2 million new full-time jobs in agriculture. These jobs will be measured more in terms of income and work opportunities than of specific employment. For instance, the spread of irrigation will make possible two or more annual harvests. Various land reclamation and minor irrigation and similar schemes will give actual new employment. Agricultural income per occupied person is likely to go up by 17 per cent.

Creating employment both in rural areas and in the cities involves, in this transition period, important decisions as to the types of development activities to be chosen for investment, in terms of the employment each may yield. It involves some choices as between those techniques using much labor and those using a higher degree of mechanization.

Compared to the need for jobs, the new large-scale industries, although they are laying the foundation for future growth, will not, over the Plan years, absorb large numbers of workers. It should also be remembered that in the highly industrialized United States, only about 17 million persons are employed in manufacturing.

The new steel and other plants, moreover, of both Government and private enterprise, are necessarily to be of the most advanced type and include some automation. For example, steel production by the end of the Second Plan will be well over three times higher than in 1956, but it will employ only about twice (30,000 more) as many workers as at present. Basic industries are so essential, however, to the ultimate productive capacity of the nation that investment in them cannot be questioned.

The principal sources of new employment outside agriculture, for India as for all developed countries, is construction. Government and private enterprise together will invest enough in construction to create almost a fifth of all the new jobs expected over the Second Plan.

In construction work, however, machinery will be used where needed for technical reasons, and also for relieving the social cost of arduous human labor and for completing the projects quickly. Rapid completion of irrigation projects, for example, with the help of machinery as well as hand labor, brings more rapidly the benefits of larger crops and higher rural incomes.

Where machinery is not needed for these reasons, in other types of construction, and in transport and communications, as well, a choice must be made between hand labor and machinery.

The principal point at which difficult issues arise in the choice between highly mechanized techniques and those using much hand labor is in production of consumer goods. For India, as noted earlier, the problem is twofold. Modern machinery is on the one hand costly in capital (usually in scarce foreign exchange), and on the other it displaces workers who have in any case to be provided employment— or a dole.

India's solution in this transition period is, as we have seen, to emphasize and encourage development of the traditional hand industries. These are of particular importance in giving new full-time and considerable new part-time employment in rural areas.

For mechanized industries producing the same goods as the traditional industries, India has had to balance the country's needs for employment on the one hand and for production on the other. Of special interest perhaps is the significant and often controversial case of cotton textiles. While the larger part of the total yardage needed over the Second Plan has been allocated to the mechanized textile mills, a substantial part has at the same time been reserved for the hand-loom and power-loom weavers. The majority of weavers live in rural areas, and about 2 million will have employment producing the cloth expected. In textile mills only 760,000 workers will produce 3½ times as much cloth.

It is interesting to recall here the classic emphasis of Mahatma Gandhi on cottage industries, and especially on hand spinning, as means of giving work to rural people.

Calling their enforced idleness India's "tremendous tragedy," he said: "The sole claim advanced on behalf of hand-spinning is that it alone offers an immediate, practicable, and permanent solution of that problem of problems that confronts India, viz. the enforced idleness for nearly six months in the year of an overwhelming majority of India's population, owing to lack of a suitable supplementary occupation to agriculture, and the chronic starvation of the masses that results therefrom." [1]

As noted earlier, every effort will be made in hand-loom production and in all hand industries to develop improved and more productive methods, including simple machinery, to assure that employment is not secured at the sacrifice of rising production.

By stimulating investment in all techniques and programs which will create employment, the Second Plan expects its 10 million new full-time jobs to develop in these activities and services:

NEW EMPLOYMENT OVER THE SECOND PLAN

	THOUSANDS
1. Construction	2,100
2. Industries and Minerals	750
3. Cottage and Small-Scale Industries	450
4. Professional and Government Services	434
5. Rural Development, Forestry, Fisheries, and allied Agricultural programs	413
6. Education	310
7. Railways	253
8. Other Transport and Communications	130
9. Other Social Services	142
10. Health	116
11. Irrigation and Power	51
12. Plus "Others," including trade and commerce (@ 52% of total 1 to 11)	2,704
13. Agriculture	1.6 to 2 million
TOTAL	9.6 to 10 million

Ten million new jobs is an enormous number to be created in five years in any country.

A comparison with the United States may give some idea of the size of the problem. The United States is not now deliberately trying to stimulate employment as India is today and as the United States did in the 1930's. But it is interesting to note that employment in the

[1] *Young India*, Oct. 21, 1926.

United States, in the present very rapidly expanding economy, rose by 2.2 million over the five years from 1951 to 1955. Over India's First Plan, that is, roughly over the same period, 4.5 million jobs were created (not counting trade and commerce); more than twice as many jobs must be developed over the Second Plan.

Ten million new jobs will be, however, just sufficient to absorb the new people who will be seeking work for the first time over the Plan years. Thus the Second Plan will not cut into the backlog of the present unemployed, but it will at least prevent unemployment from growing worse. And, through village and small industries, construction works and other short-term labor, it will provide considerable new part-time employment both in cities and in rural areas.

The Second Plan will also begin for the first time in fifty years, barring the two war periods, to increase the proportion of persons employed outside agriculture. And it will lay the foundation in industry and elsewhere which will expand employment over the future.

Regional Unemployment

In certain areas of India, chiefly those with few natural resources, or with very large populations, chronic underemployment exists, and incomes fall well below the all-India average. Migration of surplus labor is not a generally workable solution, for language differences and other reasons. Surveys of local resources, skills and facilities are being undertaken, and area employment is one of the problems which will be kept in view in regional planning.

The Educated Unemployed

A special problem for India, as for some other underdeveloped countries, is that of the "educated unemployed." The "educated" are defined as those with high-school education or better. In January 1956 a special study group appointed by the Planning Commission estimated educated unemployment at over half a million (550,000).

Nearly one out of every ten graduates, and one of six of all those with secondary education but below the college level, are unemployed. Employment surveys show that the general education level among the urban unemployed is considerably higher than that of the employed. The situation is particularly serious in large cities where over one-fourth of all the unemployed are "educated."

The problem is not a new one in India, but has been growing more acute over the last three decades. The reasons for it are several. Total college enrollment has been going up rapidly—about 80 per cent since 1950–1951 alone. The great majority of the graduates have only general education rather than technical training.

Moreover, or partly as a result, a very large number of the educated unemployed seek white-collar jobs, two-thirds of them in administrative, executive or clerical work. Relatively few seek business opportunities on their own. Their preference is for Government service, which still today, as under the British, has the highest social and professional prestige and security.

From estimates made for the Planning Commission by the Special Study Group, 1.5 million more "educated" persons will have finished their studies and be looking for work over the next five years. Adding the half-million "educated" now unemployed, there will thus be a need for 2 million jobs suitable for the educated over the Second Plan.

The Planning Commission estimates that the regular requirements in Central and State Government service will total about one million jobs. Private enterprise is expected to absorb about 200,000; another 240,000 jobs will be available through deaths and retirement. These estimates, should they be borne out, would leave a half-million educated unemployed in 1961—or no advance from the present situation.

The large group of educated unemployed represents both social waste and unrest. The Special Study Group has proposed three types of special short-term measures to provide more employment, in addition to programs of State Governments.

These are: (1) work and orientation camps, where, in useful constructive work, vocational aptitudes may be discovered and new respect gained for manual work; (2) intercity motor freight transport—a much needed service in view of India's transport shortage, for which groups of young men, organized in cooperatives, could secure Government financing; (3) increasing entry into small business, also with some Government financial assistance.

During the first two years of the Second Plan, pilot projects in all these fields are being started; those which prove most successful will be expanded.

The final solution to the problem lies of course in adapting the Indian education system to the needs of national development, and in establishing methods of training and recruitment that will use to the full the capacities and energies of India's young men and women.

As the Plan makes a direct attack on these and other specific employment problems, it will also do something else which cannot be directly measured or predicted now in terms of precise number of new jobs, but whose effect on employment will be as profound as it is incalculable. That is the stimulus it will give to the initiative and creative energies of the people themselves, to find constructive work and create employment opportunities either individually or in co-operation with others.

Clearly a very important factor in both city and village has been that the unemployed and underemployed have not had the means or in a life of bare survival, incentives for self-employment.

For example, a farmer unemployed out of harvest season might, if he had credit and technical help and stimulus, build a well or irrigation bund, or start some small enterprise, and thus employ not only himself and family but possibly other laborers besides. Similarly, if a village is assisted with some funds and technical help, with stimulus and guidance, it can give considerable voluntary or even paid employment in building schools, roads and maternity centers.

The chief effort of India's rural development program and its village and small industry programs, and indeed of the Plan as a whole, is to provide such means and stimulus to self-help and initiative. Apart from the specific rural program, its loans and technical help for farm improvements, and the loans and guidance available under the village-industries program, the Second Plan has also set aside Rs. 15 crores for local development works to be undertaken by the communities themselves.

The experience of the First Plan showed that, with such help, India's great resource of the energies, skills and manpower of its people can become a creative instrument of development, the very means by which the people can achieve their own aspirations. As yet the use of this great resource has only begun.

The powerful stimulus of India's plans for development, of growing confidence in India's future, of readily available financial and technical help, of rising incomes and production will increasingly result in hundreds of thousands of individual decisions to find constructive work, to initiate new enterprises, to create new opportunities. It is these decisions which characterize a dynamic and vital democratic society, and which in an awakening India hold a vast and incalculable promise for the use of India's potential resource—the skills and energies of its people.

TRAINED MANPOWER

At the same time that it has large unemployment, India has, like all countries today, a serious shortage of technically trained men and women. To India, the problem is of special urgency. The nation can develop and go ahead only as fast as trained people are available to man the new steel plants, the schools, the health services and the agriculture program.

Very rapid action is needed to provide trained people—not only for the Second Plan but also for the future. Every young man and woman entering technical training this year is a resource not for the Second Plan but for the Third and Fourth.

Some progress has already been made over the First Plan in technical training. But even with these gains the pace of training of the Second Plan must be much faster.

The Second Plan has launched a big program of technical education and training which will cost the Government well over Rs. 100 crores.

The chief responsibility for expanding technical education on an all-India basis falls on the Education Ministry. It has large funds

(Rs. 52.5 crores) specifically for the purpose, and will also use the major part of its university funds for technical education.

Other Ministries, such as Labor, Railways, Iron and Steel, Health and Agriculture, are also expanding and strengthening technical training in their fields to staff their own development programs.

TRAINED MANPOWER – More Skills for India's Growth

Engineers   🯅 =30,000 engineers

1950-51 ᵢ 3,758
1955-56 🯅 🯅 56,000
1960-61 🯅 🯅 🯅 🯅 118,000

Rural Extension Workers*   🯅 =30,000 rural extension workers

1950-51 Negligible
1955-56 🯅 15,500
1960-61 🯅🯅 38,000

Trained Teachers†   🯅 = 30,000 trained teachers

1950-51 🯅🯅🯅🯅🯅 🯅🯅🯅🯅🯅 🯅🯅🯅🯅🯅 429,000

1955-56 🯅🯅🯅🯅🯅 🯅🯅🯅🯅🯅 🯅🯅🯅🯅🯅 🯅🯅🯅🯅🯅 🯅🯅 633,000

1960-61 { 🯅🯅🯅🯅🯅 🯅🯅🯅🯅🯅 🯅🯅🯅🯅🯅 🯅🯅🯅🯅🯅
          🯅🯅🯅🯅🯅 🯅🯅🯅🯅🯅 🯅🯅🯅 } 1,013,000

Doctors   🯅 = 30,000 doctors

1950-51 🯅 🯅 59,000
1955-56 🯅 🯅 🯅 70,000
1960-61 🯅 🯅 🯅 82,500

Nurses   🯅 = 30,000 nurses

1950-51 🯅 17,000
1955-56 🯅 22,000
1960-61 🯅🯅 31,000

* Village extension workers for the rural development program.
† The total *need* for trained teachers in 1960–1961 will be about 1,365,000. Of these, however, only 1,013,000 or four-fifths will be *trained* teachers; the others will serve without training.

ENGINEERING PERSONNEL

The Second Plan's steel mills, transport, power and irrigation projects, fertilizer plants and heavy manufacturing industries will require very large numbers of skilled engineers—as many as 36,000 when the projects are in full operation.

Large numbers are needed elsewhere as well—in all types of construction: buildings, roads, ports, schools, and so on.

Fortunately, the shortage of competent engineers and scientists was felt early. Under the First Plan the number of trained engineers more than doubled, and many new training schools and colleges were started.

The Education Ministry will spend virtually all the funds which are provided for technical training to expand training in engineering and technology still more. By the end of the Second Plan, nearly a third more engineers (graduates and diploma holders) will be finishing training each year, or 11,000 altogether. After 1960–1961 the output will be more than double that of 1955–1956.

The Second Plan will: expand further the Indian Institute of Technology (Kharagpur), which has been brought to a high professional level over the First Plan; set up three similar institutes in west, north and south; expand the Indian School of Mines and Applied Geology (Dhanbad); increase the number of all engineering institutions from 128 to a minimum of 153; take measures to strengthen quality of training. India's total output over the Second Plan is expected to be 24,000 graduate engineers and about 30,000 diploma holders.

Even with all these measures, the Engineering Personnel Committee believes that the need for engineers will exceed supply every year of the Second Plan. By 1961 they expect a shortage of about 9,800 trained men. Other estimates indicate that the shortage will come sooner and be larger than the Committee expects, as it has in every country undergoing rapid economic growth.

A special problem for India is providing practical training for its engineers; the particularly urgent need is for training of staff for the new steel and heavy engineering plants. Over 2,000 skilled staff are needed. While India's few steel manufacturers are cooperating, the number of trainees is so large that foreign training will be necessary. Under the present plans, the United States is now training 200, and may train as many as 900; others will be trained in the United Kingdom, the Soviet Union, West Germany, Canada and Australia.

Training in irrigation and power plant construction, in production of fertilizer and DDT, and in shipbuilding will be done in the Government-owned plants and projects.

For scientists, a new scientific personnel committee has recently been set up to study India's needs now and over the future and to plan for high-quality training, and to consider, as well, the use and relationships of scientists in Government service.

Skilled and Semi-Skilled Workers

Besides highly trained engineers, India needs a vast number of skilled and semi-skilled workers. On rough estimates, it needs almost as many *new* workers of this kind over the Second Plan alone as there were in the entire labor force in 1956—750,000 *new* workers over the five years, as compared with an 825,000 total labor force in 1956.

Training this vast number is a staggering problem. Present training programs can turn out only 32,000 a year, or only somewhat more than a fifth of those required. Although all training will be expanded, it will still fall far short of need.

Vocational training is handled by many agencies, public and private. The most organized system of training is maintained by the Ministry of Labor. It turns out some 10,000 craftsmen a year.

Over the Second Plan the Ministry will triple the number trained as a "modest beginning" on the problem. Apprenticeship programs in both public and private industry will train 7,000 craftsmen each year, but steps are being taken to promote such training on a much larger scale in private industry. Evening classes, run either by the Government or by private industry, will give over 3,000 workers opportunity to train for higher levels of skill, and the program is being stepped up.

Over the future an important part of the problem is to shape secondary education so that it can help produce high-school graduates whose education includes, or can readily be supplemented by, technical training. The new multi-purpose high schools are an important step in this direction.

Craftsmen, artisans and business managers are also needed for village and small-scale industry. The Second Plan expects 450,000 new employment opportunities to be created in these smaller industries; a large proportion of the people needed must have some skill and training. Under present plans of the State and Central Governments, 30,000 persons at all levels will be trained through training-production-extension centers, polytechnics, small industry service institutes, model and mobile workshops.

AGRICULTURAL PERSONNEL

Under the First Plan agricultural education took a long jump forward. With new emphasis on the practical needs of the village farmer, no less than 130 entirely new institutions were started to train workers at all levels for the rural development program.

Three new agricultural colleges were set up; twenty-one colleges added, for the first time, some systematic extension training; five have established regular extension departments. The training of 15,000 village-level extension workers, involving the establishment of a completely new India-wide network of training centers, is one of the First Plan's outstanding achievements.

The Second Plan will require far more trained agricultural workers than the First.

Needed for rural development during the next five years are about 6,500 college graduates in various agricultural specialties; 5,000 veterinary graduates; about 48,000 rural extension workers [1] at all levels; 25,000 people to engage in expanded cooperative programs. Even these estimates may be low, and an Agricultural Personnel Committee has been set up to make a careful study of India's needs, both for the Second and for the Third Plans.

The Second Plan will increase and expand the agricultural colleges, add four new veterinary colleges and a dairy science college, run multiple shifts of trainees, raise the number of extension training

[1] Includes 11,400 group-level workers.

centers and basic agricultural schools to 160 from the present 98. India recognizes it will be a constant and real problem to improve and keep up the quality of training with such quick expansion.

INDUSTRIAL AND BUSINESS MANAGEMENT

India's new industries will need hundreds of top and middle-level managers and executives. Training men of this caliber is a major problem, both for the Government and for private enterprise. Many of the skills necessary are not only technical or administrative, but human and social skills. A government committed to democratic methods is under special obligation to see that it has enlightened and highly capable leadership at all levels in industries that it operates.

Since there is limited large-scale industry in India, there is no large pool of skills on which to draw. For example, India's steel plants are going to expand themselves, and cannot supply any important number of managers at any level for the new Government plants.

Under the Ministry of Education, a plan for management education and training, covering industrial engineering, industrial administration and business management, has been started in seven selected centers; a Board of Management Studies has been set up to coordinate training; a National Institute of Management is being established. Junior-level training in business management has been set up in Bombay, Delhi, Madras and Calcutta. Plans are under discussion for a high-level Institute of Business Administration at Bombay, and an Administrative Staff College patterned generally after Henley in the United Kingdom is getting under way at Hyderabad. The new steel and other large plants also will send top-level men overseas for management as well as technical training.

The Government has also created, as a new arm, so to speak, of the administration, an Industrial Management Service. This will be a pool of trained men for both State and Government-owned industries.

The Second Plan expects all these measures, taken together, to make at least a good start on providing top-quality business and industrial management—a problem with which both Government and private enterprise must increasingly concern itself.

HEALTH PERSONNEL

Shortage of doctors, nurses, midwives, sanitarians—indeed, all categories of health workers—is, second to cost, the major obstacle to providing even minimum health care for India's rural people.

During the First Plan years, there was one doctor to every 6,200 people in India, compared to 1 to 1,000 in Japan. The majority of doctors, moreover, practice in the cities where earnings and living conditions are most favorable.[1] Shortage of other trained medical workers is even more marked, and likely to persist longer, partly due to lack of facilities for training, in larger part to lack of candidates.

As in the West a century ago, nursing and similar health work is only slowly becoming a socially accepted or adequately paid occupation for women. In 1956 there were roughly only a fourth as many nurses and other auxiliary health workers as were needed.

For training more doctors, first priority in the Second Plan is given to expanding the present thirty-six medical colleges and their attached hospitals so that they may take at least a hundred students each; some have been able to take only half that number. In addition, ten new medical colleges will be set up.

Efforts will also be made to raise the quality of medical training. Medical colleges are now staffed, on the clinical side, by teachers who are working on a part-time basis. This has considerably affected the quality of teaching.

In order to raise standards of undergraduate and graduate education and research, the Second Plan will make it possible for departments of almost all medical colleges to have a full-time non-practicing staff. All colleges will add Preventive Medicine and Psychiatric departments; the Institute of Medical Science will be completed.

There are only 600 to 700 qualified dental surgeons in India; and only six dental colleges, all below standard. The Second Plan provides Rs. 2 crores to raise standards of dental training, add four new colleges and double total admissions.

To provide more nurses and all other health workers the Second Plan allots Rs. 6 crores for training programs which will use the

[1] In rural areas there was by 1957 only 1 doctor to 15,000.

medical colleges and hospitals, as well as establish new training centers.

By the end of the First Plan, India had only 25 per cent as many health workers (other than doctors) as it needed. By the end of the Second Plan it will have 40 per cent. This is an advance—but it shows the distance yet to go.

TEACHERS

India, like most countries the world over today, has a shortage of trained teachers. While the number of teachers (primary and secondary) increased by 40 per cent over the First Plan, over the Second Plan it must rise by at least another 30 per cent to meet the need.

For India, quality of teachers is a problem too—for over one-third of all primary and nearly half of all secondary teachers have no formal training for the job.

The Second Plan will greatly expand teacher training—a 24 per cent increase in the number of teacher training institutions, a 30 per cent increase in enrollment. Altogether some 420,000 teachers will be trained over the five-year period. This will not only be enough to man the new schools and fill vacancies, but to raise considerably the proportion of trained teachers.[1]

The future needs for teachers are enormous. Even by the end of the Second Plan only half of India's children below fourteen will be in school; and one-half the job of providing schools and teachers for them remains to be done over future Plans.

A special problem is training of women teachers. In sharp contrast to many other countries, women teachers are less than a fifth of the total in India, and girls' education lags far behind. The Third and future Plans will concentrate largely on girls' education, and the women teachers for that program must be put in training over the next five years.

ADMINISTRATIVE PERSONNEL

Government is bound to grow as the nation develops, as it has in the United States and elsewhere. In every field of Government service

[1] Proportion of trained primary teachers in 1950–1951 was 59 per cent; in 1955–1956, 64 per cent. By the end of the Second Plan it will be 79 per cent.

there is now and long will be a great shortage of men and women competent to fill the hundreds of new key posts in Government—at both senior and junior levels—and to speed execution of development plans. Competition for exceptionally able young Government servants will increase. Old personnel recruitment and training policies, keyed to a day of surplus rather than of shortage, are being revised as part of the over-all problem of administration, discussed in the following chapter.

ORGANIZATION

Within the first months of the Second Plan, the Government took the significant decision to set up a high-level Government group to form major manpower policies for the nation, and to give coordination and leadership to nation-wide manpower policies and programs.

In September 1956 a Manpower Committee chaired by the Prime Minister was established in the Cabinet, and a Directorate of Manpower Coordination formed in the Home Ministry. These will bring about more effective Government-wide action on manpower programs of the Planning Commission. The Planning Commission itself has added a new division of Technical Manpower.

The functions of the Manpower Directorate will include: assessing manpower supply and demands; framing broad policies; stimulating and coordinating the training and employment programs in the Central Ministries and States.

The Government has also moved early in the Second Plan to strengthen its public employment service. This service, begun in 1945, maintains employment exchange offices in the States. Under the Second Plan the number of local offices will be nearly doubled, to 256. The service will take the major part in collecting labor-market data, in developing employment counseling, in matching men and jobs, and in acting as the principal agency for achieving both order and movement in the labor force.

Few nations have had to solve manpower problems of such size, complexity and urgency in such a brief span of time. Even under the most favorable circumstances, these problems will challenge the best efforts of a democratic government.

CHAPTER VIII

Administration

To put the Second Plan's vast series of development programs into operation, to organize and administer them effectively, and by democratic means, is a job of immense proportions, in terms of size and speed of administrative tasks involved.

In facing these great tasks, India feels particularly fortunate that it has so strong a foundation on which to build. In contrast to some other underdeveloped nations where colonial rule left no such heritage, the British Government in India had set up an administrative system of efficiency and an administrative service of high competence and integrity. Upon Independence these could be and were at once, as we have seen, applied to the needs of the new nation. The caliber of the Indian administrative services had, moreover, attracted many able graduates, and Government work had a high level of prestige.

As a new nation India has attempted to build up an administration to a high standard. It is grateful that to some extent it succeeded in

111

doing so and will continue its efforts. A leading American public administration analyst has described India's as "among the dozen or so most advanced governments of the world." [1] Knowing how much more there is to be done, the Government does not feel it can accept this generous appraisal.

Under the British Government, Indian administration had been adapted primarily to regulative and revenue functions. While it progressively took up some development services, its chief duties were still to maintain law and order, collect taxes and administer a dependency.

The new Government had to develop not only as an independent and democratic government, but as a service government, capable of planning and putting into action an intensive welfare program, of providing effective leadership and action in meeting the needs of the people, of enlisting and fostering their partnership and participation, of acting swiftly and flexibly in a period of urgency and great change.

Early in the First Plan, and even before, the Government invited study by expert public administration analysts, both Indian and foreign, to determine how the Government structures and procedures could give efficient support to development programs.

On the basis of these early studies, both the Central and State Governments instituted important reorganization proposals in administrative structure and procedures. The imperative needs of the Second Plan give new urgency to still more rapid and far-reaching reforms and will place India's administration under heavy strain. The more so since India now looks at administration with a broader and broader view.

Today administration includes: planning itself; recruitment and training of manpower for all development programs as well as the administrative service; efficient management of Government-owned industries and enterprises; ensuring integrity of Government personnel; securing local voluntary participation of the people in planning, in development, in small savings campaigns and, where it is practical

---

[1] *Report of a Survey,* by Paul H. Appleby, (then) Dean of School of Public Administration, Syracuse University, 1953.

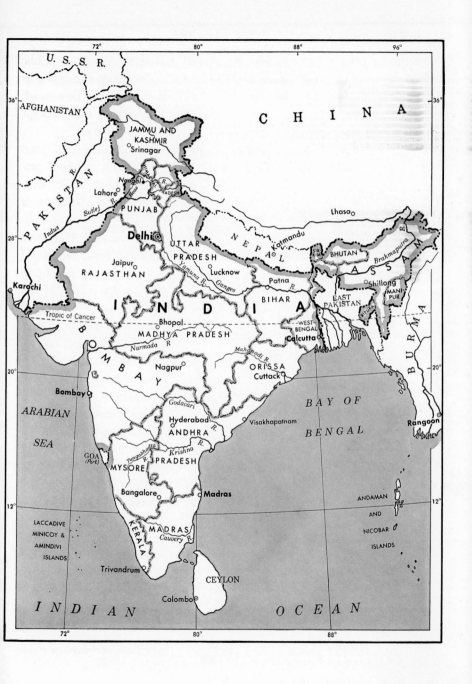

and desirable, in cooperative action. These functions are in addition to the continuous need to administer, supervise and evaluate the development programs themselves.

EXPANDING ADMINISTRATIVE PERSONNEL

One of India's greatest administrative problems—organizing manpower for development as a whole—has already been discussed.

A specific problem is how to expand, very rapidly, and without lowering of standards, the administrative service itself, to carry out the now wide variety of development programs. What is needed is to build up, with future needs in mind, an enlarged permanent corps, and provide continuing in-service training to prepare men and women to meet these needs.

Special recruitment is now under way for the Indian Administrative Service,[1] apart from the usual recruits—also an increased number—who will formally enter the Service by competitive examination for junior posts.

Under consideration as well is establishment of All-India Technical Services to which the new type of technical and scientific personnel needed for industry and similar projects may be recruited.

To staff State-operated industries and other enterprises, an Industrial Management Service has been set up, which will provide a pool of managerial talent on which all the Central Government Ministries conducting such enterprises, and the States as well, will draw.

All these new and special recruitments require the Administrative Service to be more flexible in its policies and criteria on selection and promotion, and on ready transfer between various branches of the Service. Rigidities as to recruitment and promotion, which may have developed under older conditions, have to be given up if effective administration is not to be jeopardized. Particular attention to the problems of promotion by merit, as well as by seniority, is needed so that capable new talent, such as, for example, those with valuable

---

[1] This Service was established in 1947, as successor to the former ICS (Indian Civil Service). As an all-India service, it is under the ultimate control of the Central Government; but is divided into State cadres, each under the immediate control of a State Government.

field experience in administering rural development blocks and projects, may move readily to positions for which they are qualified. Further the Government must consider how it may draw into public service persons of special experience and knowledge who do not, or may not, wish to seek careers in Government, but who have an important contribution to make to development programs.

The new administrative tasks of securing public cooperation and participation in development programs require training in new human and social skills. Rigid attitudes toward rank and status, based on an old system of values, can have no place in the administration of development programs designed for all the people. Older attitudes of "authority" must be replaced by the newer attitudes of service to the people, by techniques of persuasion and education; by an understanding of teamwork, of the discussion and interchange of ideas with workers at all levels and the people themselves.

For India, as perhaps for other older societies, these are new skills. Yet they are essential in all branches of the administration, if the fullest initiative and contribution of each individual, within the Service itself and among the people it serves, are to be evoked for the development of the nation.

Another need which India had felt early was for professionalization on a self-conscious level of public administration in India, and for a strong independent body with membership drawn from within and outside the Government, which could give continuing objective leadership and analysis to public administration, training and study programs and policies.

An Institute of Public Administration, with the Prime Minister as Chairman, was inaugurated in March 1954, as a central professional body to give leadership to a broad program of development of India's administrative services. The Institute, over the Second Plan, will set up branches in every State. Three have already been opened, in Jaipur, Poona and Bangalore.

The Institute has established a School of Public Administration to train both prospective Government administrators and those already in service. The School will be opened in 1958.

The Institute and the State and Central Governments have begun extended training programs, and expanded opportunities for in-service training both in India and overseas. Several universities have established or strengthened courses in public administration with support from their State Governments. An administrative staff college has been established at Hyderabad, and there are also training schools for the Indian Administrative Service at Simla and Delhi.

INTEGRITY IN GOVERNMENT

The Indian Government, like any government faced with new democratic responsibility, has a rightful concern to establish high standards of integrity. Any evidence of corruption arouses deep public anxiety. India has been spared at higher levels the demoralizing evil of public corruption. In several fields, however, there have been complaints of lack of integrity in the official machinery.

The Indian Government recognizes that, in the rapid expansion of its administrative services and the handling of vast development programs, some weaknesses exist and that there has to be constant vigilance against every form of corruption. While the Government welcomes criticisms, the main attack to assure integrity is the positive one of ensuring efficiency in every branch of administration—by avoiding delays, by eliminating unnecessary bureaucratic procedures, by decentralizing authority.

As India pushes ahead with development, it will exercise the most jealous watchfulness to keep up a high standard of public morality. A special vigilance division has been set up in the Ministry of Home Affairs to work with the several Government Ministries and departments, both to take speedy action in event of malpractice and, as importantly, to establish procedures which limit opportunity for it.

ADMINISTRATIVE EFFICIENCY AND ECONOMY

Efficiency of administration is one of the keys to India's growth. On efficiency depends the speed with which the Indian people and the nation will reap the benefit of development, and of the funds and effort put to their service. The people, too, will be willing to shoulder greater burdens if they feel assured that public funds and public servants are being used fully and directly for the country's progress.

Over the First Plan the Government began reforms in both the State and Central Governments, to assure greater efficiency and economy.

With the particular purpose of achieving economy in development projects, a Committee on Plan Projects was formed early in 1956 by the National Development Council. This Committee, working through specially chosen teams of officials and public members, investigates and inspects in the field selected important projects, reports on progress and needs, and makes any necessary recommendations for more efficient operation in the fields under review.

So that Government servants may be helped by efficient Government procedures to give swifter service to the people, an Organization and Methods Directorate designed to speed program action was begun during the last two years of the First Plan in the Central Government. Similar offices were set up in State Governments.

Among other reforms begun earlier, one of the most pressing for the Second Plan period is the spread of decision-making, authority and responsibility. Power and initiative have tended to be concentrated at the upper levels of administration in any department. The level at which effective decisions are made has indeed been pushed upward. This is a problem that will have to be solved. In a fast-developing nation such procedures inevitably mean either serious overwork of the few high-level officers empowered to make decisions, or delays in getting programs in action. Or often both. A studied effort must be made to assure that at each level the officials concerned have the opportunity to exercise the maximum responsibility and initiative, and in fact do so.

Another need is more emphasis on progress reporting, both to Government and to Parliament, for all development programs. The Planning Commission, in its yearly evaluation of the achievements of the Plan, in its continuous review of progress in various development fields, such as the rural program and others, has made a contribution to progress reporting, as have many administrative agencies.

More needs to be done, both in the Central Government and in the States.

ADMINISTRATION OF GOVERNMENT INDUSTRIES AND ENTERPRISES

Delegation of responsibility and managerial progress reporting are particularly urgent where Government administers industrial and commercial enterprises.

The general policy is that these enterprises must be set up so that they can be run on efficient business lines, with the fullest degree of autonomy, of swiftness of decision and action necessary for efficient management yet still consistent with the over-all responsibility of Government and accountability to Parliament. In Government-controlled enterprises already established, several forms of organization have been used—joint stock companies, statutory corporations, control boards, departmental management. For new enterprises, the Government has invited particular study of this issue by both Indian and foreign administration analysts.

Speaking to the point in Parliament, the Prime Minister said:

I have no doubt that the normal government functions applied to a public enterprise of this kind will ensure the failure of that public enterprise. . . . Every person who has advised us . . . has told us "Do not interfere with your enterprises, give them responsibility, give your executive responsibility, do not interfere. . . ."

Therefore, we have to evolve a system for working public enterprises, where on the one hand there are adequate checks and protections—that is inevitable—and on the other there is enough freedom given to that enterprise to work quickly without delay. Ultimately judge it by the results.[1]

While as yet no final decision has been made as to the precise administrative form or forms to be taken by new Government enterprises, it is generally agreed that they must be autonomous bodies, with full managerial responsibility, and subject before Government and Parliament to an "audit of achievement."

[1] May 23, 1956.

The Role of the States

A special condition for the economic and social development of India is the division of authority and responsibility as between the Central Government, the States and the 300 Districts.

Under the Indian Constitution, the Indian structure resembles that of Canada or Australia, in that it has a British-type parliamentary form at the Center, and a concurrent parliamentary form in each of the States. Compared to the United States, the States and the Central Government in India are somewhat more interdependent.

Under India's federal system, its fourteen [1] States have substantial autonomy. Administration of development and other domestic programs, such as health, agriculture and land problems, education, small industries, is almost wholly in their hands. During the First Five Year Plan, more than 60 per cent of the total expenditures for development were for projects administered by more than twenty State Governments.[2] Nearly half of the total expenditures of the Second Plan will be made by the States, not the Center. The States also have revenue resources proportionately larger than States in many other federal systems, relative to the taxing power of the Central Government.

In its relation to the States, the role of the Central Government is to shape national policies, give a national sense of direction, and build up the means by which there can be a close partnership with the States in all matters of national interest and development, a working together in the national endeavor. Each State, under its constitutional powers, interprets and applies these policies in relation to local needs and conditions.

The need for close coordination between Center and State on development programs, especially agriculture and small and village

---

[1] On Nov. 1, 1956, the previous 28 States were reorganized into 14 States and 6 centrally administered Territories, largely on linguistic lines, and with the intent, as well, of making each a more viable administrative unit. Many of the States are as large as individual nations elsewhere. Uttar Pradesh, for instance, has a population far exceeding that of the entire United Kingdom.

[2] As before Reorganization of States on Nov. 1, 1956.

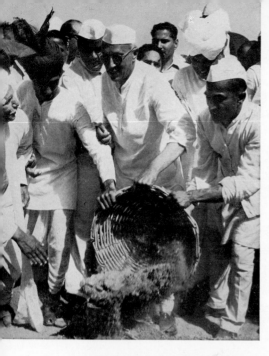

BEGINNING OF A REVOLUTION: Prime Minister Nehru (center) helps lift the first basket of earth to inaugurate on October 2, 1952, the nation-wide community projects program of village development and reconstruction. A self-help program which reached over 80 million villagers in less than four years, and which will cover all of India's villages by 1961, it is bringing about a revolution of progress to India's rural people.

REACHING THE FARMER IN THE FIELDS: A village extension worker invites a farmer to a demonstration of an improved plow, which could replace the primitive type he carries.

TRAINING FOR VILLAGE WORK: A class of young Sikhs in the Punjab, training as village extension workers, studies a simple but improved seed drill suitable for village use. Over 5,000 extension workers a year have been trained for service throughout India.

NEW VILLAGE SCHOOLS: This new school, in what was formerly a backward tribal area in Andhra State, is one of 15,000 rural schools built under the village development program by villagers who contributed up to half the cost in labor, land and cash.

industries, is urgent; new techniques of liaison with the Central Government on key programs are being evolved.

Over the First Plan, methods of working with the States were very greatly improved and strengthened. The formation of the National Development Council, as mentioned in the earlier discussion on planning, was a significant step, and the Council, which includes the Chief Ministers [1] of all States and members of the Planning Commission, with the Prime Minister as Chairman, plays an important part in the formulation of national policies and in securing common agreement and coordination for these policies.

As part of the reorganization of the States in November, 1956, five Zonal Councils were formed (northern, central, southern, eastern and western). Each is composed of the States and Territories in the zone, and acts as an advisory body to the Central and State Governments on matters of common regional and interstate interest, particularly social and economic planning.

The Councils have as their common chairman the Central Minister of Home Affairs; the vice chairman of each Council will be, in rotation, the Chief Minister of each of the States represented on each Council.

For the carrying out of development programs, the Planning Commission is particularly concerned that the Governments of the States be administratively strengthened for the heavy responsibility they must bear.

During the First Plan the States geared themselves for the new development emphasis by setting up an office of the State Development Commissioner who would coordinate and give leadership to development activities of all the State Departments of Health, Agriculture, Education, and so on. The Commissioner is given over-all policy guidance by a committee of the State Cabinet under the State's Chief Minister. The need of coordination becomes greater as development becomes more and more the business of Government.

[1] The Chief Minister relatively to the State Government is comparable to the Prime Minister to the National Government. He heads the majority party of the State Legislative Assembly. The Governor of each State is its constitutional head, appointed by the President of India.

Many States suffer from lack of enough top-level trained personnel, especially technical men. During the First Plan important State departments were without directors or senior officers; and in some small States shortages of qualified senior people was responsible for failure to fulfill program targets. The Central Government is both urging and assisting States to plan for, recruit and train adequate administrative staff, with reserves for the continually expanding needs. One strong reason for proposing the all-India technical service, the joint development and other service cadres is to provide a pool of skills which can supplement the supply on which the States may draw, and provide qualified persons to serve regions or groups of States.

District Development Administration

Below the State level, the 300 Districts (roughly comparable to the counties of the United States and Britain), today, as in British India, are considered "the pivot of the structure of administration." These Districts usually contain one or two million people; a few contain as many as four to five million, or a number equaling the population of Norway or Denmark.

The administrative head of each district is called the District Collector or District Magistrate, titles carried over from an earlier period when his chief functions were land-revenue collection and law and order. The Collector is a member of the civil service, not an elected or politically appointed official.

The District Collector's responsibilities are increasing as all development programs—and especially the rural development programs—are intensified. Standing between the State Government with its elected legislature, and the local self-governing groups in the villages, the Collector's position and potential role is of great and, as has been said, pivotal importance in a developing India.

With a strengthened and democratized administration, the Indian Government considers, indeed, the District as an agency of change toward a new social order. It must respond to the needs and aspirations of the people, and in a democratic society will be judged by the ways it finds to achieve these aspirations through the cooperation of the people and their Government.

On the one hand, it is at the District level and below that the development programs directly touch the Indian people, in the villages and countless small towns. On the other, the very choice of democratic means for India's growth, as noted earlier, makes it necessary to strengthen and, where they do not already exist, create local democratic organizations composed of and working with the people, in order to plan and carry out the work of development at the District, sub-district and village level.

Development must be carried out by these local bodies so that strong local leadership may be found and encouraged, and so that the people of each area themselves may assume, under their own leadership, the main responsibility for solving their local problems and developing their own resources.

The need for creating a well organized democratic structure of administration within the Districts is now widely felt. It is believed that local bodies at the District (and in larger Districts, at a sub-district) level should have an organic link with the popularly elected village councils and gradually assume the responsibility for local administration of development programs, with clearly assigned functions. New proposals for decentralizing local administration of development programs along democratic lines were worked out in late 1957 by a team set up through the National Development Council.

During the First Plan the District Collector began more actively to assume the functions of a District Development Officer, in addition to his regulative duties. In some areas a special development or planning deputy was assigned to his office. Under the Second Plan, the Planning Commission has urged further strengthening and staffing of the District administration, to fulfill the urgent local demands for coordination of technical staff in the Districts, to supervise, guide and evaluate all types of development works and programs of the area.

The Planning Commission also recommends District Development Councils to survey and plan for the needs of each District, and to work directly with local village groups through village self-government organizations (*panchayats*) and with the local block and project officers of the national rural development programs.

District Development Committees were established in the First Plan in all Districts for advising on rural development and on other programs. While some were effective, the majority did not function fully, largely because their role of duties and opportunities were not always clearly appreciated.

The Planning Commission suggests that each Council include not only District Collectors and the local development officers, but local representatives of the State Assemblies and national Parliament, leaders of village panchayats and other local bodies, representatives of cooperatives and local social service agencies.

A similar council at a lower or sub-divisional (*taluq*, or block) level is also recommended, with similar representatives. The role and integration of the rural development block in District administration is indeed of great importance for the future.

In general, the functions suggested to these local bodies are: local planning, reviewing and coordinating development activities in the area or District, and very particularly stimulating public initiative, leadership and participation in development activities and small savings drives, and a constant concern that the poorer and disadvantaged people of the area benefit from development programs.

Village Panchayats

In ancient India, it is believed that most villages had a form of local self-government. The common form was one in which elected elders constituted a village council, a panchayat, passing on all public affairs of the village, including private disputes. Many believe, as Prime Minister Nehru writes in his book *The Discovery of India*, that "the strength and perseverance of India in the past seem to have lain in her widespread system of village republics or self-governing panchayats."

Local self-government weakened and finally almost disappeared, as successive waves of alien rulers destroyed the autonomy of the village and imposed new laws and revenues from distant and alien authorities. Every village, however, retained its headman who, together with certain village elders, was by common consent the village's spokesman.

To some extent under British rule, and very particularly since Independence, an effort has been made to revive this old form of village government, and both the First and Second Plans have put a high priority on formation of panchayats.

While local self-government needs no justification in a democracy, it may be useful to summarize why India attaches to it so high a priority.

First, the reasons are frankly practical. If the work of village development is to get done in a democratic society which proposes no all-powerful centrally controlled apparatus, and if it is to be done, too, with maximum financial help from the people themselves, the villages must themselves organize to carry out, and contribute to, much of the work of development—the building of schools, roads, irrigation and similar projects.

The Planning Commission clearly acknowledges that rural progress depends entirely on the existence of an active village organization which can bring all the people, including those at the bottom of the social and economic ladder, into common programs and activities, using assistance from the Government, and their own contributions in labor, cash and kind.

Further, India feels keenly that the nation's strength as a democracy depends to a most important degree on building, in hundreds of thousands of villages, effective local governments through which the people can, as responsible citizens, plan and participate in their own and the nation's progress. As such, these governments are not considered merely as local municipal bodies, performing largely housekeeping or even local development chores. Rather, they are seen as essential means of fitting local and village activities into the over-all pattern of District and State plans, and as the final and essential

link in an integrated democratic administrative structure of the nation as a whole.

Further, village society is in a state of transition. Powerful social
and economic forces—land reform, wider education, rural development—are bringing great changes. These forces put strains on old
village societies which, however backward, had achieved a remarkable social stability and cohesion.

As Mahatma Gandhi, with his great insight, saw so clearly, the
social strength and cohesion of the villages is imperative to sustain
the new nation. He saw, with equal clarity, the key role of the vil-
large panchayats in maintaining that strength, and attached the
highest importance to reviving them. His teaching is reflected today
in India's recognition that a village panchayat, representing the needs
of all groups, can play a considerable part in bringing about a more
just and integrated social structure and in developing new patterns
of rural leadership. Indeed, India feels the development of local
self-government is a key part of the larger process of fundamental
reconstruction and reorganization of village social and economic
life.

The general purpose is to establish, especially in rural development areas, what is called a "statutory" panchayat to serve every village. A statutory panchayat is one formally set up and registered
under State laws which provide some financing, and which permit
the panchayat to administer certain civil and criminal suits and
adjudicate local disputes. All States now have panchayat legislation.

The number of panchayats increased considerably (40 per cent)
over the First Plan, reaching in 1956 to a total of over 117,000. Over
the Second Plan, it is hoped to double the number to 244,564—or
one for each of nearly half the villages in India. It is suggested that
for villages too small or isolated (about half the rural people live in
villages of less than 1,000 population), natural groupings of villages
may be made to provide a unit of at least 1,000 persons. One panchayat could serve this unit.

Development of village leadership which is representative of the
village as a whole is extremely important. There has been concern

that the usual election process may not always bring out leaders with the qualities most needed for village development and with constructive interest in the growth of the community as a whole. It is also recognized that unless there is comprehensive village planning, which takes into account the needs of the entire community, those groups with the least economic and social status, such as tenant farmers, landless laborers, artisans, may not benefit sufficiently from Government development programs and assistance.

The Planning Commission urges that States, as many already do, require the elected members to take in, as additional members, representatives of the Harijans (untouchables), the landless or other socially and economically depressed groups in the village; and ex officio representatives of local cooperatives. A means is also now being worked out whereby, by groups of villages, panchayat leaders can be given special training to educate them to their new functions, and to their responsibilities to the community as a whole.

How to finance the panchayats is a special problem if they are to assume wider and more important functions. Most State Governments grant them a portion of the local land taxes; panchayats may also collect small civic taxes; in some few areas they levy land taxes. So far this financing has proved inadequate. The Second Plan recommends that the States grant 15 to 20 per cent of local land revenues, plus 15 per cent more if the panchayat itself raises an equal additional amount.

The functions of the statutory panchayat generally conceived today and recommended by the Planning Commission are, in addition to the local planning and development, both administrative and judicial.

Among civic functions, the panchayat is expected under most State laws to act as the local civic authority—maintaining village roads, improving village sanitation (a very important role under India's health program), providing village lighting, and maintaining the village community hall, with its small library and, in some cases, the village battery radio set.

A key function, however, is that of local development—planning the village improvement needs, constructing and maintaining village schools, roads and so on, organizing voluntary village labor and contributions and small savings; development of cooperatives and village livestock improvement; and, very importantly, serving as the village's direct medium of contact with all development programs of the District, State and Center.

The panchayat is also seen as the essential democratic agency to carry out any eventual reorganization of land management. The Planning Commission recommends that panchayats also concern themselves with: development and regulation of use of the village's common land, forests, and reservoirs; assistance in consolidation of holdings; promotion of good land management among the village farmers.

It is also proposed that, on problems of local land reform, the panchayats be associated with decisions on tenants' and owners' rights, on determination of surplus lands and their distribution. As land reform becomes more effective, and more of a direct local issue, these functions may assume a critical significance.

In acting as a judicial body, the panchayat can provide a very real service. Where the panchayats already are active, disputes which otherwise may have dragged through District courts, impoverished the disputants and divided the villages into factions, have in most cases been readily settled. In some States a separate panchayat has the judicial functions.

The potential strength and value of village self-government to India's growth can hardly be calculated. At the very least, it provides the final and integrated link in the chain of administration where vast national and State development programs reach directly to the people to help them rise from the mire of poverty. As it does so, and at its best, it will reflect the ideal of self-governing village republics which Gandhi envisaged: "Here is perfect democracy, based on individual freedom." [1]

[1] *Harijan,* July 26, 1942.

CHAPTER IX

Financing the Plan

To pay for the Second Five Year Plan will take a supreme effort by the Indian people, by Indian private enterprise and by the Indian Government.

The total cost of national development programs, Rs. 7,200 crores (Rs. 4,800 from Government, Rs. 2,400 crores from private enterprise), looks small, of course, compared to expenditures of developed nations. The United States, for example, spends Rs. 4,800 crores every eighty days on defense alone, and Rs. 4,800 crores about every year and a half on education alone. Yet this is an enormous sum for a nation such as India, only now arising out of the mire of poverty, to raise for national development even over a period of five years.

For India, as for other underdeveloped nations, the question is further complicated. Development requires two kinds of financing or, in effect, *two kinds of money*.

It requires rupees, or India's own currency (one rupee equals about twenty-one cents) for expenditures inside the country. All rupees must, of course, be raised within India—by taxes, bonds and small savings, deficit financing, and so on.

Development also requires, however, foreign exchange—chiefly dollars and pounds sterling—to enable India to buy essential development goods from the United States, the United Kingdom, Canada, European nations, Japan, and other countries—power generators, locomotives, and freight cars, steel, heavy machinery, textile machinery, drugs and even food.

Foreign exchange can come only from outside India, raised by selling Indian exports abroad, or by foreign capital coming into India as loans, grants or private investments.

In India's Second Plan, the amount of foreign exchange needed is very high—about one-fourth of all Plan expenditures. This is because India has to import heavy machinery and other equipment to get industries expanding rapidly.

India is committed to raising its resources by democratic means. It cannot raise money by compulsory "contributions," deliveries of agricultural "surpluses" to the State, depression of living standards. The Indian Government will, to be sure, tax the people heavily— in 1957 it imposed new taxes which are heavy by any standards— but it must, as it has done, tax with the consent of the people, and with their willingness to share the cost as well as the benefits of development.

Clearly, raising funds for the Plan will require not only some very real sacrifices but the ablest economic leadership. It will require, as well, some new and imaginative answers to the problems of financing development of free underdeveloped countries, which have little capital and are short on foreign exchange.

For example, India shares, with other nations of the world, the challenge of discovering how underdeveloped countries may more freely buy from the developed nations in the period of transition before they are able to earn sufficient foreign exchange to pay for increasing imports. The flow of goods between the developed nations which can sell or lend and the underdeveloped nations anxious to buy has to be enlarged.

India also hopes to help work out some solutions to the encouragement and use of foreign capital in the underdeveloped nations, in ways that will on the one hand speed social and economic growth, and on the other furnish profitable, secure returns to attract the available capital of developed nations.

India also shares in common with other Asian nations a very special challenge in finding ways to use one of its greatest resources —the manpower, energies and skills of its millions of people—to build the nation, and to create new wealth and capital in roads, schools, irrigation projects and the like.

These are, of course, some of the long-range problems of financing the development of India, as of other backward nations. If India succeeds with its Second Plan, some new approaches to these problems may be evolved.

Meanwhile, however, India faces the harsh realities of mustering the finances needed—both in rupees and in foreign exchange—to put its development programs into immediate action.

In the first eighteen months of the Plan period, steadily rising prices in India and abroad, added to the earlier effects of the Suez crisis with its delays and higher shipping costs, have given the problem of financing the Plan a new and serious urgency. Estimates reviewed in the late autumn of 1957 indicate the cost of the Plan may turn out to be perhaps 10 per cent more than originally expected, with a large share of the increase needed in foreign exchange.

It is clear that even if India with supreme effort and the most careful management is able to muster the rupee costs of the Plan, the problem of foreign exchange is critical in the extreme.

The cost of the Plan has already been given in general; but a clearer picture is needed now to discuss some of the special problems of financing. Put briefly, again, and using the Second Plan's estimates, the Plan itself will cost the Government Rs. 4,800 crores. It will cost private enterprise Rs. 2,400 crores—that is, Rs. 2,400 crores is the amount private enterprise (which includes large and small industry, agriculture and construction) is expected to invest over the five-year period. The total then is Rs. 7,200 crores, without accounting for any rise in prices.

These Rs. 7,200 crores represent of course both rupees and foreign exchange, rupees forming the larger part, very roughly three-fourths of the total, and foreign exchange one-fourth.

Investment in the Plan

Before passing on to the urgent question of how the Rs. 7,200 crores can be raised, there are several things that must be said about the amount of *investment* in the Plan. The quick summary below reviews both Government and expected private investment over the Plan, and the proportion of each that will be put into industry, agriculture, power, etc.

The investment planned for each program—industry, agriculture, and so on—represents India's best judgment as to the amounts needed to achieve Plan targets, and to bring about the desired balanced development of large and small industry and industry and agriculture.

The Plan's production targets are high, and the investment targets are consequently also high. It is in the Second Plan and the Third, it will be recalled, that India must make proportionately its greatest investment in order to get the rate of growth necessary to cross the "threshold" from an underdeveloped nation.

Total *investment* in the Plan comes to Rs. 6,200 crores—Rs. 3,800 [1] crores from Government and Rs. 2,400 crores from private enterprise.

Rs. 6,200 crores is, as we have seen, double what was invested in the First Plan. For Government alone, it means 2½ times more, for private enterprise 50 per cent more. The ratio of Government in-

---

[1] Rs. 3,800 crores rather than Rs. 4,800 crores is given as Government *investment*. The additional Rs. 1,000 crores is technically called "current outlay" (that is, outlay for social services, and so on). The type of expenditure, while important in itself, is not investment and hence does not appear in the 'investment' summary.

PRIVATE AND GOVERNMENT INVESTMENT IN THE SECOND FIVE YEAR PLAN
(Rs. crores)

	PRIVATE		PUBLIC		TOTAL	
	Amount	Per Cent	Amount	Per Cent	Amount	Per Cent
Agriculture, Comm. Dev.	175	8.8	338	8.9	513	8.8
Irrigation	100	5.0	456	12.0	556	9.7
Large Industry (incl. Power and Mining)	617 [1]	30.8	1,077	28.3	1,694	29.2
Small Industrial and Other Enterprises	100	5.0	120	3.2	220	3.8
Transport and Communications	83	4.2	1,335	35.1	1,418	24.3
Other (Social Services, Residential Buildings, Misc.)	925 [2]	46.2	474	12.5	1,399	24.2
TOTAL	2,000 [3]	100.0	3,800	100.0	5,800 [3]	100.0

[1] Power is estimated at Rs. 42 crores, Rs. 40 crores for mining; Rs. 535 crores for industry alone.

[2] For private enterprise, this item is almost entirely for construction, including housing.

[3] Plus Rs. 400 crores for "stocks."

vestment to private investment in the Plan as a whole is roughly 3:2 (Rs. 3,800 : Rs. 2,400). Actually, private investment will probably do better.

For it should be said here that the investment figures for private enterprise can of course only be an estimate. Investment in large modern mechanized industries may, the present indications are, turn out to be larger than expected. How much small private individuals and firms will invest in agriculture, in small industries and various small trades and transport is always difficult to guess.

It should also be said that the figures given for private investment do not include investment the Indian people may make without expenditure of actual money, as, for example, the labor and materials that, without paying actual cash for them, a farmer puts into building a well.

This kind of investment, what economists call "non-monetized," is very large and important in underdeveloped rural economies, particularly in agriculture and irrigation. Some estimates put it as high as one-fourth of all investment. All of it is, of course, private investment.

A total investment of Rs. 6,200 crores means, as we have also seen, raising the rate of investment to 11 per cent by the last year of the Plan, compared to over 7.3 per cent in the last year of the First Plan. Stated another way, by the last year of the Second Plan India must be drawing off 11 per cent of its income for investment, in national development.

This, as we have seen, is a substantial increase for a country just beginning its development. Indeed, about 100 per cent more resources will have to be gathered to finance the Second Plan than the First Plan.

This shows the size of the job which the Indian Government and the people face—in organizing to raise this increased amount in taxes, loans, stocks and shares, and so on.

It is widely agreed that an investment of at least Rs. 6,200 crores is required to yield the 25 per cent increase in national production and income, and the other targets proposed in the Plan. Any lowering of investment can only mean lowering of targets, and a continuation of poverty. Indeed, it is believed that only by the most careful and imaginative management can even Rs. 6,200 crores investment expand income and production by 25 per cent.

One of the key factors in India's economic growth, it will be recalled, is how much production can be got for each rupee invested. This raises questions as to the relative productivity of projects using much capital as against those using much labor, and questions of the proper balance between Government and private investment.

The Indian Government feels it must, in so vast an undertaking as the Plan, keep itself flexible and realistic, and constantly review its first judgment—as to levels and balance between investments in different programs—in the light of actual developments and experience. While India will hold itself to the targets of the Plan, and use every means, consistent with democracy, to gather financing for it, the Government is also determined not to endanger, in doing so, India's financial stability and balance—such as by risking a dangerous inflation or exacting savings at human and social cost. The Plan, its targets, and the taxes and other financial measures necessary to achieve it are constantly under Parliamentary, press and public discussion and review. The tax and other financial measures necessary to achieve the Plan's targets are brought before Parliament, and reviewed in wide public discussion so that each measure, as well as the new burden it imposes, is paced to the capacity of the people, and adopted with their consent and support.

It is already clear that, as we have seen, some original Plan estimates have to be revised upward because of rising prices. These adjustments will require other investments to be cut down, particularly where they use foreign exchange on less essential items. But whatever adjustments are made, the needs of development as a whole will continue to be great, and some risks must be undertaken. India believes that no risk is greater than that of stagnation.

Nevertheless, all development programs are under constant review. How much to invest, in what programs, the proper balance between large and small industry, between industry and agriculture, the proper proportion of Government and private investment—these are all questions that need constant review and reappraisal, flexibility and judgment as India makes its great experiment of pushing a mixed economy ahead by democratic means.

The broad fact remains, however, that India will need at least Rs. 6,200 crores of investment to accomplish the targets it has now set. These Rs. 6,200 crores, plus the Rs. 1,000 crores which India calls "outlay," a total of Rs. 7,200 crores, is what India must raise in rupees and foreign exchange to finance the Second Plan.

It will be easiest to take the problem of financing the Second Plan in three parts: (1) how the Government will raise the rupees it needs for the Plan; (2) how private enterprise will raise its rupee needs; and (3) how the foreign exchange may be raised, by Government and private industry, for purchases abroad of development equipment and machinery.

What is immediately clear is that, while India can, with supreme effort, muster the rupees the Plan needs, the gap in foreign exchange cannot be closed without substantial foreign contribution.

1. *Financing the Government's Share of the Plan*

It will be remembered that the cost of the Plan represents to the Government only about half of the Government's total expenditure over the five-year period. Put another way, the cost of the Plan—of progress, in short—is roughly equal to all other costs of running the Government. "Government" refers both to the Central and to the State Governments.

Necessary Government expenditures *outside* the Plan include defense, normal government administration such as law and order, basic postal services, and so on, and, very importantly, the cost of maintaining the development services begun either in the First Plan or earlier.

While the non-Plan expenses, over the five Plan years, have been budgeted very closely, they have increased from the First Plan levels— in part because of the cost of carrying on the new development programs begun in the First Plan, in part because of the growth of Government services natural in a country newly independent.

Any need to increase them further, however, during the Plan period, as, for instance, if prices rose rapidly or if it became necessary, as indeed it has become within the past year, to increase defense expenditures, would obviously endanger the amount available for the Plan.

The non-Plan expenditures can be easily met by the Central and State Governments' normal tax and other revenues. The problem is to find money over and above these basic expenditures for financing the Plan, to the amount of Rs. 4,800 crores.

Part of this, the larger part, Rs. 4,000 crores, must be raised in

India; the rest must be raised externally in foreign exchange, and how this amount can be raised is considered later.

The ways by which governments raise money are common in every democratic country: by taxes, by floating loans, by considered use of deficit financing (printing more money), by stimulating the people to buy savings and other Government bonds, as, for example, the United States did during World War II with its Defense Savings Bonds.

To finance its share of Second Plan costs, the Indian Government will use all these methods to the utmost, consistent with the financial stability of the country and the social stability of its people.

The fact that the economy itself is expanding and producing more means that the yield in taxes, small savings and loans will be higher than in the First Plan.

Roughly, these were the Government's original proposals for raising the Rs. 4,800 crores needed in rupees and foreign exchange for the Plan (that is, beyond basic non-Plan needs of Government):

		ORIGINAL ESTIMATES, MAY 1956		
		Rs. Crores		
1. TAXES				
From new taxes	450			
From former taxes	350			
		800		
2. OTHER REVENUES				
Pension funds, railway profits, etc.	400			
		400		
3. LOANS AND SMALL SAVINGS				
Loans	700			
Small Savings	500			
		1,200		
4. DEFICIT FINANCING		1,200		
5. Foreign Assistance			800	
GAP		400		
TOTAL		4,000	800	4,800

All these methods are, however, interrelated, and have to be used in careful harmony, the more so since prices have been rising throughout the first period of the Plan. Deficit financing may have the effect of raising prices. A rapid rise in prices may discourage savings and bring about social unrest. Higher taxes, by reducing incomes available for expenditure, may hold down prices—but it may also reduce savings available for private investment.

Obviously, the Government will have to use extreme care and constant watchfulness in its efforts to balance and adjust methods of raising funds for the Plan.

TAXATION

As in most countries, the largest source of funds to the Government is from taxes of all kinds—income taxes, excise taxes, corporation taxes, land or real-estate taxes, import duties, and so on.

The Indian Government expects about a fourth of all the Government's needs for the Plan to be met from revenues of the State and Central Governments. When the Plan was originally issued, it was expected that Rs. 450 crores would come from new taxes. Former tax measures, the yield from which will go up because of higher incomes and an expanding economy, were expected to produce an additional Rs. 350 crores for the Plan. The total tax revenues available for the Plan, according to the original estimates, were thus Rs. 800 crores.

The Plan had, however, as we have seen in the table above, left a gap of Rs. 400 crores. According to a decision made in May 1957 by the National Development Council, this amount must now also be met largely by additional taxation. This means that India now expects to raise Rs. 800 to 850 crores in *new* taxation alone over the Second Plan. This, for India, is an enormous tax increase, and will spread the tax burden more widely and more heavily perhaps than at any time in India's history.

The Prime Minister, discussing the heavy new taxes in Parliament, said: "We must remember that if we have to make good, we have to carry these burdens. We have to produce this money from our country, because while we are prepared for the help of other countries, we are not prepared to be dependent on other countries. We want to indicate to the rest of the world that we are prepared to swallow many bitter pills to retain our independence and to maintain our progress." [1]

[2] Prime Minister to Parliament, May 30, 1957.

In raising so large a part of its Plan funds from taxes, India faces some particular tax problems. Incomes in general are extremely low and, as we have seen, concentrated in the lowest bracket (95 per cent of the people earn less than Rs. 1,500 [$300] a year). Only a small portion of the population therefore is able to pay any appreciable income tax, unless their already very low living standards are cut down even more.

The vast group at low living levels has to be reached by other types of Government taxation, such as the excise and import duties. While some of these taxes affect only the people relatively well off (such as customs duties on automobiles, foreign liquors and cosmetics, and mechanical appliances), many of the taxes—and more and more under recent tax proposals—impose sacrifices on the common man.

Yet most of the burden of the direct taxes (income, estate duty, and corporation taxes, accounting for about one-fourth of total tax revenue) must be borne by a relatively minute section of the people. The direct taxes of the Central Government actually affect only about 1 to 1½ per cent of the country's working population.

Income-tax rates for this fractional group are already high. A comparison of India's rates with those of other countries shows that while rates in India are lower for the low-income brackets, there is a steep rise on incomes from $5,000 up. Rates are among the highest in the world for incomes of $8,000 and up. Thus tax burdens are concentrated upon the people responsible for a large part of the savings in the community. If taxes are raised too high for this group, they may not have enough savings to invest as much as is needed in business enterprises.

Corporation taxes now average about the same in India as in the United States. Development rebates, and tax holidays in the case of new industries, plus generous depreciation allowances, have been given to lower the effective Indian rate, and to encourage private industry to expand.

However, taxes, as a whole, represent in India about 8 to 9 per cent of India's national income, a proportion less than that of developed and even some underdeveloped countries. For some time India has been aware that revisions in its total tax structure were essential. A Tax Enquiry Commission of leading industrialists and of Government and private economists reported in 1955 on possibilities for further taxation. Two of the major recommendations concerned the broadening of the income-tax base with lower tax exemptions, and more effective tax collection.

During the latter part of 1956 the Central Government raised taxes, reimposed a capital gains tax, and in order to conserve foreign exchange increased certain import duties and excises. In May of 1957, the newly elected Government placed before Parliament its stiff and far-reaching tax proposals. These included taxes on wealth and expenditure, a lowering of the exemptions on income, plus some relief to higher bracket incomes as a stimulus to investment, a new tax on railway fares, and still higher excise and import duties.

Taken together, all the new tax measures begun in 1956 and 1957 will alone yield about Rs. 800 crores over the Plan period. This is almost double what the Central Government originally estimated it could get in new taxes.

While this is promising, a considerable portion must be used for non-Plan purposes, including the higher cost of defense, administration and development services. There is also the possibility that the State Governments may not raise as much of their share of new taxes as expected. The States did not reach their tax targets during the First Plan. Considerably more, indeed, will have to be done by the States to increase their revenues through new or expanding taxes.

The question has frequently been raised that India takes relatively little, considering that it is so largely an agricultural nation, in land and agricultural taxes. Such taxes are the concern of the States rather than of the Central Government. Land revenue contributes only about 8 per cent of total tax revenues.

Doubtless India's land taxes could be raised somewhat, especially on lands improved by the Government through irrigation and so on. This the States are doing to some extent. It is expected that, with land reform, the contribution of land and agriculture can be increased. The urgent need, however, to sustain at least the present level of incomes of India's rural people, and to give them every incentive to increase agricultural production, makes the question of higher land and agricultural taxes one for very careful consideration.

Altogether, at this time, India's prospects of raising at least as much as it expected in taxes look fair—fair enough, it is hoped, to lessen somewhat the amount of deficit financing India may need to use. This is very important in view of the continued rise in prices.

In any event, a tax burden of at least the present size is inevitable for the Indian people. From the trend of prices and other indications, it appears that deficit financing of the size originally hoped over the Plan period will not be possible. The National Development Council feels that, to the extent that deficit financing cannot be used, the shortage must be met largely by additional taxation, and through small savings.

LOANS AND SAVINGS

The Government's prospects for raising rupees for the Plan by loans, savings bonds and the like also look reasonably bright.

The Indian people responded well during the First Plan to small savings drives. For example, in the year before the First Plan was begun, only Rs. 33 crores were collected in small savings. In the last year of the First Plan, the amount was more than double, Rs. 68 crores, and for the Plan years as a whole exceeded the target and met as much as 12 per cent of all Plan expenditures.

The Second Plan hopes to collect up to Rs. 100 crores a year, or Rs. 500 crores for the Plan period. This will call for a very energetic and effective savings drive, directed especially to the really small saver in urban and rural areas, who generally has not yet been reached. But, with all the experience and machinery now at the Government's command and with the public more and more "plan-conscious" and experiencing more and more of the Plan benefits, this is expected to be a feasible if difficult task. Recently, the interest rates offered on small savings have been raised to attract more savers; and the State Governments have been asked to get vigorous savings campaigns under way.

Aside from small savings, the Government, Central and State, also expects to float public loans from institutional and other investors, to the average of Rs. 140 crores a year, or Rs. 700 crores for the Plan period. This target looks very possible of achievement. In 1954–1955 the Central and State Governments were able to raise as much as Rs. 115 crores. In the first year of the Second Plan they were able to raise Rs. 140 crores (net).

It is true, of course, that as the economy expands—private enterprise is itself looking for bank and other loans to enable it to expand—there is likely to be a tight money market. In 1957 the program of borrowing by State Governments was substantially reduced.

The key to the success of both the savings and loan drives, of course, is how much the Indian people are willing voluntarily to put aside in savings and investments out of any new income they may earn during the Plan.

This is important not only for the success of savings campaigns, of course, but from the point of view of general inflation. If the increasing incomes are not immediately used to buy more food and clothing, prices will not rise so rapidly and deficit financing can be used more safely.

All in all, however, prospects seem generally not unfavorable for the Government to raise through small savings and purchase of Government bonds the amount it hopes and needs to get.

Deficit Financing

Deficit financing is a method of raising money used on occasion by all Governments. In times of stress—war or other emergency—Governments use it more freely. Deficit financing was for example used by the United States Government and the United Kingdom during World War II. Technically, it means spending more than is actually taken in, and is done by printing money, against loans made by the Central Bank to the Government, or by a drawing down of cash balances.

In a sense more painless than raising taxes, it is a method, however, that always must be used with great care by a nation wishing to keep its financial stability. Overused or wrongly used, it can lead to a serious price rise or inflation.

The Indian Government used deficit financing moderately during the First Plan, mostly during the Plan's last two years. About 21 per cent of the First Plan, or Rs. 420 crores, was deficit financed, while prices generally remained stable, and even, until the last months of the Plan, came down.

Over the Second Plan, the Government had originally hoped it could use deficit financing to a total of Rs. 1,200 crores—or to about a fourth of all Plan costs.

Price rises showing up early in the Plan, however, and continually throughout 1956 (the wholesale index rose by 12 per cent for the year), have made it necessary to limit the amount of deficit financing to considerably less than it had budgeted for in the coming years.

There is general agreement that an expanding economy needs some more money in circulation. Consequently deficit financing can be undertaken to some amount without causing a general rise in prices. Economists in India, as elsewhere, differ, however, on the amount by which the money supply can be increased without affecting the price level. They also differ on how much inflation it would be proper to tolerate in the interests of economic development.

In any event, the Indian Government is proceeding cautiously because it is determined to keep its financial stability. It is watching the result of its present deficit financing carefully, and is prepared to take quick action, if price rises continue, to mop up surplus purchasing power.

Rapidly increased production—of food, cloth and other goods—will, of course, hold down prices. The Government is pushing hard for increased production in every part of the economy so that prices can remain steady, and permit the Government to use more deficit financing to fulfill urgent Plan needs.

Summarizing its prospects of raising the necessary rupees for the Plan, the Government finds that, although taxes, savings and loans will yield as much as expected, it cannot rely on deficit financing to the amount it hoped.

This presents a severe dilemma. Can taxes be raised still more on top of the new heavy burden just imposed? Can still more in savings and loans be collected? The dilemma is that if the Government takes too much in taxes and loans, it will dry up money needed by private enterprise for expansion. If it takes too little, development cannot progress.

Viewed as a whole, then, the Government's task of raising its rupee needs is by no means easy. It will call for an all-out effort and the utmost vigilance on non-Plan expenditures. As a last resort, some expenditures on the Plan itself may also be cut.

The Agricultural Commodity Agreement, made between the United States and India in mid-1956, which is bringing 3.5 million tons of wheat and substantial amounts of other United States surplus commodities (rice, cotton, and so on) to India will be a sizable help. These commodities, to be sold by Government within India, will raise Rs. 137 crores in rupees for internal use. To the extent that India will not have to import so much food, cotton, and so on, they will also conserve foreign exchange.

2. *Financing Private Enterprise's Share of the Plan*

Exactly how much private enterprise will spend during the Second Plan cannot be known or planned precisely—but it is estimated at Rs. 2,400 crores, or at least 50 per cent more than over the First Plan.

A fair share—somewhat under a fourth—of this Rs. 2,400 crores of private investment will be needed in foreign exchange, particularly by those private industries which must purchase machinery, raw materials and the like from abroad.

Private enterprises depend for invested funds on the savings of individuals or on their own earnings. Individuals may invest savings directly by purchasing goods or equipment, by purchasing shares or bonds, or by depositing these savings with investing institutions.

Private enterprise as a whole is expected to need and spend a very large amount on construction and agriculture, irrigation, small industry, and so on, although just how much can only be guessed. A large part of it will be direct investment, not passing through banks; and a large share will be in labor and materials, that is, non-monetized investment, without involving cash transactions.

With the growing enthusiasm for the Plan, contributions of voluntary labor and materials, already considerable during the First Plan, to various "nation-building" activities should also increase, and in total add up to a significant amount of private investment. As noted earlier, a great challenge to planning under democracy is how this kind of contribution may be stimulated to the utmost, and use India's vast human resources to create national wealth.

Taken in all, however, the Government feels generally that, because of the rising tempo of development, the growth of towns, and the rural development program, the question of enough money for private development of agriculture and construction will not present a very serious problem over the Plan period, and that even if it were less than now expected, measures could be taken to stimulate increased use of resources among village farmers.

The chief concern is how private large-scale and medium *industry* may raise the capital it needs for expansion and growth. In view of the fact that the Plan includes development of a large number of private industries, the Government has very urgent concern that sufficient private capital be available.

The Government expects that expansion of business and industry, and of the economy as a whole, will, as we have seen, create more income and hence more savings, and encourage more investment in all new enterprises, and especially industry.

The summary on the next page shows where it is expected that private industry will be able to raise the capital. The extent to which Government or Government-facilitated capital (and foreign capital) will be needed is very clear.

Although large and well established firms have had no difficulty in selling shares in new or expanded enterprises, India's capital market is not yet so fully developed that it can readily draw upon all available savings. The Government is making every effort to strengthen the market by establishing suitable credit and financial agencies.

The Government also adjusts its own efforts to raise funds so that it does not compete with private enterprise for capital. And it grants various tax and other concessions to stimulate investment in those industries essential for development, or for manufacturing exportable goods, or which will help conserve imports.

The Government, further, has announced as its basic industrial policy that it will help essential industries find capital, both foreign and domestic, and itself make credit available.

One way it will do so is to channel funds through direct loans and various types of lending agencies participated in or sponsored by

FINANCING PRIVATE INDUSTRY EXPANSION OVER THE SECOND PLAN
(Excluding Small-Scale Industry)

	Rs. Crores	
	1951–56	1956–61
PRIVATE DOMESTIC CAPITAL		
New issues	40	80
Corporate profits and reserves available for investment (in new units and for replacements)	150	300
Other sources, such as finance from managing agents, excess profits tax refunds, etc.	61–64	80
CAPITAL FROM GOVERNMENT OR GOVERNMENT-FINANCED OR -SPONSORED LENDING AGENCIES		
Loans from industrial finance corporations, State finance corporations and the Industrial Credit and Investment Corporation	18	40
Resources from the National Industrial Development Corporation	—	55
Direct loans; indirect loans from Government, from equalization funds; State participation by Central Government; participation and/or loans by State Governments in share capital of private enterprises	26	20
	295–298	575
FOREIGN CAPITAL		
Foreign capital, including suppliers' credits	42–45	100
TOTAL	337–343	675

Government. These agencies are described in a later chapter on private enterprise.

On behalf of private enterprise the Government also is negotiating with several international lending agencies, and making a strong effort to attract foreign private capital.

For investment in large and medium industry alone, the original estimates of the Second Plan were that private industry would need approximately Rs. 570 crores—more than double what it spent over First Plan. An additional Rs. 150 crores are needed for modernization, or a total of Rs. 720 crores. With the rise in prices over the first part of the Plan, these estimates have gone up.

This total of Rs. 675 crores falls somewhat short (by Rs. 45 crores) of the Rs. 720 crores needed. But the Government reasonably expects that with the new steps it is now taking to stimulate investments and strengthen public confidence it will be possible for private enterprise to raise the additional capital it needs.

The Rs. 100 crores of foreign capital expected by private industry is part of the larger and urgent problem of all foreign exchange needs of the Plan.

3. Foreign Exchange Needs of the Plan

The Second Plan needs to raise at least Rs. 1,700 crores ($3.5 billion) in foreign exchange for carrying through both Government and private development programs, even after taking into account some possible reductions in Government programs as originally planned.

This very high figure of Rs. 1,700 crores—about a fourth of the total public and private cost of the Plan—is due almost entirely to India's effort to industrialize. The Plan requires exceptionally heavy imports of steel, machinery, power plant equipment and the like. Railway equipment alone represents nearly a third of all of the Government's foreign exchange needs for the Plan.

Clearly, as India expands and develops, it becomes a far better customer for the goods manufactured by developed nations than if it remained in backward poverty. Yet at the same time the very urgent question is how India may find the dollars and pounds sterling to buy the goods it needs, particularly if world prices continue to rise.

India realized as it drew up the Plan, with its stress on the development of industry, mining and transport, that it would mean a heavy strain on foreign exchange. The original Plan estimated a deficit of about Rs. 1,100 crores over the five years. Most of the deficit was expected to be felt in the first three years of the Plan, when the largest purchases of steel, machinery and other equipment were being made to get the steel mills and other Plan programs rapidly under way. In the latter part of the Plan period, as a number of the projects were completed, the shortage of foreign exchange was expected to lessen.

Actually in the first year of the Plan, however, India's imports of machinery and industrial raw materials exceeded original expectations, and fresh estimates of the foreign exchange gap have now been made. The amount of foreign exchange needed to equip the steel plants, for example, is likely to be considerably larger than estimated earlier. Prices of imported steel machinery and equipment have also risen appreciably. In addition, India's foreign-exchange resources are being strained by larger imports of foodgrains and by the increased cost of defense.

To pay for its essential imports India has drawn heavily upon its sterling reserves. In the autumn of 1957, India reduced the legal minimum limit for the currency reserve, in order to use its sterling reserves to the maximum extent feasible. In addition, India has obtained short-term credit of Rs. 95 crores ($200 million) from the International Monetary Fund, of which India is a member.

In early 1957 India took stringent measures to cut down its imports, especially of non-essential consumer goods, largely the luxury goods used chiefly by the rich and well-to-do. Foreign travel except for essential purposes was also restricted. To bring about even more immediate savings, in June and September 1957 further drastic import restrictions were made.

Later in 1957 a strict order of priorities was set to ensure imports of machinery and materials for the most essential Plan projects. This new order required that no new commitments involving foreign exchange be made for any projects other than those included in what is called the "core" of the Plan. This "core" includes steel plants, coal, railways, ports, and power projects which are related to other "core" projects—as for example, those which provide the power necessary to run the steel mills. It was also decided that no new programs involving foreign exchange costs would be adopted in the annual plan for 1958–1959. Further, projects and proposals which require foreign exchange but are already under way were being reviewed in order to cut the foreign exchange needs to a minimum.

It was decided that any projects requiring foreign exchange, which were outside the "core" group, would be permitted only under special conditions, whether they were Government or private projects. To be permitted, they must have a high priority and their foreign exchange costs should as a rule be covered by investments, loans or credits not involving foreign exchange payment before 1960–1961. A detailed review of non-"core" projects was being made in the last months of 1957, and an order of priorities for them was being drawn up.

The foreign exchange needs for the maintenance of the economy— that is, for purposes other than planned development programs— were also being reviewed. A large number of commitments for foreign exchange payment had, of course, already been made, and those which were outstanding, whether made by Government or private enterprise, were put under review. Where possible, arrangements were being negotiated to rephase payments. It is recognized, however, that with the large number of commitments outstanding, the first year or two after 1957 will be very difficult.

Yet even with all these restrictions, it is certainly not expected, in view of the great volume of costly imports needed for the Plan, that exports can at any time balance imports during the Plan period. Proposals for substantially stepping up exports were worked out in late 1957, to form the basis for a new export promotion program.

India's imports have greatly increased, as we have seen, since India began intensive development. Its largest imports have been foodgrains, crude and refined oil, raw cotton and jute, chemicals, drugs and medicines, electrical goods and equipment, machinery, iron and steel, and cars, trucks and other vehicles. Together these accounted for two-thirds of India's total imports in 1955–1956.

Over the Second Plan, as already made clear, the bulk of the additional imports will be machinery, vehicles, iron and steel and other metals—at a rate of about Rs. 430 crores (about $860 million) a year. About 7 million tons of steel will be imported and a large amount of other metals, especially aluminum and copper.

India will also import considerable foodgrains over the Second Plan period—between 8 and 10 million tons. This is a larger amount than originally expected, but it is now felt that because of the rising demand for food as incomes go up, adequate food supplies must be assured to keep down food prices, and have stocks in reserve against any failure in monsoon rains and harvests. The recent agreement made with the United States Government for surplus agricultural commodities (mainly wheat and rice) has considerably eased the problem of financing food imports.

India expects, as it develops, to be an increasingly heavy importer, although as its own industries grow, the type of goods imported may change. At a higher stage of industrialization it will need newer and more advanced types of machinery. As incomes and living standards rise, there will be demand for higher types of manufactured consumer goods and for the raw materials and machinery with which to make new and additional consumer goods within India as well. India expects, as it develops more fully and steps up its own production, to be able to pay for such goods, and also to repay the debts being incurred today, out of its increased national income and increasing exports. Meanwhile, however, India's export earnings will not balance the essential goods it must import, and other sources of foreign financing will have to be found.

FOREIGN PRIVATE CAPITAL

The great majority of countries which have developed in the past have done so with the help of foreign capital. The great growth of the United States over the nineteenth century was in part assisted by capital from the United Kingdom, France, the Netherlands, and other nations. Britain's industrial revolution was financed in part by profits drawn from its colonies. Latin American countries and China, for example, are now receiving considerable capital and know-how from various sources for their development.

Similarly, foreign capital is now needed in India.

A few generations ago, however, the flow of capital from nation to nation was easier in general than today. The close tie-up between political dominance and foreign investment which characterized the old colonial system has disappeared, and some new arrangements to replace the old are only slowly being worked out.

Before Independence, in India as in other underdeveloped countries, foreign capital had tended to concentrate largely on the development and extraction of raw materials and facilities for moving them— on mining, tea and other plantations, and railways. An independent country anxious to develop itself naturally hopes that foreign investors will enter into nation-building industries and enterprises, not only to supplement the country's own slender resources for such industries, but, by bringing in advanced technical knowledge, skill and methods, to encourage local capital and strengthen new competence and skills within the country itself. Foreign capital so invested can fill a strategic and integrated role in the country's advancement, as well as help create for itself a more stable and rewarding investment in a constantly strengthened and expanding nation.

Very shortly after Independence, India expressed this view, and gave assurances not only that repatriation of capital and remittances of profits would be safeguarded, but that the Government would also so frame its policy as to enable further foreign capital to be invested on mutually advantageous terms and conditions. The First Five Year Plan also expressed India's welcome to and desire to attract foreign capital and described the important role it could play. India is happy, moreover, that it has a record, since Independence, of political and financial stability that possibly is rivaled in few underdeveloped countries.

Those familiar with the outlook and attitudes of leaders of the

Indian Government, and with their earnest desire to secure rapid development through every means consistent with democracy, feel assured that private foreign investment will have an important role to play in India's future development.

A considerable number of foreign firms and investors are in India, although the number is far less than India needs and can provide profitable opportunities for. A survey recently reported by the Reserve Bank of India shows that from mid-1948 to the end of 1953 there were roughly Rs. 130 crores of (net) foreign investment over this period, of which roughly 40 per cent was reinvested profits and 60 per cent fresh investment.

Since the end of 1953 there has been considerable new private foreign investment in India—for example, in oil refineries, in drug manufacture, in dyestuffs, in truck manufacturing. There is general confidence in India as a promising field for foreign investment and in its great future as an expanding market.

The Government is actively encouraging investment in such essential industries, and freely permitting repatriation of original capital, reinvested profits and capital gains, if any. Control of capital issues and licensing of new industries are common to both domestic and foreign investors.

It is worth noting that the Government has particularly encouraged and helped investment of foreign capital in basic industries.

For example, from British, American, German and other firms there is foreign capital or technical assistance or both, in the manufacture of locomotives, trucks, heavy chemicals, and dyestuffs, electrical and heavy machinery, and essential drugs. There has also been in other fields some gradual change-over from more purely trading operations to actual manufacturing with foreign capital. Here the most important example is the setting up, over the First Plan period, of three oil refineries; a number of other proposals are under consideration.

In the Second Plan, as under the First, particular encouragement will be given to foreign capital to establish industries in collaboration with Indian industrialists, and to use Indian workmen and technicians. Several major proposals have already taken shape in which

BETTER SEED, BETTER CROPS: A Sikh farmer contrasts the finer quality cotton produced by new, improved seed with the yield from the local variety he formerly used. Improved seed varieties are an important step in increasing India's crop yields, which have been among the lowest in the world.

NEW HOMES, NEW VILLAGES: A supervisor helps advise a villager in Mysore State, on constructing his new stone house with local labor. Nearly 100,000 new village homes were built under the village development program during First Plan years, with small home-building loans advanced by the Government.

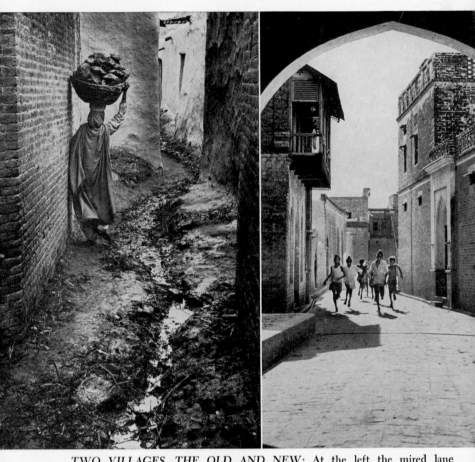

TWO VILLAGES, THE OLD AND NEW: At the left the mired lane common in Indian villages before the self-help rural improvement program began. Today thousands of villages like the one at the right have paved their streets, installed drains, and provided street cleaning and lighting services, schools and playgrounds. Rebuilding and reconstructing backward villages is a major aim of India's rural development program.

foreign and Indian capital will collaborate. These include the Atul-ICI Dyestuff project for the manufacturing of vat dyes, and the Mercedes-Benz Automobile project for manufacturing trucks and buses with Tata Iron and Steel Company, also at Jamshedpur. Production of these trucks and buses has already begun.

To explore opportunities for expanded foreign investment, the Government is underwriting a special study by the newly formed National Council of Applied Economic Research [1] on India's tax policies as related to private foreign investment in India. The Indian Government is also sponsoring an evaluation of the experience to date of foreign capital in India, with preparation of documented case material on investment opportunities.

The Indian Government has also contributed, as one of forty-eight countries, to the newly formed International Finance Corporation, whose objective is to further economic development by encouraging the international flow of private funds into private investment. The Industrial Credit and Investment Corporation (described on p. 275), is also expected to play an important role in bringing together prospective foreign investors and private entrepreneurs in India.

With all such means and encouragement, the Government shares with Indian private enterprise the hope that foreign capital will be invested in India on an increasing scale.

Over the Second Plan, the minimum expectation is for additional foreign private investment of Rs. 100 crores.

FOREIGN LOANS (NON-GOVERNMENT)

An important further source of foreign exchange for India's development is in loans from foreign lending agencies. The Indian Government has very actively encouraged and assisted such loans, both to private and to public enterprise.

The International Bank for Reconstruction and Development (the World Bank) has already provided considerable loan assistance to

---

[1] The National Council of Applied Economic Research was set up during 1956, as a private body with directors drawn from private industry and Government, to conduct economic research for Government and private industry.

India—a total of Rs. 40 crores over the First Plan—both to Government and to private enterprises.

Over the First Plan, with facilitation by the Indian Government, the World Bank made a loan of Rs. 15 crores to the Indian Iron and Steel Company (IISCO) and a loan of Rs. 7.7 crores to the Trombay Power Project of the Tata Hydroelectric Agency. A third loan of Rs. 4.8 crores was extended by the Bank in March 1955 to the Industrial Credit and Investment Corporation of India, a semi-official body making loans to selected private investors. The major part of all these World Bank loans will be drawn upon during the Second Plan period.

In 1956, with the Government's active assistance, the World Bank finalized a $75 million loan to the Tata Iron and Steel Company (TISCO) for its expansion program. This is the largest loan as yet granted by the World Bank for industry, and the largest single loan granted for any purpose to any Asian country.

The World Bank has sent two missions to India over 1956–1957 to review proposals for assisting railway expansion to relieve the expected transport shortage. The Bank announced in mid-1957 an initial loan of Rs. 45 crores ($90 million) for railway development, and further loans are expected.

The Government is also helping private enterprise to negotiate various kinds of private credit and deferred payment schemes. Early in the Second Plan the Government began to facilitate offers of short-term foreign credit, which were being made available by overseas banks to enable Indian firms to purchase capital equipment abroad.

FOREIGN ASSISTANCE

India has long realized that the burden of financing its development rests almost entirely on its own efforts—indeed, efforts beyond efforts—to raise, by higher taxes and other means, the rupees needed, and to create conditions favorable to foreign trade and foreign capital. Any assistance from abroad, however generous, can only be small compared to the vast total necessary to develop the nation and the burden that must be borne by its people.

Over the First Plan, however, the aid of foreign nations—in loans, grants and technical assistance—has helped to make up for India the vital balance in its development funds. Foreign aid and loans totaling nearly Rs. 300 crores were made available for Government development programs over the First Plan period. This assistance the Indian Government and Indian people greatly appreciate.

Many nations have contributed not only grants and loans, but have opened for India, as for other countries, their enormous store of scientific and technical knowledge, a resource whose value is beyond price.

For India, the largest single contributor was the United States. Including the United States Wheat Loan (1951) and the contribution of private United States philanthropic agencies, total United States aid to the First Plan amounted to Rs. 238 crores, or about four-fifths of all foreign assistance received by India over the First Plan period. About 55 per cent of the assistance received from the United States was in the form of loans.

Other contributors have been the Commonwealth member nations of the Colombo Plan, which provided Rs. 45 crores on a grant basis; and the Norwegian Government, which granted Rs. 6.6 million for a valuable project of developing India's fisheries and fishing communities.

Agencies such as the WHO, UNICEF, FAO, and other arms of the United Nations, and private philanthropic groups such as the Ford and Rockefeller foundations, the American Friends Service Committee and others, have made important contributions, very particularly in the field of technical assistance. The United Kingdom has contributed principally such technical aid.

All this foreign assistance has been vitally helpful in the fields in which it was largely concentrated: rural development, education, expansion of industry, mining, railways and power, and public health.

Some of the Colombo Powers' assistance, and in the last two years of the First Plan roughly half of United States development assistance, have been in the form of surplus agricultural commodities, which, as mentioned earlier, have not only supplied needed food, but helped hold down food prices, and save foreign exchange for essential imports.

India believes that as it launches its Second Plan it can look forward to some measure of foreign assistance in loans and grants.

The full extent of this aid cannot naturally be calculated in advance. Some, however, is already known. The United States Commodity Credit Agreement in August 1956 provided surplus agricultural products to the value of Rs. 137 crores in loans and grants; Britain and the U.S.S.R. have promised credits for machinery and other equipment to the value of Rs. 98 crores for the two steel plants to which they are providing technical assistance. A reasonable assumption is that the Colombo Powers will continue their present level of aid.

Summing up India's position of late 1957, there is a total foreign exchange deficit of Rs. 1,700 crores (about $3.5 billion) which seems inescapable if projects for the "core" of the Plan, and the projects on which substantial investment has already been made, are not to suffer. Against this deficit, India has financed somewhat over half—about Rs. 500 crores—from its own resources, and Rs. 450 crores through foreign assistance in loans and grants, or a total of Rs. 950 crores (about $2 billion). India can draw upon its reduced sterling reserves only very little more. It is estimated, therefore, that for the Plan to be fulfilled in its essentials, foreign assistance of about Rs. 700 crores ($1.5 billion), mainly in the form of loans, is needed.

India hopes that its own efforts to earn more foreign exchange by increasing its exports will be supplemented by nations which share its concern for the rapid advancement of the Indian people, and which produce the goods which India so urgently wishes to buy, thus finding a way to fill the gap in India's foreign-exchange resources.

The
Development Programs

SECOND FIVE YEAR PLAN, 1956–1961

SECTION I

AGRICULTURE and RURAL
DEVELOPMENT

HIGH LIGHTS

of programs to advance

INDIA'S RURAL ECONOMY AND RURAL PEOPLE

The Second Plan will spend Rs. 568 crores, or about 60 per cent more than was spent in the First Plan, on agriculture and rural development. When the costs of proposed irrigation are added, rural expenditures will be nearly one-fifth of all expenditures under the Second Plan.

Virtually every major activity of the Second Plan has, moreover, been framed to yield direct benefits to rural India. The Second Plan, taken as a whole, has these main targets for the advancement of India's rural economy and its village people:

All of village India—325 million people—covered by the rural development program.

Faster land reform and fairer land distribution.

Cheap farm credit accessible to all villages, and increased rural cooperative services.

A 28 per cent rise in total agricultural production.

A 17 per cent rise in agricultural incomes.

1.6 to 2 million more full-time rural jobs.

21 million more acres under irrigation.

Every cultivated acre supplied with improved seed and fertilizers.

A road within five miles of every village in well developed agricultural areas.

Rural electrification of 13,900 villages.

Rural postal and telegraph services expanded, with a goal of reaching within five miles of every village.

3,000 more rural health clinics and an intensified rural health program.

A nation-wide rural housing program.

Advance of village schools and rural higher education.

Strengthened village self-government, with panchayats in 244,-564 villages.

CHAPTER I

Rural India:
Problems, Progress and Targets

Rural India covers four-fifths of the total population. Its farms yield about half the total income of the nation. For nearly 250 million people agriculture is a means of livelihood; for them and over 50 million more the Indian village and rural society are a way of life.

Despite India's great cities, its industries, its proposals to intensify industry, India is now and will remain in the foreseeable future a predominantly agricultural nation. For India, as for almost all of Asia, the test of development is the advance of agriculture and of rural people.

In agricultural India crops and climate vary widely. Fruit orchards on the cool Himalayan foothills contrast with hot dry plains in north and central India, where wheat, cotton, millets and sugar cane are the principal crops. Here, aside from a few winter showers, the July-to-October monsoons are the only rains.

Toward the South, in the Deccan plateau, wet and dry lands produce cotton, millets and rice.

159

Far South, on the western coast, constant moist heat and heavy rainfall produce rice, coconuts, spices, cashew nuts; tea and coffee plantations cover the hills and mountainsides. On the South's east coast, the chief crop is rice; the rains are fickle.

Westward, in Kutch and Rajasthan, an encroaching desert produces scant wheat and millets for a sparse population. Far to the east, near the Burma border, Assam averages over 100 inches of rain a year, and produces chiefly rice, and tea on the mountain slopes. From densely settled West Bengal, and from Bihar and Orissa, the States surrounding Calcutta and sharing its steamy climate, come principally rice and jute.

For India, as a whole, about 78 per cent of cultivated acreage is in foodgrains.[1] In value, rice is the leading crop, followed by wheat, then sugar cane, ground nuts and other oil seeds, millets and grams (foodgrains and pulses) and cotton. Although the total value of jute, tea and spice crops is relatively small, they are extremely important as exports earning foreign exchange.

In spite of differences in crop and climate, throughout India rural society and rural problems are everywhere much the same.

The typical rural community is the village, a cluster of small huts of mud, thatch or bamboo, or, a few, in the mountains, of wood. There are 558,089[2] of these villages in India, 70 per cent of them with a population of 500 or less. Most of them, except in the rural development areas, are isolated and backward. Schools are few, roads, radios and newspapers rare, farming methods primitive, and the village people at the bottom of the scale in health, sanitation, literacy, income and opportunity.

In village society, in its economic opportunities and social distinctions, status and caste play a large part. Most of the villagers are cultivators, and most of these own the land they till. But 25 per cent of village families hold 84 per cent of the land, and possession of land is the common key to privilege. At the bottom of the social and eco-

---

[1] Land under cultivation is about 40 per cent of the total land area. This compares with 16 per cent in Japan and 11 per cent in China.
[2] 1951 Census.

nomic ladder are the agricultural laborers who form about a third of the rural population. Half of them are landless, and almost all are Harijans or belong to other "depressed" classes.

A rigid hierarchy, village society has nevertheless achieved remarkable social stability and cohesion. Over the centuries, India's villages, isolated and resistant to destructive wars, to famine and to alien values, have been the reservoir and guardians of India's common culture.

Earlier generations called the Indian peasant farmer "pathetically content." Today, under the stimulus of Independence, with the incentives and help of the rural development program, he has revealed aspirations long submerged, creative energies long suppressed, and a great resurgent vitality.

The typical village farm is a subsistence holding, tiny by most Western standards and certainly by those of the United States. Fifty-three per cent of all farm owners hold less than five acres. In most of India, from a third to three-fourths of all holdings—in densely crowded Travancore-Cochin (now Kerala State) as high as 95 per cent—are less than five acres. As population grows and lands are divided on inheritance, the number of small holdings is increasing. An antiquated and feudal land system has for centuries inhibited rather than encouraged farm improvement, new investment and higher production.

The small yield of Indian fields, among the lowest in the world, is both the cause and the effect of rural poverty and backwardness.

Modern knowledge of improved seeds, fertilizers, farm practices and implements has not, except in development areas, reached the village farmer from India's agricultural colleges and research stations. The improved plows and other implements which helped revolutionize agriculture in the West are in use in only a few areas. Use of fertilizers, though it increased enormously over the First Plan, is still one-ninth that of Japan per acre under cultivation.

India today has more land under irrigation from major projects than any country of the world; it must have still more. Apart from the rain-soaked Malabar Coast and Assam, irrigation is the essential of consistent agricultural production. Of the total crop area, 80 per cent depends wholly on fickle seasonal monsoons.

Yet, given improved farm practices and implements, good seeds, fertilizers and green manures, irrigation to supplement the monsoons, and dry-farming techniques, Indian agriculture has unique advantages. The warm climate, never touched by frost, can under irrigation produce two and even three harvests a year. Plentiful farm labor makes possible for many crops a type of intensive agriculture that in Japan, for example, has brought amazing yields.[1]

Farm mechanization is not necessarily considered the solution to India's low production. For India, mechanization is not always more efficient, in terms of capital or labor, nor the necessarily desirable goal. In whatever way land may be distributed under land reforms, or whatever new methods of village land management may be undertaken, the basic unit of cultivation will, for the vast majority of Indian farmers, be a small holding readily plowed by a pair of bullocks, which cost Rs. 500–750 ($100–$150), and require no fuel, and whose supplementary farm uses are of great importance.

Tractors devised in labor-scarce countries where vast acreage must be cultivated have, however, certain valued uses. In areas infested by the destructive kans grass, or in waste lands badly eroded or overrun by scrub jungle, tractors are essential to clear and to cut deep. On India's few very large farms, they have been used with efficiency.

Low rural incomes in any case leave little margin for costly farm implements or even for simple basic improvements. In some areas, perhaps as many as 80 per cent of the farmers need loans to buy seeds and other essential supplies; and in the past the village moneylender has prospered on peasant debts. Cheap, accessible rural credit is fundamental to rural progress.

The question of costly mechanization is seen in clearer focus when it is recalled that one of India's gravest social and economic problems is an oversupply of agricultural laborers, numbering (with their

[1] It is interesting to note that rice yields per acre in Japan, where cultivation is largely by hand, are among the highest in the world, and average two-thirds higher than United States mechanized rice cultivation.

dependents) about 90 millions [1] throughout India. Their per capita income is Rs. 104 ($21), less than half the nation's average. A fourth, or possibly as many as a third, of them are believed surplus to the needs of agriculture. The half of them who are also landless cannot profit from programs designed to advance small farm owners. Many of the major challenges of India's agricultural advance express themselves in their most concentrated form in the conditions and immediate prospects of landless laborers.

For a few of those who have no land or have too little, the distribution of land following land reforms and land reclamation is a way out, and as we have seen, India has planned over the future some relief of pressure on the land by creating more jobs outside agriculture.

But now and for some time to come a problem of greatest urgency is how to develop a system of efficient land management through which all village farmers—those with larger farms, but particularly those with small and fragmented holdings and little capital for investment, and those with no land or capital at all—can be helped to greater production, income, employment and opportunity.

In India's approach to developing its agriculture it strives for two basic objectives.

First, India must bring about the social and economic advance of its village people, creating and encouraging a vital, democratic, productive village society. At the same time it must rapidly increase agricultural production. The prosperity not only of the rural people but of India as a whole, and the success of the Second and all future Plans, depend on the prosperity and production of agriculture.

We have seen that in other nations under rapid development, efforts to advance rural people while at the same time sharply stepping up agricultural production have proved the crucial test of social policy, and of social and political stability.

India has deliberately chosen the democratic process, and put above all other considerations the development of the individual. India has

---

[1] Agricultural Labour Enquiry 1950–1951. The Census of 1951, taken earlier, and using a less comprehensive definition of cultivating laborer, put the figure considerably lower.

been interested in the comment of Professor Arnold Toynbee who visited India's rural development areas in the winter of 1956–1957:

The world's peasantry still amounts today to something between two-thirds and three-quarters of the world's total population. This means that the peasantry's future is going to be decisive for mankind's, and the crucial question for the peasantry is how they are to come to terms with the modern way of life that has suddenly been conjured into existence by the Industrial Revolution. In Russia, China and India alike, energetic attempts to modernize the peasantry are being made in our time; but the experiment in India is uniquely important and interesting. . . . India has chosen the harder and slower way of trying to persuade the peasant's conservative mind to opt for modernization voluntarily as a result of being rationally convinced of its advantages. It is obviously a matter of immense importance . . . that this courageous and imaginative Indian experiment should succeed.[1]

The following pages describe the methods, the programs by which India attempts to solve by democratic means this greatest of all its problems—the advance of its agriculture and its rural people.

THE FIRST PLAN'S ACCOMPLISHMENTS

On this great problem, the First Plan made an impressive beginning. Framed in the 1951–1952 period of acute food shortage, following four years of poor weather and unreliable monsoons, the First Plan gave top priority and nearly one-third of its total budget to agriculture, irrigation, and development of the rural people.

Indeed, taken as a whole, the most important single contribution of the First Plan can be said to be its vigorous and imaginative attack on India's rural problems, its long-static agriculture, its impoverished and backward villages.

The Plan achieved an actual increase of 20 per cent in foodgrain production (the target had been 15 per cent), greatly enlarged the land area under cultivation and irrigation, initiated basic land reforms and launched the dynamic rural development program which has begun the rejuvenation of India's rural people.

[1] *Hindustan Times*, May 19, 1957.

The major programs are described in detail in later chapters. A brief summary here gives a view of the First Plan's rural effort as an integrated whole.

1. *The Rural Development Program:* Of highest importance for the Second and all future Plans, the First Plan set up a fundamental organization—the rural development program and the national extension service—which for the first time in India's history could reach to the villages with the means, the knowledge and stimulation to self-help.

This program, by the end of the First Plan, had been extended to nearly one-fourth of rural India—80 million villagers in 123,000 villages—to break the barriers of rural ignorance, poverty and apathy.

2. *Land Reform:* Throughout India, the so-called "intermediaries" —the old feudal landlord and tax-farming systems—have been almost entirely abolished, with compensation. Land rents are generally much reduced, although there is considerable difference between States. In all, a positive and appreciable beginning has been made on this most difficult and urgent issue.

3. *Irrigation:* 16 million new acres were irrigated, or over a fourth as many as were put under irrigation in all India's preceding history.

4. *Land Reclamation:* For forty years preceding 1950–1951, no large new acreage had been put in cultivation. To relieve pressure on the land and increase food production, the First Plan in five years brought 7.4 million new acres under the plow by reclaiming waste and jungle lands, by tractoring out the destructive deep-rooted kans grass, by bunding and leveling eroded areas. Altogether 24 million additional acres were put into more productive use over the First Plan, by land reclamation, irrigation and other means.

Although no exact total figure is available, many thousands of acres were distributed to the landless individually and in colonizing schemes. Fifteen million acres of the new lands are planted to food crops, the remainder to commercial crops.

5. *Improved Farm Practices:* Throughout India, but especially in rural development areas, a beginning was made to spread the use of improved seeds, implements and better farming practices. Although

not enough work was done, there was some progress. The so-called Japanese method of rice cultivation was introduced on 2.1 million acres, with an average increase of 80 per cent above previous yields. By education and propaganda, the use of fertilizers was more than doubled (610,000 tons at the end of the Plan as against 275,000 tons in 1950–1951). In the last years of the Plan, demand for fertilizers ran ahead of supply in spite of a sharp rise in production.

6. *Agricultural Education and Research:* A significant advance was made in expanding and strengthening agricultural education and for the first time relating it, with extension training, directly to the practical needs and problems of village farmers. The setting up of a nation-wide rural system of village extension training for rural development workers at all levels is one of the outstanding achievements of the First Plan years.

Yet apart from these specific achievements, without question the First Plan's greatest contribution was a new, resurgent spirit in rural India. The rural problems that remained were immense and staggering still. But rural India's awakening brought a fresh and vital confidence to all of India. It brought a new assurance that solutions to rural problems, which have for centuries depressed the economy and the nation, can be found in the democratic process, in the awakened energies of the village people.

PROGRAMS OF THE SECOND PLAN

The Second Plan's rural programs are framed with an even greater awareness of the close interdependence of agriculture and industrial development, the sharper knowledge that a dynamic, productive rural India is essential as a base for India's economic growth. Increasingly and acutely, India realizes that without a swift rise in agricultural production the Plan itself cannot be fulfilled.

In general the Second Plan will continue, expand and redouble the substantial efforts and progress begun over the First Plan. No new major program is introduced. The important new targets are the raising of agricultural production by 28 per cent, the effort to find some solution to efficient land management and the problem of the landless laborer, the expansion of the rural development program to cover all India, and its intensified integrated use as the key instrument for carrying out all programs of rural advancement.

CHAPTER II

Community Development:
The Silent Revolution

On October 2, 1952, the anniversary of Mahatma Gandhi's birthday, India launched a program whose purpose was no less than a rural revolution.

What it proposed was to transform the social and economic life and outlook of the rural people, raise farm production and incomes, and create from stagnant backward villages a vital, progressive rural community. It proposed to do all this, not by coercion, but, as the "essence of the program," by self-help and participation of the people themselves.

The community development program, as it is called, was based on the knowledge that the advancement of India's millions of people in the villages is imperative to the nation's social, political and economic development. It was based on the knowledge that if these people have in the past seemed apathetic, or "pathetically content" with poverty, it is because they were for so long not permitted to participate in programs for their own improvement.

It was based on the faith, already justified, that if they were given the opportunity for self-help they would respond with their skills, enthusiasm and energies to achieve their own advancement. It was also based on the knowledge that no program for the advance of India's villages could succeed unless it had the wholehearted cooperation of the rural people themselves.

The program proposed, under a unique form of organization, to bring the people the means and stimulus of self-help in every aspect of rural life—village schools, roads, community centers, safe drinking water, better seeds and plows, knowledge of improved farming, methods of health and sanitation.

But "the community projects," said the Prime Minister as the program was being shaped, "are of vital importance not only for the material achievements they will bring about, but much more so because they seek to build up the community and the individual, and to make the latter a builder not only of his own village center but in a larger sense of India. . . . The primary matter is the human being involved, the man who is going to work, the man who is going to feel it and translate that feeling into action." [1]

The program began in October 1952 in 25,000 villages; at the end of the First Plan in April 1956, it had reached 123,000 villages and 80 million people, just under a fourth of all villages in India.

The program's possibilities were soon widely recognized.

"For the first time, it may be said with truth that we tackled the rural problem in a realistic way," said the Prime Minister in 1955. "This was not merely from above but rather by inducing the people themselves to solve their own problems. Something life-giving went to them and their eyes brightened and their arms began to function and their muscles became stronger. A process of rejuvenation set in." [2]

The program's approach and methods are based largely upon experiments made by Rabindranath Tagore, by Mahatma Gandhi, and

[1] Prime Minister Nehru, at the First Development Commissioners' Conference, May 7, 1952.
[2] Prime Minister Nehru, Message to the Fourth Development Commissioners' Conference, 1955.

others, Indian and foreign, who had attempted over the past fifty years to tackle the urgent problem of rural reconstruction.

What distinguishes the community development program from efforts of the past is its organization and scope, its methods, and its purpose.

Under the program, "blocks" of roughly a hundred villages (about 60,000 to 70,000 people) are taken as a development unit, an area for intensive effort. Concentrated in each block, under a block development officer, are the technical specialists and the funds to bring the villagers both the knowledge and the means to advance in every aspect of their life—education, health, agriculture, animal husbandry, village industry, housing.

What early experiments had made clear was that all aspects of rural life are so interrelated that there could be no permanent advance in health, for example, or agriculture, if each were dealt with separately. Every block therefore makes an intensive coordinated approach to raising the level of rural life *as a whole*—stressing the building of a new school as much as the introduction of improved seeds and fertilizers, improved sanitation as much as the building of new roads or wells.

The agency of community development is a national rural extension system. India's national extension service was founded in 1953 and is regarded as one of the most significant achievements of the First Plan years. The service drew for inspiration on the experience of rural constructive workers stimulated by Tagore and Gandhi, and on the agricultural extension system widely used in the West and in Japan. Its essential method is education and persuasion; never coercion or dictation. Its incentive is the advancement both of the individual and of the community.

The key agent at the village level is the multi-purpose village extension worker, a young man, usually with high-school education or better, who has been especially trained in rural extension work. Young women are beginning to be used to do home extension work with farm wives and families.

Living in one of a 'circle' of the eight to ten villages under his care, the worker goes from village to village, from farmer to farmer, using all the techniques familiar to extension work in the West—field demonstrations, individual talks and group discussions, audio-visual teaching, approach to villagers with help on felt needs in order to awaken new needs and interest in change.

Trained as a multi-purpose worker, he brings help and information on improved methods of cultivation, on health care and sanitation, on cattle diseases and their prevention, and so on. Working through village leaders, he enlists the interest and participation of the village as a whole in change and progress.

As needed, he calls upon the funds and technical specialists from the block headquarters. Each block has specialists in agriculture, animal husbandry, cooperatives, and so on, provided by the respective State departments; and may also draw upon the District specialists in health, education, public works and the like.

The essence of the program is its dependence, its insistence, on self-help and participation of the people in their own progress. Early experiments in rural improvement had shown that "unless people feel that the program is theirs and value it as a practical contribution to their own welfare, no substantial results will be gained." [1] Its revolutionary character lies precisely in that it has succeeded in awakening this participation and organizing it on a national scale.

On the one hand, participation is individual. New seeds, plows, fertilizers are made available (free in experimental amounts, at cost for larger amounts) to the individual farmer; he is shown how to use them, and makes his own decisions to adopt them on his field to better his yield and income.

Participation is also of the group—the village. An eminent rural sociologist of the United States, who recently studied the program, points to one of the most significant aspects of the program when he suggests that "India's community development extension program is based on the knowledge that adoption of improved practices by

[1] *First Five Year Plan* (Government of India, 1952), page 223.

individuals will be more rapid if organized groups assume responsibility for the spread of these practices." [1]

The village is encouraged to build a new school or road, with the "block" paying part of the cost, and furnishing building plans and engineering skill. The village itself, however, must make the final decision to build the school and, moreover, put up its share of the cost in cash, labor and materials.

To stimulate the desire and courage for change, to aid the village in pooling its energies and abilities, the village is helped to form a representative democratic body, a panchayat or village council. It is the council's responsibility to collect the village's share of the cost of building the school or road, and supervise the construction. By these means the village itself, through its leaders, brings the people together as participants in their own progress.

An important point of distinction with rural programs followed in several countries is that in India's program, while various measures of social reform are pursued, all classes are urged to participate—the landowner and the landless, the village teacher and the Harijan. The rich man often gives land for the school, the poor man labor to build it; the children of both attend it.

The community development program is national. Its organization in four years to reach 80 million people, with a total staff of 80,000 persons, was an enormous administrative task. And this is but the first stage to covering the entire countryside of 325 million people.

Over-all coordination of policy and of planning of the program is in the hands of a newly formed Central Ministry of Community Development.[2] Direct administration of the program lies with the States in the office of each State's Development Commissioner. The Commissioner appoints block administrative staffs and the village

[1] A Critical Analysis of India's Community Development Program, Dr. Carl C. Taylor, Community Projects Administration, July 26, 1956.
[2] Created Sept. 1956 from the former Community Projects Administration which was within the Planning Commission. The program is carried on under the general guidance of a Central Committee which is composed of the Chairman and members of the Planning Commission and the Ministers of Food and Agriculture and Community Development.

extension workers, and secures and coordinates for the blocks in his State the technical services of the various State departments, such as Agriculture, Health, and so on.

The District Collector, as we have seen, has the responsibility of coordinating all development activities in the District. He is the leader of a team composed of representatives of various development agencies. To a large extent the District plan is woven round the community development program. This program itself has already gone a long way in integrating the work of all the agencies in the District, and in securing popular cooperation in carrying out their programs.

District Deputy Collectors have been given special training to serve as what are called project officers, who closely and directly supervise the work of all block development officers in the blocks under their jurisdiction.

At the District and State and block levels there are advisory committees composed of public citizens as well as of officials who review and suggest development policy. The need to strengthen these public advisory bodies has already been mentioned.

There are now two types of blocks—the intensive and the less intensive, called, respectively, the Community Development (CD) Blocks and National Extension Service (NES) Blocks. The organization and methods and purpose of both are identical; the intensive Community Development Blocks have more funds for health and education and for rural arts and crafts. The NES Block represents the normal and permanent pattern. During the Second Plan at least two out of every five NES Blocks are to be converted into intensive (CD) blocks, mainly on the basis of achievement.

By the end of the First Plan, there were 1,200 blocks, of which a fourth were "intensive"; by the end of the Second Plan, 3,800 new blocks will be added, of which nearly a third will be intensive.

Funds for the program are provided in the plans of States, and the Central Government contributes to this as to other development programs in the States.[1] Under the Second Plan, when the program

[1] Seventy-five per cent of all non-recurring expenditure and half of the recurring, with the States providing the balance.

is to cover all of India, the Planning Commission has allocated Rs. 200 crores, almost all of which—Rs. 188 crores—is provided by the States. Over the First Plan the expenditure by State and Central Governments was only Rs. 6 (about $1.25) for each of some 80 million people to whom it brought opportunity and means of advancement.

A new and nation-wide training system had to be set up to meet the needs of this vast development program.

Some specialized training was of course required for the thousands of multi-purpose village-level workers needed. Extension training centers, giving a six-month course in extension methods, agriculture, rural health, literacy, animal husbandry, and practical village work, were set up all over India. By the end of the First Plan there were forty-three, which together had trained 15,865 [1] village workers.

In 1955 twenty-five centers for training women for village extension work were set up, as more and more development workers realized that an approach must be made to village women if rural family living standards were to be raised. Simultaneously, to guide these women's centers, an office of Home Economics Extension was set up in the Central Food and Agriculture Ministry—India's first organized national bureau of home economics.

Regionally throughout India, centers were set up for training, in two- to six-month courses, other kinds and levels of workers: block and project officers, rural health workers, the social education organizers who are concerned with group organization and literacy teaching. Five agricultural colleges added extension departments, so that new agricultural students might learn the extension approach needed, henceforward, in all agricultural posts.

As the development program progressed, it became clear that the village extension workers needed more general agricultural training before their six-month special extension work, and forty-eight "basic" agricultural schools were set up for the purpose.

Under the Central and State Ministries of Health, midwives, nurses, lady health visitors, rural health workers of all levels began

[1] As of March 31, 1956.

training at forty-two centers. Inter-State seminars, in-service training programs, field-study tours were organized for top-level as well as for lower echelon development officials and workers to help stimulate the exchange of experience, ideas and criticism essential to make the total program constantly dynamic, refreshed and growing.

Under the Second Plan 200,000 new workers will be needed at all levels. To help train them, the number of extension training centers will be brought up to sixty-one, the basic agricultural schools to ninety-five.

ACCOMPLISHMENTS OF THE PROGRAM

India's community development program has been subject within India to continuous review and evaluation by the Programme Evaluation Organization, especially created in the Planning Commission for this work in 1952. It has also attracted the interest and study of rural sociologists, extension specialists, official and non-official community development experts from many countries.

Some visiting students of India's rural program have said it is "the most significant experiment in economic development and social improvement in Asia at the present time." India was also interested in the comment of Professor Toynbee: "The practical idealism of this great Indian enterprise may be going to bring about one of the most beneficent revolutions in the peasantry's life that have been known so far in history."

While India is too aware of the human and organizational problems yet to be solved to accept such comments without reservations, it is commonly agreed that the community development program has so aroused the enthusiasm and participation of India's villagers as to constitute a genuine people's movement, a true, if silent, revolution. As the Prime Minister said: "Something life-giving went to them. . . . A process of rejuvenation set in." Many villagers have been heard to say: "We were dead, and now we live." "We were slaves, now we are free."

Statistics give only a mechanical, partial view of what the program has done in the villages, but these are none the less revealing. Throughout India villagers have placed schools high on their scale of values, and 15,000 new schools have been started. School attendance in some areas is two to four times as high as before. A million people have attended literacy classes. While improvement in health and sanitation has generally lagged, over 1,000 health and maternity centers were set up, 101,000 wells built or renovated, 92,000 new homes built and another 33,000 improved.

Some 56,000 miles of village roads have been built or improved, providing in some cases the villagers' first road links to the outside world.

To improve crop yields, over 9 million maunds (321,429 tons) of fertilizers and 4½ million maunds (160,714 tons) of improved seed were distributed. Nearly 2 million acres were brought under irrigation either by sinking new wells or by minor works.

Villagers have joined in community activities, many for the first time. Ninety-five thousand community centers, 69,000 village clubs and organizations of farmers, of young farm people, and of women have been started, and some 34,000 panchayats and village councils have been created as actual or potential village governments.

Every road, school, health or community center has been built in large part by the people themselves through contributions in cash, labor or kind. The total contribution of these villagers to building and all activities under the program equals one-half the total contribution of the Government.

Some blocks have, of course, done more successfully than others. In the best, the considered opinion is that living conditions are now tending toward favorable comparison with those of small towns in terms of education, health and other amenities.

Striking as these achievements are, careful analysis by the Programme Evaluation Organization and independent specialists, Indian and foreign, emphasizes that the program needs strengthening on important fronts.

While the new roads, schools and health centers fulfill real needs and are valuable symbols to the people of their own advancement, India's leaders of the program believe there has been overemphasis on these physical accomplishments. More emphasis is needed on developing the people, and specifically on developing local leadership and organizations which can guide responsible group action in a dynamic people's movement.

The Indian Government is also concerned that the program has not done enough for increasing farm production and rural employment. More needs to be done to help the landless and the rural unemployed, the socially disadvantaged. The program also has shown up the need for closer, more effective coordination of the State technical specialists and departments with the community program, for strong technical cadres at every level, and more of them closer to the villages.

PROGRAM FOR THE SECOND PLAN

Under the Second Plan the community development program is to be extended to all of rural India. Its organization will be used as the principal medium for carrying out all important efforts designed to increase agricultural production and assist the rural people.

In view of the Second Plan's high priority on a very rapid increase in agricultural production, village extension workers will in turn put their highest priority on agriculture. Definite targets of production will be set for each group of villages under the worker's charge.

The development program throughout will work in closest integration—"a kind of marriage"—with the agricultural departments and other revelant Ministries on these further rural goals of the Second Plan: the development of cooperatives; strengthening of panchayats as organizations actively responsible for village development and, as further experience is gained, for land management; consolidation of landholdings; development of village and small-scale industry; special programs for the weaker sections of the community—landless laborers, artisans, the small farmer; more intensive work with women and young people and tribal peoples.

An experimental village-industry program has already been launched in twenty-six development blocks throughout India. Under discussion is a pilot experiment in cooperatives; cooperative farming will also be undertaken in selected blocks, and a coordinated effort on rural housing has already been initiated in development areas. A program has been started for training 34,000 rural schoolteachers as village leaders in development work.

As the community development program grows in scope and activity, it presents a tremendous challenge in organization to the Indian Government and to the Indian people. It is of highest importance that, more and more, the program stimulate and guide the villagers themselves to take initiative, to assume leadership and responsibility for their own development.

For India, as for other underdeveloped nations, the community development program is not an end product, but an instrument of development placed in the hands of the people. It is the means through which the rural majority can gain new strength, skill, productivity, self-confidence and the democratic vitality essential to push ahead the nation as a whole.

The success of community development therefore determines to a greater degree than may be realized the prospects of achieving both economic progress and social and political freedom.

As India extends this program over all of rural India, it does so in the conviction expressed by the Prime Minister:

I think that the most significant development of these years has been in the domain of Community Projects and the National Extension Service. Apart from the practical results which have been achieved, and these are both visible and considerable, there is something even more important, even though it cannot be measured and weighed. This imponderable factor is the spirit of the people, the removal of inertia in thought and action, the development of a team spirit in national work and the sense of partnership of the people in great undertakings.

This represents the new dynamism which is so essential to all progress.

It means a social revolution in our ways of life and work which is creeping gradually but surely over the vast land of India.

It is because of this that the Community Projects and the National Extension Service have become, more than anything else, the symbols of the resurgent spirit of India.[1]

[1] Prime Minister Nehru, to the Fourth Development Commissioners' Conference, Simla, May 1955.

Land Reform

However great the achievements of the rural development program, without doubt the greatest challenge for India, as for other Asian countries, is how its land, so scarce, so precious, so vital to the lives and livelihood of the people, may be most fairly shared and most efficiently used.

In an old country the land system is a product of history. It reflects the rise and fall of kingdoms, dynasties and tribes. Until the second half of the nineteenth century, from time to time the peasant farmers in different parts of India had to bear the burden of wars between rival nobles and chieftains. During times of peace peasants prospered; when peace was disturbed there was much suffering. Yet during those centuries there was enough land to go round; in every part of India groups of farmers could find new land on which to settle and form new villages.

However, with the rapid increase in population, introduction of

Western ideas of property, the growth of commerce and the development of communications, land and the produce from it grew more
valuable, and landlords and moneyed men made harsh exactions from
the tiller of the soil, in spite of early efforts to protect him. As it developed in many parts of the country, the land system impoverished
the farmer, weakened his initiative and held back agricultural progress. For years before Independence, "land to the tiller" was a widely
accepted platform.

A few facts will set the picture of India's chief land problems:

First, while India is a land of small peasant owners, and though
there were few very large estates, nevertheless there was much inequality of landownership. As a rule, some three-fourths of all farms
are of less than ten acres. On the other hand, though there are differences in each State, perhaps a third of all land is held by a few large
owners in farms of thirty acres or more.

Second, until recently many of the larger owners did not themselves cultivate or manage their own farms nor did they invest in
improvements. In some States as much as one-half, in others up to a
third or a fourth, of the area held by landholders who owned more
than sixty acres was cultivated by tenants. Unlike the small owners,
who worked their own land, more and more of these larger owners
went to the cities as absentee owners, their farms worked by tenants,
sharecroppers and laborers.

Third, there have been insecurities and injustices in the rights of
India's many tenant farmers and sharecroppers, and since Independence almost every State has enacted new legislation aimed at
giving them security and a fair livelihood. Most tenants have had to
pay in rent or crop shares up to as high as 50 per cent of their harvest,
and some even more. In densely populated rural areas many tenants,
on the will of the owners, could be deprived of the land for the next
harvest season.

Further, the average holding for most farmers, whether owner or
tenant, is, as we have seen, too small to be economic—that is, to yield
enough crops or income—and is constantly made smaller and more
fragmented as land is divided by inheritance. Over the greater part of

India, depending on the population and the intensity of agricultural development, about two-thirds of the farms are of less than five acres and together account for less than a fifth of the cultivated area. Among these, an average farm seldom exceeds two acres.

Further, while redistributing land will help farmers share more equally, there is too little land to go round even if it is fairly divided, and only a small proportion of the landless can hope to benefit.

Finally, land in India, as elsewhere in Asia, is the main source of wealth, of income, of status, of opportunity. Those with no land or with too little are not only at the bottom of the social and economic scale but lack essential means by which they can rise up the ladder.

What India hopes for is an agriculture based primarily on fair and healthy peasant ownership and served by various voluntary cooperative societies. In a nation dedicated to the advancement of all its people, and pressed to provide social justice under democracy—and where, moreover, every incentive must be used to increase farm production—land reform takes on a crucial significance.

In 1949 the Prime Minister told the United States Congress:

> One of the main causes of social instability in many parts of the world, more especially in Asia, is agrarian discontent due to the continuance of systems of land tenure which are completely out of place in the modern world. In a country of which agriculture is still the principal industry, land reform is essential not only for the well-being and contentment of the individual, but also for the stability of society.[1]

Land reform is indeed, for India, the question where the issue between the "haves" and the "have nots" demands the most urgent attention. At perhaps no point in India's economy is there more clear conflict of interests than between the larger landowners on the one hand and the tenants, sharecroppers and landless laborers on the other.

India is aware that history's record of peaceful land reform is scant. In most countries in the past, deep-seated wrongs in the ownership of land, and in the power exercised by landlords, led to political up-

[1] Washington, D.C., Oct. 13, 1949.

LEARNING A CRAFT: A young villager gets a lesson in chair making at a craft training center in southern Bombay State. Chair making, leather and metal work and weaving are among the principal crafts taught at these industry centers.

YOUNG FARMER'S PRIZE: Farm youth groups, patterned on the 4–H clubs and similar groups in the United States and elsewhere, are being formed in many Indian rural development areas. This Sikh member of a young farmers' club in the Punjab proudly exhibits the potatoes which won him first prize in a District contest.

RECREATION FOR VILLAGE YOUNGSTERS: A village extension worker, in Bidar, Mysore, teaches games to a children's recreation club. He has helped organize the club as part of a village development program's effort to enrich rural life. Clubs formed for older boys are active in social service as well as in sports and games.

INTRODUCING IMPROVED POULTRY: To improve farm diet and incomes, better breeds of hens, cattle and other livestock are being introduced into village areas. Here a veterinary extension officer shows Rhode Island Reds, and an improved type of poultry pen, to two Mysore villagers.

CLEARING JUNGLE FOR FARM LAND: During the First Plan period, 7,400,000 acres of land were reclaimed for farming from waste and jungle areas and from land formerly covered by destructive kans grass. Here equipment of the Central Tractor Organization clears jungle in Madhya Pradesh, near Bhopal.

heavals; the breakup of feudal land systems was often accompanied by much conflict and suffering. In most Western nations in the past, land reforms followed only on independence struggles or civil revolutions.

India has rejected class conflict both as a philosophy and as a method of achieving social and economic change. India has chosen the democratic process and the peaceful democratic way. On land reforms, this decision means that India must work out entirely new approaches to an issue long linked to conflict and violence.

In evolving these new solutions, India will, to use the Prime Minister's words, follow "the way Gandhiji taught us—that combination of firm adherence to principle and objective and yet a friendly approach even to those who differ and whose interests clash with that objective." [1]

It may be true that, at first, such methods will bring less rapid progress on land reform than methods of violence. But India believes that democratic change, won by non-violence, is more successful in gaining the acceptance of the people, and thus more enduring and more successful from the point of view of final results.

The land reform efforts begun since Independence and even earlier, and carried on over the First Plan period, have been aimed at changing the worst features of the antiquated land structure which had been in large part responsible for the plight of the small farmer. They have been aimed as well at a reorganization of agriculture for more efficient and economic farming.

Since India's land system is very different from that of most countries, at least a brief and oversimplified picture will be needed of some of its peculiarities, so that the meaning and importance of recent land reform measures may be understood.

It should first be said that in India, under a tradition extending back over many centuries, the State is considered the "ultimate owner" of the land. Actually and in fact, until the end of the eighteenth century, the individual farmers who tilled the land were

[1] Prime Minister Nehru, letter to Presidents of State Congress Committees, March 3, 1955.

the only real owners. The right to own land of which the State was the ultimate owner was—as it is today—unquestioned.

Whether large or small, the owners had recognized and relatively secure rights to transfer, inherit, rent out and even mortgage the land. They did, however, have to pay rent to the State as the "ultimate owner." These rents were to all effects a kind of land tax. Until the latter part of the eighteenth century, the rents were usually moderate.

Another peculiarity of India's land system is not only that so large a part of the land is tenant-farmed but that tenants traditionally had relatively secure rights to the land, whether they rented it from landlords or directly from the State.

The origin of India's present land reform problem lies in the so-called "permanent settlements," which the East India Company made in 1793 and superimposed on the old system of peasant ownership under the State. As a political and administrative expedient, the Company created a new class of landlords with whom they made these "permanent settlements." These *zamindars*, as the new landlords were called, were installed as *intermediate owners*, or landlords *over* the small owners and actual tillers of the soil, and authorized to collect the rents for the State.

What inevitably happened was that the zamindars, given power over large areas, usually raised the rents so that they could take a bigger share for themselves, and the peasant farmer staggered under a double burden. The zamindars, moreover, with their special privileges and position were able to break down the customary and heritable rights enjoyed by tenants and reduce them to rent-oppressed tenants with no security but the zamindar's favor.

While the first "permanent settlements" were made in Bengal, Bihar and Orissa, the zamindari system and various modifications of it spread, and in 1947 covered nearly half of India.

Similarly, at different times, in some princely states such as Hyderabad and Rajasthan, various kinds of feudal "tax farmers" had been created, as princes and maharajas bestowed upon their supporters the right, virtually in perpetuity, to collect the rents, usually oppressively high, from large tracts of villages.

Zamindars and other superior landlords and tax farmers are known as "intermediaries," that is, intermediate between the owner or tenant and the State as "ultimate owner" of the land.

It was these various "intermediaries" and superior landlords whose links with the rural people and with farming itself gradually weakened, and who were or became by and large the non-cultivating and absentee landlords who have characterized much of Indian agriculture. It was their sub-owners and tenants, with layers and layers of intermediaries on their backs, who had neither the money nor the incentive left to improve their farms or crops. In general they could farm only for subsistence. Many owners, falling behind in their rent or into debt, lost their lands to become tenants or sharecroppers.

At the same time, throughout India, outside the zamindari and tax-farmed areas as well as within, as population and demand for land increased, myriad forms and systems of ownership, sub-ownership, tenancy and sub-tenancy grew up, complex in the extreme, and differing in detail from area to area. All served generally, however, as in the zamindari areas, to make the tenant more insecure and burdened with rent. Here too many owners lost their lands to village moneylenders, and more and more land passed into the hands of the larger landlords who did not till the soil.

Any effort at land reform had first of all to deal with the evils of the zamindari and the tax-farming systems, and to protect the tenants. Indeed, the British Government began some reforms in Bengal as early as 1859, and later made even more vigorous efforts, as the evil system showed itself in an increasingly depressed and impoverished rural people, and in abnormally low yields per acre.

Some of these reforms were successful, and by 1947 many tenants of the intermediaries had acquired at least permanent and heritable rights, often rights of transfer as well; some rents were also regulated. In some of the princely states, however, feudal tax-farming systems continued; extortionate rents and evictions were common.

For the new and independent India, land reforms, and first of all the abolition of the intermediaries, became a matter of highest priority.

The problem had to be tackled within the framework of the new India's Constitution and the property rights it guarantees. Moreover, under the Constitution, land legislation falls under the jurisdiction of the States, and the major burden of reform on the State administrations and legislatures. The role of the Central Government and the Planning Commission has been to develop a common approach, having popular support, which could be adopted in each State as part of the national Plan, with due regard to local needs and conditions. The accent of the approach was a positive, not negative, one, emphasizing the need for increasing agricultural production, and bringing about more equality and social justice.

Even before the First Plan was issued, however, several States had adopted legislation for the abolition of intermediaries—Bihar, Bombay, Madhya Pradesh, Madras, Uttar Pradesh, Hyderabad and PEPSU. Carrying out of the legislation in Uttar Pradesh and Bihar was, however, delayed because the zamindars vigorously contested its validity.

The First Plan, which came into operation in April 1951, laid down the basic principles of land reform for the entire country.

The main land reform recommendations of the First Plan were:

1. Abolishing, in zamindari areas, the intermediaries between the State and tillers;

2. Tenancy reform, to reduce rents and give tenants an opportunity to acquire permanent rights over the land by payment of fixed compensation, subject to the landlord's right to resume a certain area for his personal cultivation;

3. Fixing ceilings on holdings;

4. Reorganizing agriculture, by consolidating small holdings and preventing further fragmentation, and by the development of cooperative village management and cooperative farming.

A Central Committee for Land Reform was constituted by the Government in May 1953, consisting of the Chairman and members of the Planning Commission, as well as the Ministers for Home Affairs and for Food and Agriculture, to guide examination of reform proposals of the State Governments. A Panel on Land Reforms, including non-official leaders, was appointed by the Commission in May 1955 to review progress and make recommendations for the Second Plan.

On the whole, the First Plan made measurable progress in land reforms, though not as far-reaching or as rapid as was hoped and as is necessary. The achievements of the First Plan years and the Second Plan's recommendations may be summarized as follows:

Abolition of Intermediaries: The former "intermediaries" of the old zamindari and other tax-farming systems had by the end of the First Plan been almost entirely abolished. Only a few small spots remain where further action is needed.

In bringing about this basic reform, India has proceeded legally and with widespread public support. No confiscation was involved. All intermediaries have been awarded compensation for the giving over of their lands—to a total of Rs. 615 crores.[1] The payments, usually fixed at a multiple of the intermediary's former annual net income from his holdings, are generally being made in negotiable and transferable bonds payable over twenty to forty years. Some payments are also being made in cash. Generally, home-farm lands were left with the intermediaries; their "common" lands (waste lands, forests, and so on) were transferred to the Government.

All other land which was formerly under the control of the intermediaries is now held directly from the State by the small owners and tenants who had been farming it. The intermediaries are no longer on their backs.

Here a point should be made clear. All landowners, whether large or small, new or old, continue to pay the State rent on the land, as a form of land tax. With the intermediaries abolished, however, the owners pay their rent directly to the States instead of to the intermediaries as before; and in some cases the new payments have been reduced from the former rents. It is out of the rents of the newly freed owners that the States are now paying compensation.

Rights of Owners: With the intermediaries gone, the many former complex varieties of tenancy and sub-tenancy have not only been

[1] Fifty-three per cent of this is in Uttar Pradesh and Bihar.

greatly reduced, but for the most part tenants who held land under the intermediaries have either become owners of the land or have the right to do so.

For these new owners the present need is for some uniform pattern throughout all the States, determining their rights and obligations. Measures are needed, for example, to enable them to mortgage the land to obtain loans from Government or cooperative credit organizations with the land as security, and also to lease it out under special circumstances. In some States these rights are not now permitted.

Another particularly important need is for some regulation to prevent further fragmentation of small holdings, as lands are divided upon inheritance. Some States have such laws, but they have found it difficult to enforce them.

Tenancy Reform: While many former tenants-in-chief of the intermediaries have become owners, a very large number of tenants and sub-tenants remain. Some, as in Delhi State and Uttar Pradesh, have been given permanent rights and security. In India as a whole, however, protecting tenants against eviction and giving them some secure rights in the land are now considered among the most pressing land reform issues. In the past several years such evictions have demanded attention. The reasons for them, and the measures proposed for control, are discussed below.

India has made some progress in assuring tenants of fairer rents. The First Plan had recommended that a fair land rent should be one-fourth to one-fifth of the gross produce. While some States (Bombay and Rajasthan) have revised rents to as low as one-sixth, rent legislation is very uneven and some States lag far behind. For example, in Madras State the rent is still high—one-third to two-fifths of the produce; in the Punjab and Bihar, a third; in Andhra, West Bengal and parts of Kerala up to one-half.

Measures to help tenants become owners are also urged in the Second Plan. Here progress has been slow, and few tenants who have had the option to buy have exercised it. One of the reasons is sheer inability to pay.

The Second Plan recommends that rents be reduced,[1] so that tenants can, as they pay the reduced rents, pay an additional sum as an installment against purchase. The combined rent plus installment payment should be held to one-fourth or one-fifth of the produce.

Absentee and Non-Cultivating Landowners: The abolition of *intermediaries* does not mean the abolition of all landlords. Large and middle-sized landholders continue in India, as mentioned earlier. Many of the large holders, moreover, and even some smaller owners as well, have, as we have seen, either been absentee owners or did not themselves cultivate their own land, but very commonly had it farmed by tenants.

Nearly all land reform proposals in India as elsewhere recommend that land go to the actual tiller, since bona fide personal cultivation of land by its owners is important and desirable. But in India the issue is a thorny and difficult one, and raises real problems as between India's many tenants, who have some traditional rights in the land, and the landowner who wishes to cultivate personally.

Two key questions thus arise: How *much* land should a single landholder be entitled to resume for personal cultivation? And what if any protections may be given the tenant whom he may displace? If nothing is done, the big landlord will stay big, although at least he will be actively cultivating or supervising his own farm. But the tenant would lose out entirely, to become a landless laborer. In short, as far as the small tenant farmer goes, land reform would have hurt rather than helped.

Today, under public pressure and expectation of legislative action, large owners try to establish their role as actual farmers, taking over for personal cultivation the land formerly leased to tenants. As a result, in certain areas there have been some evictions. These sometimes take the form of "voluntary surrenders" of tenancy rights—a

---

[1] To make this possible the Second Plan also recommends that all tenants, of lands which are not to be taken over for cultivation by the landlords themselves, rent directly from the State. This has already been done in Delhi, U.P., and Bombay.

practice open to doubt as bona fide. In some cases all members of a joint family who ordinarily would own a single property jointly have separately taken over or resumed separate parts of the family's land, so that each might be classed as an individual cultivating owner.

Definitions of "personal cultivation," and rules for resumption of land and protection of tenants, are therefore of urgent importance. As a solution to the first of these problems, the Planning Commission recommends that personal cultivation be defined so as to provide that the *entire risk of cultivation* is borne by the owner, and that the owner at least *personally supervises* farm work and resides in the village the greater part of the agricultural season.

Next, the Commission recommends that some ceiling be set on the amount of land a landholder may resume for personal cultivation, with distinctions for large and small owners. If there is a tenant who would be dispossessed, even when this ceiling is observed, the ceiling should be lowered to leave the tenant, where possible, with at least a "basic holding." [1] Where the farm is so small that the tenant would be left out altogether, or left with too little land, the Second Plan suggests that the States find land for the tenant from reclaimed lands and so on, to give him at least a basic holding.

The Second Plan also suggests that some time limit be set on the period in which a landlord may exercise his right to resume. The recommendation is six months to apply, five years actually to resume, dating from the time the resumption becomes effective.

To protect tenants against eviction, legislation has been passed in various States. On the whole, it has not been effective or well enforced. The Planning Commission recommends that evictions should be stayed except on non-payment of rent or misuse of land; that all evictions over the past three or four years be re-examined; that all "voluntary" surrenders be considered valid only if duly registered; and that a landlord may take possession only of as much land as he has a right to resume under whatever ceiling is or may be imposed.

The Planning Commission also recommends to the States that, on

---

[1] "Basic holding," a term used in land legislation, defines a minimum area needed for profitable cultivation.

lands not to be taken over by landlords for personal cultivation, tenants should have continuing possession, the right to inherit, and sufficient right to mortgage the land to obtain farm credit with the land as security.

Ceilings on Holdings: Without doubt, the most controversial land reform issue is the recommendation, made officially in the First Plan, and again in the Second Plan, that there should be a ceiling on the amount of land any individual may hold, so that the amount above this ceiling may be re-distributed to tenants and landless farmers, and bring about more fair and equitable ownership.

The proposal has a long history, and was one of the major reforms recommended as India became independent.

Here again two questions arise: What ceiling should be imposed on *future* land acquired? What ceiling should be imposed on *existing* holdings? Even before the First Plan, Uttar Pradesh had set a ceiling of thirty acres on all future lands acquired. Other States have since adopted similar legislation, with varying ceilings. In general the principle of limiting *future* purchases is widely accepted.

Not unnaturally, the possibility of imposing ceilings on existing holdings has evoked apprehensions among large landholders. Already efforts have been made, as we have seen, to escape a future ceiling by distributing ownership of large holdings among individual members of joint families who ordinarily hold land in common.

It is generally agreed, however, that the supply of land is so limited in relation to the ever growing number of people seeking it that a ceiling on individual holdings would make for a more fair and progressive land system.

There are considerable technical, as well as social and political, difficulties in imposing land ceilings. What is required at the start is a clear definition of what ceiling is not only fair but economic.

Ceilings must necessarily differ for different regions, for various kinds and qualities of land, irrigated or non-irrigated lands, and so on. It is generally believed that the ceiling should consist of three "family holdings," or roughly three times a work unit for a family of average size.

Expert study and analysis are needed to define, for various types of land, what would be a fair family holding, both as to work unit and as to income yield. This study is now being made.

Certain types of holdings should, it is generally agreed, be exempt from ceilings. Among these are the large tea and coffee plantations, orchards, cattle-breeding farms—all of which are generally more integrated operations; large sugar-cane farms run by sugar factories; and large, compact, efficiently managed farms whose breakup might lead to lower production.

When ceilings are imposed, land left over is to be acquired and paid for by the Government, generally in compensatory bonds. The lands will be redistributed to new small owners, who should pay rent to the State not to exceed the recommended fair rent of one-fifth to one-fourth of the produce. The compensation to the former land-owners will be made out of these rent payments.

In redistributing lands acquired by the State by this or any other means, the Second Plan recommends that farmers with uneconomic holdings and landless workers be given first preference, in the interest of social justice.

Ceilings on existing holdings have now been imposed in six States; for example, West Bengal has set a ceiling of twenty-five acres, Assam of fifty acres, PEPSU and Himachal Pradesh thirty. Enforcement on a national scale is clearly something that will come gradually, as democratic pressure and persuasion continue to reconcile the large holders to the seemingly inevitable sharing of land, and as a climate is created for effective compliance.

It is for this latter reason that there has been particular interest in the *bhoodan* land reform movement led by Acharya Vinoba Bhave, a social reformer and a disciple of Mahatma Gandhi. The movement began in 1951 in the Telangana area (then in Hyderabad State, now Andhra) where an oppressive tax-farming system had impoverished the peasants. It has since spread over much of India, especially where the land problem is acute.

Vinoba Bhave, walking from village to village, has asked in each that large landowners give a land gift (*bhoodan*) for the landless.

He has asked that they treat the landless as a "sixth son," and deed one-sixth of their land for redistribution. Later, gifts of whole villages (*gramdan*) have been asked from the landholders, large and small, who own land in villages.

By mid-1957 more than 4 million acres of land had been so given and some 2,000 villages, the largest number being in the tribal areas of Orissa. About half a million acres had been distributed to the landless. The movement, by high-lighting anew the Gandhian approach of social justice, of the responsibility of the privileged to the underprivileged on which India's land reform is based, has unquestionably helped produce a climate of acceptance of peaceful and orderly reforms, in keeping with India's traditions and its highest hopes.

The administration of land reform, not only where lands are redistributed, but in all its phases, is a question of especial urgency. It demands efficiency, human and social skills and personal integrity of the highest order. Among the tasks demanding all these qualities to the utmost are the maintenance of correct and up-to-date land records needed as prerequisite to fair land reform; the assessing of new and fair rents on lands recovered from the intermediaries; the fixing of just compensation; discovering and righting forced evictions or transfers of land which are not bona fide; enforcement of ceilings; fair and rapid re-distribution of lands to those most deserving.

Proper administration also requires a land census (this has now been virtually completed), basic studies in landownership and tenancy to supplement present partial surveys, analysis of what constitutes most fairly a basic or family holding, and the like. Here the universities and other research institutions which have begun land reform studies have a great contribution to make.

In summary, India's land reforms are progressing; but they must go more rapidly. There must be more equitable distribution of land, greater security and protection of tenants, more uniform reduction of rents, more action in a number of States, more wholehearted enforcement, and more effective administration.

These problems are as great a challenge to a democratic government as their solution is essential to the advancement of the rural people in income, production and opportunity.

LAND MANAGEMENT

Land reform is but one step of India's approach to its agrarian problem. The next step—intimately involved with land reform—is how the land may be re-organized for most efficient use and most productive management.

Fair distribution of land is necessary, and must be carried out in the interest of social justice and of social and political stability. But India recognizes that even thoroughgoing land reform is capable only of wiping out the worst features which have condemned some of India's farmers to a below-subsistence level of existence. Land reforms in themselves will not break the vicious cycle of more people and less land, and rural poverty. They can at best prepare the way for other needed reforms.

Land reform will create larger and larger numbers of small peasant owners. Many of their holdings are and will remain so small as to be uneconomic.

Many small holders, moreover, who have so long farmed for bare survival, without knowledge or means to try improved farm practices, need not only credit and technical help but guidance on land management in order to get efficient diversified production.

The now landless—who are to receive lands—will need such help even more, since they have had no previous experience in managing a farm.

While such help and guidance can be given through the rural development programs, and there is considerable scope, as noted earlier, for intensive small-farm cultivation, it is clear that as long as the small holding, often uneconomic or fragmented, remains the unit of management (as distinguished from the unit of *ownership* or cultivation), the possibilities are surely lessened for higher agricultural production, for adequately diversified farming, for use of all the culturable waste lands and common lands for village pasturage, woodlands, fodder crops, and so on.

With every passing year this problem grows and will grow more acute. It is necessary here to look at India's land problem in a broad perspective.

We have seen that the total amount of land is limited and that even if today it were distributed with perfect equity each family would have a holding only of less than subsistence size. As population rises, continued fair distribution among larger and larger numbers— though it might be necessary for social justice and stability—would simply assign each small holder to permanent and increasing poverty.

Further rises in farm production would become more and more difficult, if not impossible, as holders of tiny fragments of land lived on the edge of survival. Yet higher crop production is India's necessity, its hope of both survival and progress. And higher rural incomes and living standards are of equal necessity, for social stability and justice.

Further, there is now and will remain in the foreseeable future the problem of unemployed and underemployed agricultural laborers, half of whom as we know are landless and nearly all of whom are from the socially and economically depressed groups. However many —and it will be only a fraction at best—receive lands under land reform, there will still be millions who remain landless and for whom productive work must be found.

We have seen earlier that India's effort to develop employment off the land is a solution which can be effective only over the long run, and that industry will not, certainly at this stage of necessary emphasis on heavy industry, create adequate non-agricultural employment. Village and small industries will help give more full- and part-time work; so too will major large construction projects, flood control schemes, and so on. But India faces the clear fact that it is up to agriculture and allied occupations in rural areas to absorb, and use productively, a vast number of rural farmers and laborers, now and for the foreseeable future.

Here again, as in the question of agricultural production, it is clear that as long as small fragmented holdings remain the unit of management, the possibilities of expanding the village economy to create enough employment and enough kinds of employment are strictly limited.

India's dilemma—what Gandhi called India's "problem of problems"—is, therefore, how India can, by democratic means, organize a system which can use land, rural capital and rural labor to secure higher production, higher incomes, higher employment.

On this issue there is little experience in the history of the democratic nations, to draw upon for guidance. Indeed, no democracy has ever before faced a similar problem. Western nations by and large have not had the excessive, densely crowded, rural populations common in much of Asia. Although China's own political and economic systems differ, India has studied with considerable interest the agrarian organization methods used in China, where the pressure on land is similar to India's. Since India has deliberately chosen the democratic process, it remains for India to evolve its own agrarian system, which would conform to Indian principles and traditions.

As India now views its problems of land management and reorganization, these consist of four aspects: consolidation of landholdings; legislation enabling and requiring good land management practices; cooperative farming; and finally, as the goal toward which the village economy should be organized, cooperative village land management.

Consolidation of Landholdings

The first step—voluntary, legal consolidation of fragmented holdings into workable single holdings—can be and already is being undertaken. Land consolidation saves time and labor (some fragmented holdings consist of tiny sections miles apart), encourages and makes possible land improvements such as irrigation, contour bunding, construction of service roads, and so on.

Some States have made appreciable progress in land consolidation; [1] for example, in the Punjab over 4 million acres have been consolidated; in Madhya Pradesh 2.5 million, in tiny PEPSU 1 million. In Bombay and Delhi whole villages—1,060 and 210 respectively in each State—have been consolidated. Other States, however, have lagged in this useful reform, and the Planning Commission has made studies of the best existing experience available to encourage others, and urged that land consolidation be made a task of primary importance in the rural development areas.

Land Management Legislation

As a second step, whatever the size and compactness of a farm, every holding should be efficiently managed. India earlier considered an approach to this through a legislation similar to that which has been used successfully in the United Kingdom. The First Plan had recommended, with large farms chiefly in mind, that the States enact legislation requiring the efficient use of land. Since then the Panel on Land Reforms advising the Planning Commission has considered legislation in a wider context, since many small holders are now involved.

On the basis of the Panel's study, the Second Plan views any legislation in terms not of coercion but of *encouraging the conditions* of efficient management—assuring tenancy rights, provision of certain facilities (credit, improved seeds, and so on) and of setting up some minimum standards of good land management and cultivation. The Planning Commission also recommends to the States that any legislation be applied first to rural development areas which do provide the necessary facilities and incentives, and that it be carried out by the village panchayat, with supervision.

Cooperative Farming

Among the many people over the years who have studied India's agricultural problems, there has been general agreement that some form of joint or cooperative farming might facilitate the solution to the

[1] As of March 31, 1955, and before the States' Reorganization in November 1956.

poverty and backwardness of the individual peasant farmer, to the uneconomic size of landholding, to the excess of rural laborers.

Mahatma Gandhi believed that cooperative farming "based on strict non-violence," and carried on by the owners and tillers of the land, could "change the face of the land and banish poverty and idleness from their midst." [1]

Other leaders and groups in the Independence movement, likewise, felt that "while individualistic farming and peasant proprietorship should continue, progress in agriculture as well as the creation of new social values and incentives requires some form of cooperative farming suited to Indian conditions." [2]

Giving expression to these long-held views, the First Five Year Plan asserted that "the State on its part should do everything in its power to encourage the establishment of such (cooperative) farms and to promote their satisfactory working afterwards."

A small financial provision for experiment in farm cooperatives was made in the First Plan, but no specific targets were set; it was hoped that with the help of successful experience in a fair number of cooperative farming societies India could "proceed more confidently" to expand that pattern of cultivation in the Second Plan. On the whole, only preliminary action was taken during the First Plan.

Over a thousand cooperative farming societies, formed voluntarily by groups of individuals, are now functioning throughout India. Some of them have been successful, although many have had practical difficulties which technical guidance and further experience could help.

The increasing number of small peasant landholders, the urgency of higher agricultural production, and the persistent problem of surplus rural labor give a new urgency to discovering whether cooperative farming might be vigorously and deliberately encouraged as a productive and effective method of organizing land, rural capital and rural labor.

The Second Plan asserts that "the main task during the Plan is to take such essential steps as will provide sound foundations for the

[1] *Harijan*, March 9, 1947.
[2] *Congress Party Election Manifesto*, Dec. 1945.

development of cooperative farming so that over a period of ten years or so a substantial proportion of agricultural lands are cultivated on cooperative lines."

Both in the Second Plan and elsewhere, the Indian Government makes clear that it does not define cooperative farming as involving sacrifice of ownership of land, but only as the pooling of the land for cultivation under joint management. The Second Plan considers that this pooling may be accomplished by various methods, and feels that at this stage there should be flexibility as to methods. Several should be tried out, through considerable experimentation, to discover which seem most adapted to Indian conditions and traditions. The Second Plan states that the first stage of cooperative farming might very likely involve family holdings supplemented by joint work for specific purposes.

Among the essential steps suggested by the Second Plan to determine the possibilities of cooperative farming, one is that a study be made of India's present cooperative farming societies to determine causes of success and failure. This study has been recently undertaken.[1]

The Indian Government is also considering some pilot projects in cooperative action in rural development areas. There will be two important features of these pilot projects. One will be the education of the village people in the meaning, techniques and advantages of cooperation, so that any cooperative action grows out of the people's own interest in and desire for it. The other will be the effort to discover how under democratic self-government cooperative action, not only in farming but in credit and other fields, can play a role in all-round village progress in India.

Among other ways of encouraging cooperative farming suggested by the Second Plan are to give voluntary groups forming such cooperative societies preferences in supplies of credit, seed, technical assistance, allocation of reclaimed lands, and so on; and to see that new settlements made on newly opened lands or *bhoodan* lands may be cooperatively organized.

[1] By the Programme Evaluation Organization.

As in all cooperative action proposed for India, the need exists for training of cooperative organizers and managers, with emphasis on human and social, as well as on technical, skills.

Cooperative Village Management

What India hopes eventually to achieve is that each village as a whole will plan and manage the use of village lands and resources as if it were a single unit.

Consolidation of agricultural holdings and cooperative farming will specially benefit those who own a fair amount of land. But for owners of very small and uneconomic holdings such measures will do little. They will also be of small help to landless agricultural workers, who have practically no share in the land or much hope of regular employment. It is, therefore, felt that the village economy should be reorganized in the direction of cooperative village management.

Village management of land, irrigation and other resources should offer a way to provide more employment for the landless or the near landless, in constructing irrigation works, developing waste lands, and so on. The village is seen as part of the rural economy as a whole, in which agricultural production, village industries, processing industries, marketing and rural trade are organized more and more as cooperative activities.

As India sees village management, it would be voluntary cooperative management on a base of peasant ownership.

Individual farms would continue to be owned by the individual farmers, but management of the land and other resources of the village as a whole would be planned and supervised by the village as a whole through its panchayat.

The Second Plan recognizes that in the transition stages, the land in each village would include individually held lands cultivated by their own peasant owners, lands held by such voluntary cooperative farming societies as may have pooled their lands and/or labor, and any community-held lands, such as common grazing grounds, and so on. In short, the village would include an individual, a cooperative and a community sector. Cooperative village management is seen as one direction in which development will continue to take place, rather than as a fixed or rigidly determined stage in the growth of rural economy.

The Second Plan suggests that the ways to achieve cooperative village management and to assure sustained, practicable measurable benefits to the village as a whole will be through the following: the rural development and other agricultural programs; strengthening and training of the panchayats; emphasis on the other cooperative activities such as credit, marketing, warehousing, and so on; village industries programs which increase employment; voluntary cooperative farming societies; development of community-held grazing lands and similar community activities yielding positive benefits to the people as a group.

It is recognized that there will be real problems of education, of organization and training, of managerial and technical efficiency in establishing such cooperative villages.

There will also be many human and social problems. The development of cooperative village management is therefore likely to be a gradual process. Many practical problems have to be resolved, efficient organizations built up, extension workers fully oriented to the tasks of cooperative development, and a movement with purposeful leadership developed at the village level.

The forms which cooperative village management assumes and the progress toward it will depend on the experience and initiative of the people in each area and their success in carrying out rural community development programs. The approach has therefore to be both forward looking and adapted to the needs of the people of each area. The reconstruction of the entire national economy on democratic principles depends on the village becoming vital, progressive and largely self-governing, and one in which the present social and economic inequalities derived from inherited property, caste and status no longer exist.

CHAPTER IV

Rural Credit and Other
Cooperative Activities

Cooperative farming is but one of the many possibilities of cooperative action that can help India's farmers and villages.

One of the earliest recognized uses of cooperatives, and still the most urgent, is supplying farm credit to small holders who otherwise fall into the toils of the moneylender. Cheap farm credit was, and still is, indispensable to getting higher food production and to creating a vigorous, independent farm community.

The cooperative movement in India may be said to begin with the passing of the Cooperative Credit Society Act of 1904. This Act provided for credit societies only, and was followed by an Act in 1912 permitting formation of multi-purpose and other societies, and, very importantly, of central and provincial banks to help supply credit to cooperatives. In 1919 cooperation became a subject for action by the States, under the control of an elected Minister.

Cooperatives continued, however, to put their main emphasis on farm credit. An Agricultural Credit Department was set up in the Reserve Bank in 1935, and a later study (1949) urged the Reserve Bank to provide greater assistance to cooperatives.

Cooperatives of all kinds were at the same time increasing very rapidly in number. By 1950–1951, the eve of the First Plan, there were 181,000 cooperative societies against 2,000 in 1906, with a present working capital of about Rs.2,800 million against Rs.7 million. Membership was eighty-four times higher.

The overwhelming majority of these cooperatives were agricultural and more particularly credit societies. There were, however, quite a few producer and marketing societies, the most successful being those of hand-loom weavers. In Madras, for example, a fourth of all the hand looms of the State were cooperatively organized. Consumer cooperatives had not developed to any extent.

The First Plan called the cooperative form of organization "an indispensable instrument of planned economic activity in a democracy," and urged that an increasing measure of responsibility for organizing and financing rural economic development be shouldered by cooperatives. The Second Plan reaffirms this view, and with greater emphasis.

India hopes, as we have seen, to develop an economy in which, as in Sweden, there is a strong cooperative sector, as well as private and public enterprise sectors. Building this cooperative sector India considers one of the central aims of national planning. India believes in part that this cooperative sector will offset unhealthy concentration and centralization of power in the hands of the State and of private enterprise.

As importantly, India's advocates of cooperatives feel that cooperation is a way to enable the little man to hold his own and gain strength and opportunity, and a way to provide incentives beneficial to the welfare of the community as a whole.

They believe also that cooperatives, like village panchayats, are valuable agencies for achieving social cohesion in a period of rapid social change. They feel there can and should be evolved a system of cooperative community organization that touches on all aspects of village life, helps the weaker groups, and develops services and benefits for the community as a whole. This is the underlying approach in setting cooperative village management as the main direction of reorganizing the rural economy, and in establishing all rural cooperatives.

In 1954 the Reserve Bank issued a comprehensive and authoritative survey on cooperatives, the *All-India Rural Credit Survey*. The survey analyzed some of the basic troubles with Indian cooperatives and the cooperative movement, which had for some time caused concern and had been the subject of many earlier studies both of the colonial and national governments and of independent groups.

One of the most significant findings made by the survey is that credit granted by cooperatives and government agencies was only 6 per cent of the loans used by cultivators. For the rest (94 per cent) of their credit needs, the village farmers had still to resort to money-lenders and to other means.

Rigidity of lending rules in credit societies, over-high standards of credit-worthiness and shortage of working capital had resulted in making many types of loans unacceptable and many individuals in-eligible for loans. Even where credit societies have been most success-ful, only 30 to 40 per cent of rural families can qualify for loans.

Another problem pointed out by the survey was that the vast major-ity of cooperative societies were "uneconomic as business units," [1] with so high a percentage of overdues outstanding that the system was "not a system of credit likely to attract funds on its own merits and in the normal course of business." [2]

While some States used cooperative credit effectively, in general State cooperative banks had "yet to become effective units of a coordinated structure of cooperative credit." The survey also pointed out that the more fundamental cause of failure is the socio-economic structure of the village, in which lack of education in general, and of education on cooperation in particular, is an important factor.

The survey, however, expressed the "conviction that there is no alternative to some form of cooperative association as the all-important base of agricultural credit. Success, promise of success and the condi-

[1] *All-India Rural Credit Survey*, II, 216.
[2] *Ibid.*, p. 232.

tions on which these are dependent may be discovered in several instances of striking achievement in Madras, Bombay, Punjab, U.P. and certain other States." [1]

The Committee of Direction of the Rural Credit Survey made a series of valuable recommendations, the main proposals of which have been accepted in broad principle by the Government, the Reserve Bank and by representatives of the cooperative movement. The most important principle—and departure from earlier proposals—was that the State should enter into partnership with cooperative institutions at various levels, especially at the apex and central bank level, and large-sized credit cooperative societies. Partnership is not to imply interference or control.

Some of the survey's recommendations were put into effect immediately, in the latter years of the First Plan, and as a whole the survey helped to form the Second Plan's programs for cooperatives.

In the First Plan agricultural credit was provided to a total of Rs. 80 crores, to be distributed by Government and cooperatives with the help of the Reserve Bank, for short-term, medium- and long-term loans. Some additional credit was provided for cottage and small industries, preferably cooperatively organized. Rs.1 million was provided for a training program for cooperative organizers and managers, and some funds by the Reserve Bank and the States.

It is notable that 59,000 new cooperative societies were formed over the First Plan years, again chiefly rural credit societies, although many were also formed of cottage and small industries.

One of the first major steps taken on the survey's recommendations was the creation in July 1955 of the State Bank of India (converted from the Imperial Bank). The Bank now has branches in all States and most District headquarters, and is developing many smaller units, following the survey's recommendations that the credit institutions must be brought into more direct relation to the people in order to extend remittance and credit facilities to cooperatives and other banks.

The Reserve Bank has established a National Agriculture Credit Fund, with an initial credit of Rs. 10 crores, plus Rs. 5 crores per

[1] *All-India Rural Credit Survey*, II, 245–252.

annum over the Second Plan. The Central Government has also established a National Cooperative Development Fund from which States may borrow to enter into partnership with non-credit cooperatives.

From the recommendations of the survey and other studies, the Second Plan sets down three basic aspects of successful cooperation. First, credit is only the beginning of cooperation; from credit, cooperative action should extend to other activities. Further, every family in the village should be a member of at least one cooperative society. And finally, the cooperative movement should make every family in the village credit-worthy.

The Second Plan also recommends linking credit and non-credit cooperatives, as suggested by the survey, so that farmers can first get supplies and later help to market their produce. Large-sized credit societies should be formed to serve groups of villages and be affiliated with marketing cooperatives in the market towns. An "apex" marketing cooperative serving the State as a whole should be formed to which the smaller societies should be federated.

To make more small farmers credit-worthy, the Second Plan suggests that loans be advanced on the basis of proposed production and anticipated crops; and that, as far as possible, to prevent misuse of loans, loans be given in kind—seeds, fertilizers, and so on—and that where cash is required, it be given in installments.

Since warehousing is tied to efficient marketing, a Central Warehousing Corporation with parallels in the States will be set up, functioning under a National Cooperative Development and Warehousing Board. Large warehouses will be set up at one hundred important centers.

The Second Plan's targets for cooperative credit are to be achieved both through existing and through new societies. It is hoped to raise the membership of cooperative credit societies nearly three-fold, from less than 6 million to about 15 million.

While non-credit cooperatives, except in a few activities, have not made any large impression, the Second Plan believes there is considerable scope for them in village and small industries. Second Plan programs for these are discussed in the chapter on small industries.

Consumer cooperatives have so far failed to develop and the Second Plan sets no targets. But the Plan recommends that the problem be studied and a program worked out as a means to help raise rural incomes, living standards and employment. Organizing of rural labor on cooperative lines is also suggested; it has been tried with some success in some rural development areas for construction and similar works.

The Second Plan's principal targets for all cooperatives are as follows:

CREDIT

Number of larger-sized societies	10,400
Target for short-term credit	Rs. 150 crores
Target for medium-term credit	Rs. 50 crores
Target for long-term credit	Rs. 25 crores

MARKETING AND PROCESSING

Number of primary marketing societies to be organized	1,800
Cooperative sugar factories	35
Cooperative cotton gins	48
Other cooperative processing societies	118

WAREHOUSING AND STORAGE

Warehouses of Central and State corporations	350
Godowns of marketing societies	1,500
Godowns of larger-sized societies	4,000

The key point to the success of any sound cooperative movement is training. In the narrower sense, this means training of the administrative, technical and other specialists, of whom 25,000 will be needed over the Second Plan, to assure efficient, business-like management. But it also means their training in the human and social skills so keenly needed in any voluntary cooperative venture.

In 1953 the Government and the Reserve Bank jointly formed a Central Committee on cooperative training, and an India-wide system of training has been set up, with a Central College at Poona for executives and managers, five centers to train intermediate grades of workers, and special centers to train four thousand block-level workers in cooperatives for the rural development programs. Costs are shared by the States and by the Central Government. Most States are also conducting training classes for employees of State Cooperative Departments. The training of individual members of cooperatives will be organized by the All-India Cooperative Union together with similar bodies in the States.

The Second Plan also urges strengthening of the State and District cooperative staffs, and their liaison with agriculture and rural development workers to determine local credit and other cooperative needs.

While these training programs are essential, many students of Indian cooperatives believe that even more important is education of the village people to the methods and advantages of cooperation. Successful voluntary cooperatives can only arise out of the needs and interest of the people. For this to happen, the people must be sufficiently informed of these benefits, and of the technique of cooperation, and must want to work together for these benefits using the techniques that assure success.

Although the Government can stimulate and assist, cooperation can succeed only if it is a genuine people's movement. Indian leaders believe, however, that the great potential of cooperation for helping rural India carry out economic and social development and maintain its social cohesion, means that every effort should be placed on education and stimulation of the people in the use of this valuable instrument.

The total allocation of the Second Plan for cooperatives is Rs. 47 crores, as against Rs. 7 crores in the First Plan.

First Plan   Rs. 298 crores

Second Plan   Rs. 341 crores

HIGH LIGHTS
of programs for
AGRICULTURE

The Second Plan will spend Rs. 341 crores, or 43 per cent more than the First Plan, to advance India's agriculture and irrigation production, in addition to the community development and irrigation programs.

The main targets are:

A 28 per cent rise in total agricultural production.

A 35 per cent rise in foodgrain production.

A 56 per cent rise in cotton production.

1.5 million acres of land reclaimed.

8 million acres of eroded land rehabilitated.

Every cultivated acre covered with improved seed.

Every cultivated acre supplied with fertilizers and manures.

Strengthened agricultural research and training.

An All-India farm-marketing news service, and warehousing system.

Improvement of village livestock, and a 20 to 40 per cent rise in milk production in "key villages".

A 33 1/3 per cent increase in fisheries production.

Rehabilitation of 350,000 acres of degraded forests.

Flood control and soil conservation programs.

First Plan	Rs. 238 crores
Second Plan	Rs. 341 crores

HIGH LIGHTS
of programs for
AGRICULTURE

The Second Plan will spend Rs. 341 crores, or 43 per cent more than the First Plan, to advance India's agriculture and agricultural production, in addition to the community development and irrigation programs.
The main targets are:

A 28 per cent rise in total agricultural production.

A 25 per cent rise in foodgrains production

A 56 per cent rise in cotton production.

1.5 million acres of land reclaimed.

3 million acres of eroded land rehabilitated.

Every cultivated acre covered with improved seed.

Every cultivated acre supplied with fertilizers and manures.

Strengthened agricultural research and training.

An All-India farm-marketing news service, and warehousing system.

Improvement of village livestock, and a 30 to 40 per cent rise in milk production in "key villages."

A 33 1/3 per cent increase in fisheries production.

Rehabilitation of 380,000 acres of degraded forests.

Flood control and soil conservation programs.

CHAPTER V

Agriculture

The awakening of India's village people through rural development, and the great issues of land reform rely, to a very large degree, for their final solution and success on how quickly crop yields go up and how far and how fast India's agricultural services can improve farming methods.

India has under way an extensive agricultural program for rapidly stepping up crop yields, for improving animal husbandry, for forestry, fisheries and soil conservation, for improving agricultural training and research.

For these programs as a whole, over the Second Plan, India will spend 43 per cent more than over the First Plan, or Rs. 341 crores. Where they must reach to the farmer in the field, they will be carried out chiefly through the rural development program.

AGRICULTURAL PRODUCTION

The new target of the Second Plan is a 28 per cent increase in agricultural production above 1955–1956 levels. This is more than half again as high as the goal originally set by the Second Plan. The new target was fixed in the autumn of 1956, after an anxious re-examination of India's agricultural needs, principally for food and for export, over the next five years.

Rising prices, especially of food, from early 1956 onward, had made such a review essential. Demand for food had gone up more swiftly than expected. Because of good crops since 1953, reserves of food stocks and food imports had been cut down. The rise in food prices which resulted brought into sharp focus the need for very big increases in food production over the Second Plan to ward off further price rises and, as well, to meet the rising demands for food expected when incomes and employment rose under the stimulus of the Plan.

Acute shortage of foreign exchange also made it necessary to plan to push food production up so that over the Plan years imports of food could be reduced and save India's scant dollars and pounds sterling for machinery and other essential development goods available only outside India.

Re-assessment of consumer and national demands not only showed the need to set the new and higher target of a 28 per cent increase, but showed that over the next ten or more years India must aim at a doubling of agricultural production, to meet the needs of the national economy and to raise agricultural incomes.

The revised Second Plan targets for individual major crops are given on the next page.

Before these targets are achieved, some imports of food and other agricultural commodities, such as cotton, continue to be necessary. Further, as India develops and new needs arise for food and for raw materials like cotton, India will supplement its own production with imports to the extent required.

Since relatively little new land remains to be brought under cultivation, the overwhelming part of the 28 per cent increase must come

AGRICULTURAL PRODUCTION TARGETS
(Revised as of November 1956)

COMMODITY	ESTIMATED PRO-DUCTION 1955–56	REVISED TARGETS FOR PRODUCTION BY 1960–61	% INCREASE IN INDEX OF PRODUCTION
Foodgrains (million tons)	65.0	80.4	24.6
Oilseeds (million tons)	5.5	7.6	37.0
Sugar cane (million tons)	5.8	7.8	33.9
Cotton (million bales)	4.2	6.5	55.6
Jute (million bales)	4.0	5.5	58.1
Other crops			22.4
All commodities			27.8

from more intensive, efficient and profitable methods of agricultural production, that is, raising yields per acre. Achieving the large increase of 28 per cent by intensive cultivation, the Government believes, is now, as it was not at the start of the First Plan, a practical possibility.

Study of the 19 per cent rise in crop yields over the First Plan has shown that, although there have been marked differences between the increases in yield for one kind of crop and another, between increases in various States and regions, and between yields from year to year of the Plan, there was nevertheless apparent a basic upward trend in production over the First Plan as a whole, independent of the favorable rains and weather of the Plan years.

Detailed and sufficiently precise statistical studies are not available to judge to what degree each of many factors was responsible—how much was due to increased irrigation, to land reclamation, to use of fertilizers, and so on. What is known, however, is that the increase in crop yields took place even though programs for some of these improvements—particularly those for green manures, for spreading the use of improved seeds, implements and of all improved farm practices—were not carried out to the degree hoped. Effective India-wide programs on these problems, therefore, still promise in themselves considerable scope for increasing yields.

Psychological factors—the new initiative and enthusiasm of the farmer following upon land reforms and rural development—were undoubtedly important in increasing crop yields over the First Plan, and will certainly be so over the Second. Many of the areas under rural development, compared with non-development areas, have recorded higher crop yields.

Moreover, in various regions of India and in plots selected for crop competitions, yields of certain commodities such as rice, under new and intensive modes of cultivation have shown yield increases of eight to ten times the average. While such large yields are still exceptional, taking all factors together the Government feels that the substantial Second Plan increase of 28 per cent over all is obtainable, and with only small increases in the expenditures originally proposed in the Second Plan for agricultural development.

A very high degree, however, of coordination and organization and detailed and systematic planning of all programs and Government measures is an essential key to the problem. Organizationally, it will also mean that the scientific and technical agricultural services must apply themselves very intensively and directly to the problems of the village cultivator, with a new attitude to field rather than desk work. It will mean, too, administrative recognition in status and salary of the high value of competent technical men.

Systematic planning must take into account efficient land management, long- and short-term targets, price policy and the closest integration of all programs with the rural development program.

The following measures are proposed:

1. THE RURAL DEVELOPMENT PROGRAM

The key instrument in bringing the knowledge and means of intensive cultivation to the village farmers will be the community development program, which has proved an effective means for reaching the villages. As this program is expanded to cover all rural India, it will expand first into those areas where the most rapid increases in crop yields can be achieved.

Village-level workers will give top priority to agricultural production, and definite targets of production will be laid down for each

LEARNING TO WRITE: A young farm wife (right) in Uttar Pradesh, near Allahabad, is helped in a Hindi writing lesson by a trained woman village extension worker. Homemaking, health and child care, as well as literacy, are taught to village women.

NEW ROADS TO LINK THE VILLAGES: Village leader (right) discusses with a Government engineer a point on construction of the new road being built by his village. Villagers contribute up to half the road's cost, and supply all labor as a voluntary community activity.

MAKING MACHINE TOOLS: The Hindustan Machine Tool Factory, Bangalore, was set up with foreign technical assistance early in the First Five Year Plan.

LAUNCHING AT VISAKHAPATNAM: India is expanding her own shipbuilding facilities in both Government-owned and private yards, in addition to purchasing ships abroad. This Visakhapatnam yard is on India's east coast.

group of villages under the worker's charge. There will be closest integration of this program with the Ministries and Departments of Agriculture at the Central, State and local levels.

2. Increased Irrigation

Twenty-one million more acres of land will be put under irrigation (12 million from large and medium irrigation schemes; 9 million from minor irrigation schemes, including tube wells). This will bring India's irrigated area up to 26 per cent of the total area under cultivation. Increased irrigation alone is expected to give an additional 4.9 million tons of foodgrains.

3. Expanded Use of Fertilizers

In every State an effort will be made to supply every acre of cultivated land with fertilizers and organic and green manures. Special staffs will be provided in every rural development block to encourage use of fertilizers, compost and manures. Use of nitrogenous fertilizers is expected at the end of the Plan to be three times that of 1955. To meet demand, the Government proposes to build three, and possibly four, new nitrogenous fertilizer plants and to increase production of phosphatic fertilizers. Fertilizers and manures are expected to yield 3.8 million additional tons of food grains.

4. Improved Seeds

Every acre of land under cultivation is to be covered with improved seeds. Forty-three hundred seed multiplication farms of twenty-five acres each are to be set up by the States, or one to every one hundred villages in the rural development blocks. Each block will also be served by a cooperative seed store with smaller stores in every group of twenty villages. Use of improved seeds is expected to yield 3.4 million tons more of foodgrains.

5. Improved Farm Implements and Practices

Both the Center and State Governments have proposals for designing and introducing improved types of plows and other implements, and for making them cheaply available to farmers.

Acreage under the highly productive "Japanese" method of rice cultivation will be doubled, to a total of 4 million acres. General improvement in all agricultural practices as a whole, aside from those itemized above, is expected to yield 2.5 million tons more of food-grains than in 1956.

6. DISTRIBUTION OF FARM SUPPLIES

To supply farm implements, seeds and fertilizers to each of over half a million villages at the right time in the sowing season poses an enormous task of organization. At present few supply outlets exist, except a limited number of cooperatives. Setting up, rapidly and effectively, the needed outlets—within a bullock cart's distance from every village—is the high-priority distribution job of the agriculture and cooperative services and the rural development program.

7. LAND RECLAMATION AND SOIL CONSERVATION

One and a half million new acres of land are to be reclaimed, or virtually the full extent of land that remains to be brought under cultivation. Another 3 million acres which are seriously affected by soil erosion will be put under a concerted program of improvement for intensive cultivation. For areas without irrigation, soil and water conservation methods, contour-bunding and dry-farming techniques will be stressed, with efforts to enlist local participation and community action. Nearly a million more tons of food grains are expected to result from this work.

8. PLANT PROTECTION

While valuable work on a State and national level has been done, especially in locust control, new stress will be put on insect or pest control by the individual farmer on his fields. The four centers for plant-protection equipment set up over the First Plan will be strengthened; and five new ones set up.

9. AGRICULTURAL RESEARCH AND TRAINING

Research in improved plant and seed varieties, and on problems arising from actual experience and needs of the farmer in the field, is urgent. Improved strains of millets, the commonly used food-grain of the villages, are particularly needed throughout India. The Second Plan provides Rs. 14 crores for agricultural research by the Ministry of Food and Agriculture, by the special commodity committees (for sugar cane, cotton, tobacco, oilseeds, jute, and so on), by the Indian Agricultural Research Institute, and by the several Central Research Institutes (for potatoes, rice, sugar-cane). Two new centers for research on agricultural economics will be added.

The Second Plan's considerable efforts to expand and strengthen agriculture education and training with especial emphasis on extension education and research have been discussed in an earlier chapter on manpower training.

10. AGRICULTURAL MARKETING

The lack of accurate and up-to-date market information places both the farmer and the Government at a disadvantage. The Second Plan provides for the setting up of an all-India market news service, mainly for farmers, to be established in collaboration with the States. During the Plan the number of regulated markets under the Agricultural Produce (Markets) Act will be doubled, from 450 to 900. A program for compulsory grading for export of a number of commodities is in progress. The new nation-wide warehousing scheme, already noted as a Second Plan cooperative program, will add to efficient marketing service.

11. RURAL CREDIT

Cheap farm credit, to buy improved seeds, fertilizers, implements, and so on, is indispensable to enable farmers to adopt these improvements and raise yields. The nation-wide cooperative credit system, described earlier, is intended to make cheap credit accessible to virtually every village. It is felt, however, that very special measures will be needed to achieve and improve upon the present loan targets.

12. PRICE POLICY

Many analysts of India's agriculture problem believe that it is necessary to guarantee minimum prices in order to assure higher crop production. Even in a period of generally rising prices, village farmers, who have no margin of surplus funds to risk, hesitate to spend for fertilizers, improved seeds, and so on, against uncertain future prices for their crops. As long as shortage continues to be India's problem, overproduction will not be a concern as in the United States. Any surplus would be marginal, temporary and manageable.

In May 1957 the Government announced, as an assurance to growers, that it would not allow prices to fall below economic levels and would take such steps as were necessary from time to time to prevent any such price drop.

ANIMAL HUSBANDRY AND DAIRYING

FIRST PLAN	Rs. 22 crores
SECOND PLAN	Rs. 56 crores

HIGH LIGHTS
of programs for
ANIMAL HUSBANDRY

The Second Plan will spend about two and a half times as much as the First Plan on animal husbandry programs, with these main targets:

A village livestock improvement program to yield a million improved cows, about a million improved bullocks, and 22,000 improved stud bulls.

A rise in milk production of 30 to 40 per cent in next ten years in "key village" areas.

36 new safe milk-supply systems in the cities.

Eradication of rinderpest, India's chief cattle disease.

1900 new village veterinary dispensaries.

50 per cent more up-graded hens, and five times more egg production, in selected areas.

The Second Plan's very much larger program for animal husbandry and dairying has a twin purpose: to increase the supply of
milk, meat and eggs for better diets; and to provide more efficient
bullock power for farming. Assuring the supply of wool, hair, hides
and skins is another consideration, since these are important to the
economy as a whole.

Animal husbandry and dairying could be a very important factor
in raising farm incomes and in the whole rural economy of India.
As yet only a fraction of its possible contribution is being realized.
India's major problems are excessive numbers of cattle, poor quality
and scrub breeds, low milk yields, and the need to improve fodder
supplies and quality.

Cattle fulfill a multiple function in India and are second only to
land as the principal source of rural wealth. They not only provide
milk, but "horse" power for all farm implements and transport, for
lift irrigation, for threshing and other farm machinery. In many areas
they are virtually the only source of rural fuel—the dung is dried for
burning. Many believe that it is because cattle are so essential to
rural life that they have been since ancient times objects of religious
veneration.

The Planning Commission expresses concern in the Second Plan
with the expected increase in surplus cattle. Total cattle population
in India is roughly 200 million head, of which about 25 per cent are
water buffaloes. In relation to fodder supplies, at least one-third of
the cattle population is already considered surplus. Overgrazing has
helped bring about soil erosion; and grazing areas, hitherto the main
source of food, are rapidly decreasing as more land is needed to grow
food for human beings.

The surplus will be increased as famines and cattle diseases, such
as rinderpest, are brought under control. It will grow larger, too, if
there are further bans on cow slaughter, on the lines of legislation already enacted in several States.

The Planning Commission recommends that those additional
States where a ban on cow slaughter is being considered take a realistic view of the shortage of feed, and also of how voluntary organi-

zations might take responsibility, with Government and popular support, for maintaining unserviceable and unproductive cattle.

In the First Plan *gosadans* were proposed—enclosures for aged and unfit cattle, usually in sparsely settled areas. This proposal did not make satisfactory progress and a new scheme has been introduced for the Second Plan period. The size of the gosadans has been made smaller, and facilities are being provided at each gosadan for better use of hides, bones and other products.

The Second Plan programs for cattle improvement include:

CATTLE BREEDING PROGRAM

There are twenty-five well defined breeds of Indian cattle and six of buffaloes. A large majority are best for draft, and are poor milk producers. What India hopes to do in all its cross-breeding programs is to improve both draft and milk-production qualities.

The major effort of the Second Plan, as of the First, is to improve breeds in the villages, by means of what is called a "key village" scheme, initiated by State Governments. Under this scheme, which evoked wide and keen cooperation among villagers, 574 "key villages" and 144 artificial insemination centers were set up during the First Plan.

In each "key village" a quality breeding bull was stationed to serve surrounding villages; and scrub bulls of the area were castrated. Part of the program, to increase and improve fodder supplies and organize cooperative marketing of animal husbandry products, was less successfully tried in a pilot scheme of the First Plan.

The Second Plan will set up 1,258 "key villages," with 245 insemination centers and about the same number of veterinary extension centers. The program is intended to produce 22,000 improved stud bulls, 950,000 improved bullocks, and a million improved cows.

DAIRYING AND MILK SUPPLY

Average milk yields in India are one-half to one-third those of Western countries. Per capita consumption is five ounces daily as compared with a minimal nutritional requirement of fifteen ounces.

Increasing supplies of milk are extremely important in India, since milk is one of the few protein-rich foods acceptable to the large vegetarian population. A general objective is a 30 to 40 per cent rise in milk production over the next ten to twelve years—in the areas in the "key-village" scheme. Pedigree breeding stations in addition to those of the key village schemes are proposed.

Urban milk supply has become an urgent problem, as cities have grown rapidly in population. Bombay and some other towns have a safe, protected milk-supply system; but these serve only a small part of the population. During the Second Plan thirty-six milk-supply schemes, twelve cooperative creameries and seven milk-drying plants will be organized. The drying plants will be located in rural areas and will produce butter, *ghee*, and skimmed milk powder.

Collection of milk from rural areas will be organized under the control of milk boards. Calcutta, Delhi and Madras are establishing milk colonies similar to that at Aarey serving Bombay.

DISEASE CONTROL

In the past, diseases took a heavy toll of cattle, rinderpest alone accounting for 60 per cent of cattle deaths. The Second Plan proposes to eliminate rinderpest over most of the country, using methods successfully tried in a pilot scheme of the First Plan.

Veterinary dispensaries, which increased from 2,000 in 1951 to 2,650 by the end of the First Plan, will be increased to a total of 4,550 and will include 145 mobile dispensaries.

Other Programs

SHEEP

There are 38 million sheep in India, producing 60 million pounds of wool annually, more than half of which is exported. Since local breeds yield only two pounds per head, and improved breeds can yield six pounds, the Second Plan proposes 396 sheep and wool extension centers and three new sheep-breeding farms.

POULTRY

Good poultry can provide considerable extra income and better nutrition to rural families in India, as elsewhere, if India's local hens, which are poor layers, are replaced by pure-bred stock. Local Indian hens yield fifty eggs a year, compared to 120 in most countries. Poultry breeding and keeping is an important part of the program for rural development areas, and three hundred poultry extension centers supported by four regional farms will be set up.

It is hoped, in selected areas, to increase production of upgraded hens by 50 per cent, and raise per capita supplies of eggs from four to twenty per year.

Veterinary Research

Programs of animal husbandry development have to be based on extensive scientific research, organized at three levels—national, regional, and State. The Indian Veterinary Research Institute and the National Dairy Research Institute, which undertake fundamental research work on problems of all-India importance, are to be strengthened and expanded. Further, four regional research institutes will be established by the Central Government.

FISHERIES

FIRST PLAN	Rs. 4 crores
SECOND PLAN	Rs. 12 crores

Fish are plentiful in India's offshore waters, if fishermen have the kind of boats and equipment to reach them. Inland lakes, rivers and water reservoirs also, if stocked and used, are a good potential source of supply.

India began early in the First Plan to try to develop its fisheries— in part to get more food for better balanced diets, but in large part,

---

HIGH LIGHTS
of programs for
FISHERIES

The Second Plan will spend three times as much as the First Plan on developing India's fisheries, with these main targets:

A 33 1/3 per cent increase in the fish catch from the offshore and inland sources.

Mechanization and development of deep-sea fishing.

New and improved fishing harbors.

Improved fish storage, marketing and transport services.

---

as well, to help advance its impoverished fishing communities. Indian fishermen and their clusters of huts along the shores usually lack even the meagerest health care, sanitation, schools, or other services. Raising their incomes and living standards, helping them and their communities to advance as a whole, and to share, like the rural people, in the nation's progress, is the important human and social side in fisheries development.

While the Second Plan proposes general development of inland fisheries, especially in West Bengal, Orissa and Madras, the greater part of the program is for marine fisheries. Technological development and research will be important; yet the main approach will be similar to that of the rural development program—a coordinated approach to the social and economic life of fishing communities. The Indo-Norwegian Fisheries project set up under the Colombo Plan has developed an imaginative and significant program of the kind in Travancore-Cochin (now Kerala State).

Where under various programs of the First Plan, fish production rose by about ten per cent, over the Second Plan fish production is expected to increase by one-third more. An increase of 50 per cent over the next ten years is considered possible and practical.

In the development of sea fisheries, the tasks to be undertaken are broadly of four kinds: (1) improvement of fishing methods, (2) development of deep-sea fishing, (3) the provision of fishing harbors, and (4) the organization of fish transport, storage, marketing and use of fish.

With the craft now in use, the activities of fishermen are confined largely to a coastal belt of about seven to ten miles. Mechanization of fishing craft and improved fishing methods are essential for increasing production in offshore waters. The Second Plan will expand existing programs and activities along these lines.

Other measures include expansion of the extended operations at the Deep Sea Fishing Station at Bombay, the charting of fishing grounds beyond the forty-fathom line, exploratory fishing and charting of fishing grounds on the west coast and the east coast and the establishment of three exploratory fishing stations at Cochin, Visakhapatnam and Port Blair.

The Second Plan also will develop new fishing harbors and berthing facilities at existing harbors. For developing transport and cold-storage facilities, twenty refrigerated railway wagons for long-distance transport will be procured and a number of ice and cold-storage plants erected, some of these being set up at important centers to be operated by cooperatives. Steps have also to be taken for the further development of fishery by-product industries.

The Plan includes a large program for research and training on inland fisheries, on designing and manufacturing fishing nets and other gear, on storage, processing and use of fish, and the establishment of commodity standards and grades.

FORESTS

FIRST PLAN	Rs. 9.6 crores
SECOND PLAN	Rs. 27 crores

Compared to the United States of America and the Soviet Union, which have one-third of their area under forest, Indian forests cover

---

HIGH LIGHTS
of programs for
F O R E S T R Y

The Second Plan will spend nearly three times as much as the First Plan on development of India's forests, with these main targets:

Rehabilitation of 380,000 acres of degraded forest.

115,000 acres planted to commercially important species—teak, matchwood, wattle and blue gum and medicinal plants.

Demonstration timber-treating and seasoning centers.

Construction and improvement of 7,400 miles of forest roads.

---

only 22 per cent, and a considerable portion is scrub jungle or forest in name only. Yield per acre is substantially below that of Western countries, and wood supplies generally are so scant that wood can never be used freely as a basic construction material.

Industrialization will, however, bring increased demand for forest products, for paper, plywood, packing and construction. Forests, moreover, through their effect on flood control and soil conservation have an important bearing on agricultural production.

Forest development has, therefore, been given special importance over the Second Plan. Emphasis is both on long-range development and on the meeting of immediate and increasing demands for timber.

During the First Plan a number of programs for afforestation, forest communications and formation of village and small-scale plantations were undertaken. Over 75,000 acres, the vegetative cover was restored by afforestation or planting. Over 3,000 miles of forest roads were constructed or improved.

More than 20 million acres of forest land which, under private ownership or management, had been degraded came under State control. Matchwood plantations have been raised at the rate of 3,000 acres per year. Considerable expansion of the work at the Forest Research Institute, Dehra Dun, was also undertaken.

Second Plan's Programs

The Second Plan proposes a considerable step-up in forestry programs.

One of the special needs is to build up plantations of commercially important species. The Second Plan will plant 50,000 acres of forest land anew with commercially important species like teak; 50,000 more acres of matchwood; 13,00 acres with species of wattle and blue gum; 2,000 acres with medicinal plants.

Other programs include rehabilitation of about 380,000 acres of "degraded" forest areas which have come under State control during recent years; and plantations along canal banks, in roadside avenues, shelter belts and on village waste lands.

The Central Government will set up three or four demonstration timber-treating and seasoning centers, with a view to upgrading secondary timbers and utilizing them fully. State Governments will set up about ten similar small-scale plants. Forest resources surveys, including a timber-trends survey, construction or improvement of 7,400 miles of forest roads, adoption of better techniques for timber extraction, such as improved "logging" methods, are other activities planned.

It is proposed that, with close and sympathetic guidance from forest departments, more forest labor cooperatives be established for working the forests, so that the profits which now go to contractors can go more fully to forest workers.

The program for forest research during the Second Plan includes a number of projects at the Forest Research Institute, Dehra Dun, and a new regional research center, with units at both Coimbatore and Bangalore.

A Forestry Commission has been recommended to coordinate forest development and management, and to undertake such tasks as the improvement of forest statistics, market studies, grading of timber and other forest produce.

The conservation of wild life is an integral part of forest management, especially in view of the urgent need for protecting India's rich heritage of wild life, which is now finding its last refuge in the national forest reservations. In order to conserve wild life, forestry programs in the Second Plan include the establishment of eighteen national parks and game sanctuaries, besides a modern zoological park in Delhi.

SOIL CONSERVATION

FIRST PLAN Rs. 1 crore	
SECOND PLAN	Rs. 20 crores

HIGH LIGHTS
of programs for
SOIL CONSERVATION

The Second Plan will spend twenty times as much as the First Plan on soil conservation, with these main targets:

Direct rehabilitation of 3 million eroded acres, 2 million of them on agricultural land.

Conservation measures started on 750,000 acres in hills, river valleys, ravine and waste lands.

Education in soil conservation methods for villagers, and especially tribal peoples.

For about 50 to 60 per cent of India's cultivated area, irrigation is not possible, and soil conservation measures offer the most hopeful possibility of raising agricultural production.

Erosion by monsoon, floods and wind is widespread and serious. For example, in the black cotton-soil fields of Sholapur (Bombay), it is estimated that 37 tons of soil *per acre* is lost each year in the monsoon rains. In U.P., Punjab and the North West Frontier area, one estimate is that 5,000 square miles are completely useless gullied land.

For India as a whole, it is estimated that one-fifth of the area in hilly regions, pastures and waste lands are in an advanced state of erosion. Overgrazing, destruction of forests, poor agricultural practices have been the important reasons for the loss of these lands to use for crops, forests, or soil and water protection.

The Second Plan has allocated Rs. 20 crores to soil conservation. Work is to be undertaken in a concentrated manner over 3 million acres of land in areas seriously affected by soil erosion, and will include 2 million acres of agricultural land.

In the villages, on lands now being farmed, the Extension Service under the rural development program is to be the chief agency to teach soil conservation methods as part of good farm management. In rural areas, block and village workers will stimulate local leadership, as has been done in the United States and elsewhere, in organizing community action to put soil conservation measures into effect on eroded village common grazing lands and forests, and to help set community standards for land management for individual farmers.

Steps for the control of shifting sand dunes are to be undertaken over an area of 350,000 acres, principally in Kutch and Rajasthan. In important river valleys, hilly regions, ravine and waste lands, measures such as afforestation, fire control and contour bunding will be carried out on a total of 750,000 acres.

A Central Soil Conservation Board was set up in 1953, and almost all States now have their own Boards. The Central Board has circulated to the States a model bill for soil conservation legislation.

Five research-and-training centers in soil conservation have been established at Dehra Dun, Kotah, Vasad, Bellary and Ootacamund, and a research station at Jodhpur for studying different groups of problems. These stations are engaged in developing effective practices acceptable to farmers and conforming to the required technical standards. Reconnaissance surveys on a regional basis are also to be undertaken.

A major problem and possibility, however, is educating the villages in soil conservation methods, in control of erosion and overgrazing, in contour bunding, afforestation, and so on.

Many of the people concerned are nomadic tribal peoples who cut down forests to practice a destructive shifting cultivation. Education may include their resettlement. The National Extension Service and community development programs, which reach to the villages, are the most effective media for approaching, educating and, as needed, resettling these tribal peoples.

FIRST PLAN	Rs. 690 crores
SECOND PLAN	Rs. 913 crores

HIGH LIGHTS
of programs for
IRRIGATION AND POWER

To provide water for Indian fields, power for India's industries, homes and villages, the Second Plan will spend Rs. 913 crores, or 32 per cent more than the First Plan for development of irrigation and power. The main targets are:

IRRIGATION

Twenty-one million more acres irrigated, or nearly a third more land under irrigation than in 1956.

One million more acres irrigated by tube wells.

Half of all irrigated lands put under permanent reliable types of irrigation.

POWER

A 100 per cent increase in power production and consumption.

Electrification of all towns with 10,000 population or over.

Electrification of 86 per cent of towns with 5,000 to 10,000 population.

Electrification of over 2 1/2 times more villages, or a total of 13,900.

CHAPTER VI

Irrigation and Power

IRRIGATION

FIRST PLAN	Rs. 384 [1] crores
SECOND PLAN	Rs. 416 crores

Irrigation is the lifeblood of Indian agriculture. Unreliable rainfall and inadequate water supply have been major causes of India's scanty harvests, crop failures and, in the past, of famine. Yet, where irrigation is available, most farm lands in India's warm climate can grow two or even three crops a year instead of one, and give considerable additional farm employment.

India has, therefore, practiced irrigation since ancient times through wells, "tanks" (reservoirs), and canals. In the nineteenth century an extensive canal system was installed, principally in North and South

[1] First Plan Allocation.

India, and undivided India had in 1947 the largest area under irrigation of any nation of the world.

On the Partition of India in 1947, however, nearly half of all the irrigated lands of undivided India went to Pakistan, and at the start of the First Plan little more than a sixth of all farm land was irrigated. Irrigation became a top priority of the new Government, and one of the achievements in which independent India takes particular pride is the ten millions of new acres it has brought under irrigation.

The First Plan alone increased the area of irrigated land by nearly a third over 1950–1951, and when the irrigation projects of both the First and Second Plans are completed more land will be under irrigation than in all of India's centuries of history.

India has abundant sources of water, principally from its great rivers. In 1950–1951 only 5 per cent of the river supply was being used for irrigation. Incomplete surveys indicate that there is also a very substantial amount of underground water, chiefly in North India, and in Bombay State. Storage of monsoon rains is another source of supply.

Although a full survey of India's total water resources is still under way, it is now estimated that about half of all farm land can be brought under irrigation.

Planning of several great multi-purpose river valley projects, which would supply irrigation and power, and provide for water storage and flood control, began even before Independence under the stimulus of a series of disastrous floods, droughts and famines in the 1940's. Work was started in the Damodar Valley (Bihar and Bengal), at Hirakud (Orissa), at Bhakra-Nangal (Punjab and Rajasthan). Plans for other projects had been drawn up by many States.

The First Plan allocated over 16 per cent of its total budget to develop irrigation alone; 28 per cent for irrigation and power combined. Most of these funds went to speed work on the major river valley multi-purpose projects, including those on which construction had already been started.

Some of the most important of these projects are the following:

BHAKRA-NANGAL: Sutlej River, Punjab

This is the largest of the projects, and includes the highest poured concrete gravity dam in the world. On completion (about 1960) the project will irrigate 3.6 million acres in Rajasthan and the Punjab, by means of 3,000 miles of canal system.

The Nangal canal system opened in 1954, and is already irrigating 1.2 million acres. About 1.1 million more acres will come under irrigation over the Second Plan. The first of four powerhouses was opened in 1955; the project's ultimate power capacity is 594,000 kw. The estimated cost is Rs. 160 crores.

DAMODAR VALLEY: Damodar River, Bihar and West Bengal

"India's TVA," this project, begun in 1948, will on completion irrigate 1.1 million acres, and deliver 254,000 kw. of power. Two large dams, an irrigation barrage, and a thermal power station (at Bokaro), one of the largest in Asia, have already been completed. Two other dams are under construction; both will have hydel stations attached. An eighty-five-mile irrigation canal will provide a navigable route for boats and barges between Raniganj coal fields and the Hooghly River in Calcutta. The estimated total cost is Rs. 86 crores.

HIRAKUD: Mahanadi River, Orissa

Serving an area of considerable mineral and forest wealth and industrial potential, this project when completed will irrigate 1.8 million acres and deliver 232,500 kw. of power from five powerhouses. It contains the largest earth dam in the world. The dam was completed and inaugurated in January 1957. The estimated total cost is Rs. 86 crores.

KOSI: Kosi River, Nepal and Bihar

This project, designed to tame the most destructive of Indian rivers (the River of Sorrows), will ultimately include a barrage in Nepal (which is cooperating with India in the project) and two canal systems and protective embankments for control of flood waters.

Construction was begun in January 1955 on the embankments, with the help of thousands of villagers under voluntary organizations. On completion, the project will irrigate 1.6 million acres in Nepal and Bihar. The estimated total cost is Rs. 46 crores.

TUNGABHADRA: Andhra and Mysore

This project calls for a dam, two powerhouses and a canal system ultimately irrigating 700,000 acres, and delivering 63,000 kw. of power. The dam was inaugurated in mid-1953, and 47,000 acres have already been put under irrigation. The power station opened in January 1957. The estimated total cost is Rs. 60 crores.

Other important irrigation and power projects are *Chambal* (Rajasthan and Madhya Pradesh), which will irrigate 1.1 million acres and generate 176,000 kw. of power; *Lower Bhavani* (Madras), 207,000 acres; and *Nagarjunasagar* (Andhra), 1.9 million acres.

Second Plan Irrigation Programs

The Second Plan will provide Rs. 381 crores for new irrigation, or about the same amount as the First Plan. Rs. 35 crores in addition is allocated for projects to use India's share of the water of the Indus River System. Total Second Plan outlay on irrigation will thus equal Rs. 416 crores.

About half of this will go to completion of projects begun under the First Plan. With the remaining funds 195 new projects will be started, with emphasis on those of medium rather than of large scale. Only seventeen of the projects will cost more than Rs. 5 crores.

From these projects alone, the irrigated area [1] will be increased by 2 million acres a year in the first three years of the Plan, and by 3 million in each of the last years. In all, 21 million new acres will be brought under irrigation from all projects, including 9 million acres from minor irrigation works (wells, and so on) which will be built under agriculture development programs.

[1] In addition to 6.3 million acres put under irrigation from these projects over the First Plan period.

Tube wells, though relatively costly, are an important source of irrigation in some areas of India, particularly in the Indo-Gangetic plains in the North. A tube well is a single hollow tube or cylinder about 16 inches in diameter which is driven down to an average of 300 feet to reach underground water. A Diesel or electric pump pulls the water to the surface. One tube well can irrigate 300 acres.

Relatively few tube wells (2,500) were installed prior to 1951, and those chiefly in Uttar Pradesh. Under the First Plan nearly double this number (4,422) were installed, bringing eventually 2 million acres under secure irrigation, in North India, Bombay and Bihar. The Second Plan allocates Rs. 20 crores (under its agriculture "minor works" budget) for tube wells to irrigate an additional million acres, in the same States, plus Madras.

IRRIGATION BY TUBE WELL

	As of 1951	As of 1956	As of 1961	INCREASE 1951–61
No. of tube wells	2,500	6,922	10,503	320%
Total acres irrigated	1 million	3 million	4 million	300%

As shown in the chart below, India's total area under irrigation will have more than doubled under projects started in the First and Second Plans, when these are completed. Viewed another way, this means, as noted earlier, that in about fifteen years independent India will have put more land under irrigation than all its previous history. The proportion of irrigated land to total cultivated area will rise from 16 per cent in 1950–1951 and 20 per cent in 1955–1956 to 27 per cent when First and Second Plan schemes are completed.

India's achievement is also important in terms of *quality* of irrigation. In 1951, only 20 of the 51.5 million irrigated acres were under a first-class permanent type of irrigation, that is, a permanent, secure canal and reservoir system that will provide water regardless of rainfall. Most of the new irrigation being installed under First and Second Plan projects is of permanent character. The total area put under secure irrigation will be 57 million acres, or about three times as much as in 1950–1951.

PROGRESS IN IRRIGATION: FIRST AND SECOND PLANS
(*Millions of acres irrigated*)

	1950–1951	END OF 1ST PLAN (1956)		END OF 2ND PLAN (1961)		ON FULL DEVELOPMENT	
		Acreage Added	Total	Acreage to be Added	Total	Acreage to be Added	Total
By all previous Irrigation Systems	51.5		51.5		51.5		51.5
By First Plan Irrigation Projects							
Major and Medium		6.3	6.3	9.0	15.3	6.7	22.0
Minor (including tube wells)		10.0	10.0		10.0		10.0
By Second Plan Irrigation Projects							
Major and Medium				3.0	3.0	12.0	15.0
Minor (including tube wells)				9.0	9.0		9.0
	51.5	16.3	67.8	21	88.8	18.7	107.5

LONG-TERM DEVELOPMENT

While new surveys are now in process to determine the full extent of possible future irrigation of all types, rough estimates indicate that 150 to 160 million acres, or about half the total area under cultivation, can be irrigated. The Government expects to put half of this area under permanent systems.

Development of water and land resources must, however, be paced together. Major and minor works which are complementary in character and scope must be carefully balanced; and medium and large-scale projects phased rightly in their relation to each other.

A special need is to secure cooperation of local communities in building and maintenance of medium and minor works, and in using water efficiently.

A very important point made clear by the experience of the First Plan was that canal and distribution systems must be built and ready at the same time as the reservoir, so that water stored and available can be carried without delay to the farm fields. It is also important that through the rural extension service and other means, farmers have their lands ready for wet crops and know the new cultivation techniques that must be used.

COST OF IRRIGATION

Costs of installing permanent irrigation vary from Rs. 250–300 per acre in the North to Rs. 600–650 in the South, where irrigation provides for rice cultivation. To help the Government finance this high cost, a betterment levy—a capital tax on lands brought under irrigation by Government schemes—has now been accepted in principle, and legislation has been passed in nearly all States. The exact levy, determined by each State, is generally related to the increase in land value, and may be paid in cash, either in a lump sum or over a period of fifteen years, or in land.

RESEARCH

Many of the States were hampered in proposing Second Plan irrigation projects by lack of complete and accurate supporting data. The Government is aware of the need for detailed investigation and surveys on the most desirable location and type of irrigation, on area water requirements and resources, and on soil types as well as desirable cultivation patterns under irrigation; and a research plan has been drawn up for the Second Plan. A Central Research Station in Poona and twelve State Research Centers set up in recent years have been conducting comprehensive research on irrigation works, hydraulics and soils. An additional research station is proposed under the Second Plan.

FLOOD CONTROL

India has historically been subject to continued and often disastrous floods. The floods of 1954 and 1955 caused damage estimated at $1.2

to $1.9 billions, respectively, to land, crops and property, as well as great human misery. These losses are especially severe for a nation which needs to conserve its funds and energies for development.

As many of the rivers cross more than one State, the problem of flood control is necessarily an inter-State problem. A Central Flood Control Board was set up in 1954 to draw up a coordinated flood control program and to consider projects proposed by the States. A tentative program of works to be carried out during the First Plan was prepared, and Rs. 16.5 crores was made available as loans to States for flood control proposals.

Essential data needed for drawing up comprehensive plans for flood control projects are now being gathered. Until surveys have been completed and the necessary data collected, protective works of an immediate nature will be carried out which will eventually form part of comprehensive plans. Rs. 60 crores has been made available in the Second Plan for immediate and short-term measures.

POWER

FIRST PLAN	Rs. 260 crores
SECOND PLAN	Rs. 427 crores

To pump irrigation waters to the fields, to turn the wheels of its new and expanding industries, to raise living standards in the villages as well as in the cities, India must have an adequate supply of power.

Fortunately, India has one of the highest potentials for hydroelectric power in the world, roughly 35 million kw.[1] Less than 5 per cent of this is now developed, in spite of the tremendous expansion over the First Plan years.

Together with other power generated by coal and oil, the na-

---

[1] This is over 2½ times the total electric generating capacity of Japan, a big user, in 1954–55, and about 1½ times that of Great Britain at about the same period.

tion's total power resources are now believed sufficient for a fairly long period. India is also working toward development of atomic energy as a supplementary source of power, especially in areas, such as Central India, removed from hydro and coal resources.

The First Plan acted vigorously to increase power capacity and production, chiefly through hydroelectric stations in large multipurpose projects such as the Damodar Valley, Bhakra-Nangal and others throughout India. Installed capacity in 1956 is 50 per cent higher and electric energy production 67 per cent higher than in the beginning of the Plan. Most of the increase came from Government-owned plants.[1]

As a result of these First Plan efforts, power consumption has virtually doubled in India over the First Plan years, measured either in per capita terms or in the number of towns and villages electrified.

The Second Plan will greatly step up power development, not only to meet India's immediate needs but to prepare for those of the Third and later Plan periods. What the Second Plan now proposes is to more than double installed capacity, production and consumption by 1961, and over the Third Plan more than double these again. Total installed capacity is targeted at 15 million kw. in ten years (by 1966). The number of towns and villages electrified over the Second Plan alone will increase by more than 2½ times over the present number.

Emphasis will be on hydro, rather than thermal, installation; of the forty-four major new public projects proposed, twenty-four are for hydro generating schemes. About 8 per cent of India's hydro capacity will have been developed by 1961.

Over the Second Plan, as over the First, and in keeping with the new Industrial Policy Resolution, the major portion of the new capacity and production will come from Government-owned utilities. However, there will be considerable increase in private capacity, from privately owned utilities and from private industrial power plants.

[1] State-owned capacity increased 133 per cent, private 18 per cent. Production from State-owned utilities went up 114 per cent, from private 43 per cent.

The Second Plan also proposes substantial expansion of grid system and transmission lines to supply power to industrial centers and to rural areas lying along the routes.

Rs. 427 crores is allocated for power development in the Second Plan, as compared with Rs. 260 crores [1] over the First. Part of this will be used to continue power projects initiated over the First Plan, and to start projects which will yield results over the Third Plan.

The Rs. 427 crores will be spent as follows:

	Rs. Crores
Generation	235
Transmission	92
Distribution in urban areas	25
Small towns and rural electrification	75
	427

It is expected that private utilities will invest roughly one-tenth this amount, or an additional Rs. 42 crores.

The following table illustrates the progress in power production from pre-Plan years through the Second Plan:

PROGRESS IN POWER: FIRST AND SECOND PLANS
(Energy generated (kwh in millions))

	1950–1951	1955–1956	1960–1961	% Increase During the Second Plan
By Public utilities				
State-owned	2,104	4,500	13,500	200
Company-owned	3,003	4,300	5,300	23
By Private utilities (Self-generating industrial establishments)	1,468	2,200	3,200	45
TOTAL	6,575	11,000	22,000	100

[1] Allocation. Total expenditure Rs. 274 crores.

Small Town and Rural Electrification

To raise living standards, to make pump irrigation possible, and to increase employment and production in village and small industry, the Second Plan proposes an intensive program of small-town and rural electrification. All towns over 10,000 population will be electrified; 86 per cent of all towns from 5,000 to 10,000 population.

Although as yet only a tiny fraction of Indian villages are electrified, the progress over the First Plan was measurable, and will be markedly stepped up over the Second Plan. Somewhat under a sixth out of all Second Plan funds allocated for all power development will go to rural electrification. By the end of the Plan, 2.5 per cent, or 13,900 villages, will be electrified—still far too few, but over 2½ times as many as in 1956.

PROGRESS IN TOWN AND RURAL ELECTRIFICATION:
FIRST AND SECOND PLANS

POPULATION	NUMBER OF TOWNS AND VILLAGES ACCORDING TO 1941 CENSUS	PER CENT ELECTRIFIED AS OF MARCH 1951	NUMBER OF TOWNS AND VILLAGES ACCORDING TO 1951 CENSUS	PER CENT ELECTRIFIED AS OF MARCH 1956	PER CENT ELECTRIFIED AS OF MARCH 1961
Over 100,000	49	100.0	73	100.0	100.0
50,000–100,000	88	100.0	111	100.0	100.0
20,000–50,000	277	86.6	401	91.2	100.0
10,000–20,000	607	42.8	856	40.9	100.0
5,000–10,000	2,367	10.9	3,101	38.7	85.8
Less than 5,000	559,062	0.5	556,565	0.95	2.49

The costs of distribution of power to villages are very high—an average of Rs. 60,000 to 70,000 per village, owing to their distance from power sources. Rural electrification therefore must be on a planned basis, the first villages served being those near towns already electrified, or near transmission lines.

To reduce costs to village consumers, the Second Plan recommends that the State take surplus revenues from urban and industrial users; and promote village cooperatives which could help contribute construction labor for village electrification systems, irrigation pumping, motor and pump maintenance, and so on.

The Central Government has also made long-term loans to State Governments to initiate local Diesel generating stations and expand distribution, and will continue doing so over the Second Plan.

SECTION II

INDUSTRIAL DEVELOPMENT

CHAPTER I

Policies, Priorities and Targets

As India builds a strong, vital democratic agricultural society, producing more and more food, and more informed and able rural citizens, it will at the same time build up basic industries.

As we have seen, the dynamism of the Second Plan and the "grand strategy" in its war against poverty lie in this program of rapid, basic industrialization. As all advanced nations show so clearly, industry is an essential means to higher incomes, production and employment, and an expanding economy.

The Second Plan is India's first concentrated effort to industrialize. It hopes to lift industrial production to 64 per cent above that of the end of the First Plan, or virtually to double it from pre-First-Plan levels.

Well over half of all investment, public and private, made in India over the Second Plan will go to industrial development, if power and transport are included.

244

In large and small industries alone, investment by both private enterprise and Government will equal three-fourths as much as the Government spent for all purposes in the First Plan, when major emphasis was on agriculture. Private investment in large industry and mining alone is expected to be more than double that of the First Plan.

1. THE INDUSTRIAL POLICY RESOLUTION

Rapid industrialization will have far-reaching effects not only upon India's present economic pattern, but on India's culture, on its political and social future. As India stands on the threshold of its industrial revolution, therefore, it has deliberately and carefully drawn up basic policies to ensure that its industrial growth may be orderly, effective, and may be accomplished, not at human and social cost, but to the benefit of the Indian people.

The most important of these policies are contained in India's revised Industrial Policy Resolution,[1] which the Prime Minister read before Parliament on April 30, 1956, only a few weeks before submission of the Second Five Year Plan.

The Second Plan specifically states that "it is within the framework of this new Industrial Policy Resolution that rapid industrialization has to be carried through in the coming years."

The Resolution, a revision of an earlier one announced in 1948, significantly takes as its starting point the Constitution of India. It cites the Constitution's important "Directive Principles of State Policy" under which the State is directed to work toward securing social, economic and political justice, toward securing adequate means of livelihood for all citizens, equal pay for men and women, protection against abuse or exploitation of the health and strength of workers—men, women and especially children.

The Resolution cites further the directives that enjoin the State to work toward securing that "ownership and control of the material resources of the community are so distributed as best to subserve the

[1] The full text of the Resolution is given in the Appendix.

common good"; [1] and "that the operation of the economic system does not result in the concentration of wealth and means of production to the common detriment." [2]

The Resolution makes clear that these Constitutional principles— "which were given a more precise direction" when Parliament accepted, in December 1954, the socialist pattern of society as the objective of social and economic policy—must govern India's industrial policy even as they govern other policies.

The Resolution clearly sets forth India's decision to take advantage of every possible way of growth consistent with democratic principles, using public, private and cooperative enterprise.

What has been of particular interest within and outside India is not only the Resolution's reaffirmation that social and human concerns will guide industrialization, but, as well, its classification of industries into three categories, in relation to the part which the Government or private enterprise will play in each of them.

The Resolution's first category (Schedule A) consists of seventeen industries "the future development of which will be the exclusive responsibility of the State."

These are principally the basic heavy industries, which the Government alone, at this time, has the financial and organizational resources to establish and expand rapidly enough for the nation's fast development. They include iron and steel, coal and all essential and strategic minerals, oil, aircraft and ship building, power, heavy foundries and engineering. They also include the industries which have for some time been government-owned—the defense industries, atomic energy, railways and air transport,[3] communications.

In the second category (Schedule B) the Resolution lists twelve industries which will be "progressively State-owned." These include a mixed group of essential industries—machine tools, essential drugs, aluminum, basic chemicals, sea and road transport. For these, the

---

[1] Constitution of India: Part IV: Directive Principles of State Policy, Article 39, Section (b).

[2] Ibid.: Section (c).

[3] Air transport was made a Government monopoly in 1953.

State will generally take the initiative in establishing new undertakings, but private enterprise will also be expected to supplement the effort of the Government, and will have the opportunity to develop such industries either on its own or with State participation.

The third category includes all other industries. The further development of these will, in general, be left to private initiative.

With India's effort to be flexible and pragmatic in the development of its economic structure, these categories are not intended to be rigid or watertight. Even for industries listed in Schedule A, for instance, the expansion of existing privately owned industries is not precluded. The Government is free to secure the cooperation of private enterprise in setting up new units "when the national interests so require." The Government has very early begun to do so. For example, it has already energetically assisted private steel plants to get capital and technical help to expand.

To give freedom to private enterprise, and to help public and private industry to work "in unison, as parts of a single mechanism," private industries may also produce, to meet their own requirements or as by-products, goods falling within the first category.

Further, the Government expects that some of its own heavy (Schedule A-type) industries will procure parts and materials from private industries. Private industries in turn may rely for many of their needs on Government-owned plants.

The Resolution repeats the distinct advantages that small industries offer toward solving unemployment, toward more equitable distribution of income; toward mobilization of skills and capital that might otherwise remain unused; and toward helping decentralize production, thus avoiding the problems of unplanned growth of industrial cities.

The Government also hopes to help and encourage small industries to supply parts for, and to use the by-products of, large industry, so that they can become more vital and self-sufficient and more integrated into a general pattern of industrialization, as going healthy businesses.

The new Resolution further makes clear that all regions of India will be helped to advance together, so that those now lagging behind in industry and employment can begin to catch up. The Resolution also makes clear the Government's duty to mobilize and train technical and managerial personnel for industry, and to provide good working conditions, social services and incentives for all industrial workers. Government-owned enterprises must set an example in this respect.

The Resolution emphasizes the need to decentralize authority in Government-owned industries and to have sound, business-like management. Profits of the Government enterprises are to go into public revenues, but public enterprises should be "judged by their results" and have the "largest possible measure of freedom."

The Resolution also stresses throughout that "the principle of co-operation should be applied wherever possible," so that more and more private enterprises are developed on cooperative lines.

2. INDUSTRIAL PRIORITIES

Such then are the general policies underlying India's effort to set up and encourage industry. India has also found it necessary to set some order of priorities, in view of its limited funds, and especially of foreign exchange, on the industries to be pushed first and fastest.

Three principal considerations for setting priorities have been kept in mind. The industries which are to be emphasized most are: those which will give the Indian economy the biggest push forward; those necessary to raise the living standards of the Indian people; and those necessary to help India earn its urgently needed foreign exchange.

The following are among the top priorities:

First Priority: stepping up production of *iron* and *steel, heavy chemicals* (including nitrogenous *fertilizers*); and developing heavy *engineering* and *machine-building* industries.

Second Priority: expanding capacity to produce *aluminum, cement, chemical pulp, dyestuffs, phosphatic fertilizers*, and *essential drugs*.

Third Priority: modernizing and re-equipping of important existing industries, such as *jute* and *cotton textiles*, and *sugar*.

Fourth Priority: using to the full all existing plant capacity now unused.

Fifth Priority: expanding capacity for consumer goods production, in both cottage and small-scale industry, and in medium and larger industry.

This does not mean that *all* needs for first-priority industries must be met before funds or effort is put into those of lower priority or into any other programs. Rather it means that, in balancing total investment and effort, the emphasis given within each group of heavy and other industries will follow this order of priority.

The priorities are meant to guide not only Government-owned industry, but private enterprise as well. This is handled through consultation with Development Councils of major industries (there are twelve of these Councils), and through requiring licensing for all "scheduled" industries, that is, those scheduled under the Industries (Development and Regulations) Act of 1951, which includes all industries of an essential nation-building character.

The reasons for selecting these priorities are, briefly:

The requirement for steel by the end of the Second Five Year Plan will be very large; continual big imports of iron and steel would require large amounts of scarce foreign exchange. India, moreover, has the resources for efficient, low-cost steel production.

Dependence on imports means uncertainties of both price and delivery. India foresees, however, that as the economy expands, demand for steel will continue to require imports. India hopes, at the same time however, to expand its export with trade in steel and iron to earn more foreign exchange.

Heavy engineering and machine building industries are naturally tied to iron and steel production. India's present emphasis on these industries arises not only from this fact, but from a desire to produce within the country the bulk of the nation's needs for capital equipment and the machinery required for development. At present India almost entirely depends upon foreign countries for heavy machinery like power plant equipment, furnaces and rolling mills to build steel plants, and other basic industries. India must begin the manufacturing of some of such heavy machinery although an expanding economy will continue to require imports for a long time to come.

Cement ranks next to iron and steel as an essential for a growing nation—to build more irrigation works, houses, factories, schools, roads, and so on. Production of cement must be more than tripled to meet Second Plan needs.

The reason for the high priority on fertilizers is obvious, in view of the urgent need for bigger crop yields, and of the intensive agricultural programs which have been planned. Total fertilizer needs by 1960–1961 will be 2.5 million tons,[1] or over 6½ times 1955–1956 production.[2]

Jute and cotton textiles are India's most important exports and earners of foreign exchange. If India is to keep its competitive position in foreign markets, modernization of obsolete equipment is imperative.

The Balance of Consumer and Heavy Industries

As we have seen, India is determined that industrialization shall not, even at this beginning stage when very heavy investment is needed, be carried out at the cost of cutting down production of consumer goods. The whole object of the Plan is to increase the living standards of the Indian people. The only question is how fast standards may increase, given the people's needs, availability of capital and know-how, and the cost, particularly in foreign exchange, of providing adequate equipment to produce and transport the needed goods.

Striking the correct balance, within the Plan period, between the size of investment in heavy industry and in consumer industry is admittedly extremely difficult. For India this is particularly true in the

---

[1] Phosphatic and nitrogenous fertilizers.
[2] 1955–56 production, 396,000 tons.

matter of cotton textiles, the industrially produced consumer item most important to the Indian masses.

In general in fixing the individual targets for production of manufactured consumer goods, the Planning Commission made them adequate to meet all now foreseeable demands. At the same time, as mentioned earlier, the Commission had to keep in view that some restraint on such consumer goods might be necessary, especially where the machinery or raw materials needed to produce them must be imported at the cost of scarce foreign exchange.

Fortunately, compared to advanced countries, there are relatively few points where decisions have to be made. Industrially manufactured consumer goods form a very small part of the average Indian family's budget. The exceptions are cloth, and to a lesser extent sugar, bicycles, sewing machines, footwear, all of which can be made both by cottage and by small-scale industry as well as costly modern factories.

Cars, radios, refrigerators, even modern medicines are not common consumer and "cost-of-living" goods in India as they are in some advanced countries. They are not therefore goods which compete, as in advanced countries during World War II, for scarce steel and similar raw materials. Such goods are luxuries available only to a tiny fraction of the people in the highest income groups, and far beyond the reach of the vast bulk of a population whose per capita income is $56 a year. The mass of the Indian people must spend 60 to 70 per cent of their family earnings on food and clothing alone.

Cottage and small-scale industries, whose production can be stepped up at relatively small cost, are being counted upon to provide an increasing portion of the consumer goods other than food. They are expected to meet a substantial share of the *increase* in demand that will arise over the Second Plan as incomes and employment go up. Hand looms, for example, are expected to provide about two-thirds of all the additional cloth that will be required over the Second Plan period.

As mentioned earlier, the production of consumer goods from large and medium industries is expected to go up 18 per cent, and the output of small industry and enterprises (nearly all of it consumer goods and services) to go up by 30 per cent.

Balancing Large and Small Industries

The need to encourage small-scale and village industries raises a special problem with several important types of consumer goods, notably cotton textiles, which are in India produced both by large-scale, highly mechanized industries, and by the most simple cottage industries.

For reasons already mentioned and to be discussed more fully in a following chapter, the Government's desire is to protect small producers. To do so, it has been following in a few fields what it calls a "common production program." This is a policy of: (a) restricting expansion in the large-scale industries which directly compete with small-scale and cottage industries; (b) of setting quotas of production as between small and large industries; and (c) of taxing competing large industries to help pay for programs of support to small industries. The Industrial Policy Resolution has reaffirmed this policy.

The principal industries under "common production programs" are cotton textiles, matches, soap, vegetable oils, tanning and leather footwear. Although the common production program has not been applied in full to any industry, in cotton textiles, for example, certain varieties of cloth commonly used by villagers [1] were reserved for the hand-loom industry and a cess, or excise duty was applied to mills, which is used to help small industry get on its feet.

The policy has evoked considerable interest, and some criticism, outside as well as within India. It is said by some that the policy restricts industrial expansion and production, blocks technological progress, and, moreover, removes from protected small industries the healthy stimulus and risks of competition in serving the Indian demand and market.

For India, protecting small producers is, as we have seen, one as-

[1] Such as saris using dyed yarn, dhotis with borders (over a certain width), lungis, sarongs, etc.

pect of the larger problem of orderly transition from a traditional pre-industrial economy to one which is modern and technically advanced. It is seen also as an inevitable compromise while unequal levels of technology remain within a given industry, while dependence for new employment as yet falls so heavily on small industries, and while small industries are helped to gain strength.

The Indian Government feels that assigning certain kinds of production to small business will help small manufacturers organize to supply parts or perform certain processes for large industry, and thus to take their rightful place in a more industrialized economy.

Limiting expansion or production of large industry admittedly raises many issues. It has to be handled so that on the one hand shortages are avoided, and on the other hand, small industries produce enough to supply the larger market thus set aside.

For example, to protect hand looms, practically no additional mill looms had been authorized since 1955, and the Second Plan had originally proposed none. Cloth shortages in mid-1956, and the urgent need to modernize textile mills so that they may compete successfully in the export market, have forced a revision of policy, and some new looms have been sanctioned.

At the same time it is clear, however, that regardless of how much mill expansion may be possible over the Second Plan, hand looms will for some time to come continue to contribute a necessary and important share of all cloth produced.[1]

The Government's policy is, as has been noted, to press as rapidly as feasible in this transition period for adoption of technological improvements and high production methods for cottage and small industries. The shortage of cloth has given this Government decision added strength and support, having clarified for the Indian public more sharply than any other issue might, that India's newer problem is not dividing a restricted market, but organizing to produce for an expanding one.

[1] See Village and Small-Scale Industries, p. 285.

Regional Industrial Development

The need for immediate industrial progress means that, for the most part, new industries must be located in areas where adequate raw materials and transport facilities are already available—in short, in areas already developed to some degree.

The Planning Commission hopes, however, over the course of the Second Plan, to work toward some solution to the problem of the serious inequalities in development between various regions of India. A start has been made, in so far as possible, in the location of the new industries which have an important part to play in regional development as a whole. Two of the three new steel plants are being put up in the relatively underdeveloped areas of Madhya Pradesh (at Bhilai) and Orissa (at Rourkela). A heavy electrical engineering plant is also to be set up in Madhya Pradesh (at Bhopal). In Madras State, which has no coal resources, an important lignite project was begun in early 1957, in South Arcot.

Surveys for mineral resources in other areas, research on manufacturing processes and products which can be carried on by decentralized industries, will make it possible over later Plans to help all regions advance.

3. TOTAL INVESTMENT IN INDUSTRIAL DEVELOPMENT

The total amount that the Indian Government and Indian private enterprise will invest in industry (small and large industries and mining) over the Second Plan is expected to come to Rs. 1,465 crores.[1] This is nearly 4½ times as much as actual investment for these industries by both Government and private enterprise over the First Plan.

Private investment alone is expected to be more than double, Government investment about nine times, that actually made over the First Plan period.

[1] Exclusive of investment of Rs. 150 crores in plant modernization.

INDIA'S INVESTMENT IN INDUSTRIAL GROWTH 1956–1961

Rs. Crores

	Private Invest- ment [1]	Public Invest- ment	Total
Large and Medium Industry and Mining	575	670 [2]	1,245
Large and Medium Industry	535	600	1,135 [4]
Mining and Mineral Development	40	70 [3]	110
Village and Small Industry	100	120	220
TOTAL	625	790	1,465
Power	42	407	436
TOTAL	717	1,197	1,914

[1] Excludes National Industrial Development Corporation NIDC funds of Rs. 35 crores. See p. 275.

[2] Includes Rs. 32 crores on State Governments' projects, some of which, through State Financial Corporations, will assist private enterprises, etc.

[3] Excludes estimated current expenditures.

[4] This figure differs from the total outlay in the table given in the following pages on Medium and Large-Scale Industry, which deals *only* with direct expenditure, and excludes some items like those mentioned under Note 2 above.

In keeping with India's industrial policy and its agreed-on order of priorities, virtually all the proposed Government investment goes to such basic industries as iron and steel, coal, fertilizers, heavy engineering and electrical equipment.

Similarly the large portion of all private investment goes to these heavy industries (for example, one-fifth, or Rs. 115 crores, to iron and steel alone).

It is particularly interesting that, in keeping with the Industrial Policy Resolution, the Government is in the national interest seeking the cooperation of private enterprise in essential industries. Private enterprise will in fact be investing two-thirds as much in these industries as Government, as the following table shows:

SECOND PLAN PATTERN OF INVESTMENT BY TYPES OF INDUSTRIES
(*Excluding Small-Scale and Village Industries*)

INVESTMENT IN Rs. CRORES

	By Govt. Industry [1]	By Private Industry	Total
Producer goods	463	296	759
Industry machinery and capital goods	84	72	156
Consumer goods	12	167	179
TOTAL	559	535 [2]	1,094

[1] Includes new investments of NIDC.

[2] On certain projects involving the use of NIDC resources, decisions have yet to be made whether they will be handled by Government or private industry.

4. INDUSTRIAL PRODUCTION TARGETS

India has set itself some very high production targets for industry over the Second Plan. The increase in production expected is higher for industry than for any other part of the economy—a 64 per cent increase for all industries taken together. This means, as mentioned earlier, that by the end of the Second Plan industrial production will have almost doubled over the levels of 1951, the last year before India began pushing its economy forward.[1]

Some targets for specific industries are very high indeed—3⅓ times more steel and aluminum; six times more phosphatic fertilizers; fourteen times more newsprint; three times for machine tools, 2½ times as many electric motors; three times as much cement; twice as many Diesel engines, sewing machines. The list on the next page gives some of the targets for these and other industrial products.

The Second Plan targets have been set after consultations of the Planning Commission with representatives of important industries and the Industrial Development Councils; by recommendations made by the Ministries of Commerce and Industries and Agriculture; by reviewing the actual rate of investment over the First Plan; and by

[1] 1951 index of industrial production = 100; 1955–56 = 130; 1960–61 = 194.

PRODUCTION TARGETS IN MAJOR INDUSTRIES
(Government and Private Enterprises)

Industry Product	Unit	Production 1955–56 Estimated	1960–61 Target	% Increase
1. Iron and Steel				
(a) Finished steel (main producers)	Tons	1,300,000	4,300,000	231
(b) Pig iron for foundries	Tons	380,000	750,000	97
2. Structural Fabrications	Tons	180,000	500,000	178
3. Heavy Shops Foundry-cum-Forge				
(a) Steel foundries	Tons		15,000	
(b) Forging shops	Tons		12,000	
(c) Cast-iron foundries	Tons		10,000	
4. Ferromanganese	Tons	N.A.	160,000	
5. Aluminum	Tons	7,500	25,000	233
6. Locomotives	Nos.	175	400	129
7. Automobiles	Nos.	25,000	57,000	128
8. Heavy Chemicals				
(a) Sulphuric acid	Tons	170,000	470,000	177
(b) Soda ash	Tons	80,000	230,000 [1]	188
(c) Caustic soda	Tons	36,000	135,400 [1]	276
9. Fertilizers				
(a) Nitrogenous (fixed nitrogen)	Tons	77,000	290,000	277
(b) Phosphatic (as P_2O_5)	Tons	20,000	120,000	500
10. Shipbuilding	GRT	50,000 [2]	90,000 [3]	80
11. Cement	Tons	4,280,000	13,000,000	204
12. Refractories	Tons	280,000	800,000	186
13. Petroleum Refining (in terms of crude processed)	Million tons	3.6	4.3	19
14. Paper and Paper Board	Tons	200,000	350,000	75
15. Newsprint	Tons	4,200	60,000	1,329
16. Rayon				
(a) Rayon filament	Million lbs.	15.0	68.0	353
(b) Staple fiber	Million lbs.	13.2	32.0	142
(c) Chemical pulp	Tons		30,000	
17. Diesel Engines (below 50 HP)	HP	100,000	205,000	105
18. Bicycles	Nos.	550,000	1,000,000 [4]	82
19. Electric Motors (below 200 HP)	HP	240,000	600,000	150
20. Cotton Textiles	Million yards	6,850	8,500	24

[1] Represents gross production. Since part of the output will be used within the plants for conversion to other products, quantities available for sale will be 135,000 tons of soda ash and 106,600 tons of caustic soda.

[2] 1951–56.

[3] 1956–61.

[4] 250,000 bicycles are expected to be produced by small (decentralized) industries so that the total production would be 1,250,000.

257

the plant capacity already available and the new plants which will be built and approved.

For the Second Plan, the most important export commodities include cotton, rayon, and jute textiles, bicycles, coke, salt, vegetable oils and hydrogenated fats, ferromanganese, titanium dioxide. Specific export targets have been set for all these products and in the original Second Plan for finished steel also.

While over-all industrial production will increase 64 per cent, the amount of producer goods turned out (such as steel forges, power plant equipment, and so on) will go up 73 per cent, of capital goods (such as textile machinery, machine tools and the like) 150 per cent. It has already been mentioned that consumer goods production by medium and large-scale industries will go up 18 per cent, and that production by small enterprises (most of which is consumer goods) will go up by 30 per cent.

HIGH LIGHTS
of programs for
MEDIUM AND LARGE–SCALE INDUSTRY

Over the Second Plan, the Government and private enterprise will together invest Rs. 1,135 crores to expand and develop India's large and medium industries. Some of the main targets are:

A 64 per cent rise in all industrial production.

A 150 per cent rise in production of capital goods, with strong emphasis on heavy and basic industries.

Stimulation and encouragement to private enterprise and foreign capital investment.

Three new steel plants, with 231 per cent more steel production, including doubled private steel capacity.

Three new fertilizer plants, and 300 per cent more fertilizer.

Expanded machine-tool factories and a 200 per cent rise in machine-tool production.

Production at least doubled of electrical equipment—electric motors, transformers, cables, etc.

Production doubled or nearly so of essential manufactured consumer goods—bicycles, sewing machines, electric fans, automobiles.

Expanded production of atomic energy materials, and stepped-up atomic research.

CHAPTER II

Medium and Large-Scale Industry

1. INDUSTRY DEVELOPMENT BY GOVERNMENT

The Indian Government realizes that it faces a tremendous job in setting up basic industries on the scale proposed and getting them rapidly producing for the Indian economy and the Indian people.

Fortunately, the Government gained a background of valuable experience during the First Plan, although on a small scale, in constructing industrial plants and in producing capital goods.

Important State-owned factories, for ammonium sulphate fertilizer (at Sindri), for locomotives (Chittaranjan), telephone equipment (Bangalore), coaches, cables and penicillin, set up during and just prior to the First Plan have had a good production record. If others, such as machine tools, cement and superphosphate fertilizers, did not get under way so fast or produce so much as was hoped, they gave some useful lessons in the problems of launching industries in an underdeveloped nation.

During the First Plan, the Government also went far along in laying the foundations for more rapid progress during the Second Plan. For example, all preparatory work for the new steel plants, which included detailed planning and negotiation for foreign financial and technical assistance, was virtually completed by the beginning of the Second Plan.

The Government realizes that administering a large group of new and important industries requires top-level organization and policy direction. Assuring their effective business-like management is a matter that has the Government's particular concern. In addition to its own study of management of public enterprises elsewhere, the Government has invited the analysis and opinion of foreign specialists in administration to help work out the most effective result-producing types of administration. While the exact form of management of Government enterprises is yet to be determined, the Government clearly favors decentralization of authority, and the largest possible measure of autonomy, freedom and responsibility for individual plant management.

The New and Expanded Industries

The exact industries in which the Government will invest are summarized in the list on the opposite page, and show clearly the priority on steel and other heavy and basic industries.

Steel: Steel will be the Government's biggest single production program.

Three complete new steel plants will be built which will have a combined capacity by the end of the Second Plan of 2.3 million tons of finished steel. This will compare with a total output of 1.3 million tons in 1955–1956. Three entirely new townships are being built to service these plants and house their workers.

Fifteen thousand skilled workers are needed, and 2,200 technicians, engineers, managers and supervisors. Nearly all of them must be trained abroad, since private steel plants in India, although cooperating fully, are too small and too few to train more than a small

GOVERNMENT INVESTMENT IN INDUSTRY OVER THE SECOND PLAN
(*Large and medium industry only*)

Rs. Crores

I. IRON AND STEEL
Rourkela plant	128.0	
Bhilai plant	110.0	
Durgapur plant	115.0	
Total, including expansion of the Mysore Iron and Steel Works		356.00 [1]

II. HEAVY MACHINERY
Manufacture of electrical equipment	20.0	
Expansion of Hindustan Machine Tools plant	2.0	
Heavy machinery and allied projects of the National Industrial Development Corporation	35.0	
Expansion of Government Electrical Factory, Bangalore	1.2	
		58.20

III. FERTILIZER AND FUEL RESOURCES
South Arcot lignite project	52.0	
Nangal fertilizer factory	22.0	
Rourkela fertilizer factory	8.0	
Expansion of Sindri fertilizer factory	7.0	
Durgapur coke-oven plant, West Bengal	5.25	
		94.25

IV. HEAVY ENGINEERING
Expansion of Visakhapatnam shipyard	9.8	
Expansion of meter-gauge coach factory (plus another new unit)	10.0	
Railway engineering shops	7.0	
Expansion of Chittaranjan locomotive factory	5.0	
		31.80

V. MISCELLANEOUS		18.70
		558.95 [1]

[1] This includes only direct investment on the specific industries; it does not include supplemental investment outlays needed, such as building new steel townships, etc.

number. Arrangements have already been made, as mentioned earlier, to train two hundred men in the United States, and others in the United Kingdom, the Soviet Union, West Germany, Australia and Canada.

Originally the Second Plan had provided Rs. 350 crores for the three steel plants, or well over half of all Government expenditures for large and medium industry. This figure includes the amount which is expected to come from foreign assistance in capital, long-term credits for plant and machinery and other forms of credit. According to the most recent estimates, the three plants will take, over the Second Plan alone, a total of Rs. 497 crores. This will include the cost of building the new townships, iron ore development at Bhilai and Rourkela, and so on.

The Government is also providing funds for expansion of the State-owned Mysore Iron and Steel Works.

The first of the large steel plants, at Rourkela (Orissa), will cost about Rs. 128 crores during the Second Plan alone. It will produce 720,000 tons of flat products of steel, hot and cold rolled. It is being designed to operate the L.D. process,[1] a decision reached after careful study of the method in Germany, Canada and the United States. The hydrogen from the coke-oven gases will be used to manu-facture nitro-limestone fertilizer, also at Rourkela.

Planning and technical assistance on this plant has been obtained through the West German combine of Krupp and Demag under an agreement negotiated in 1953.

The second plant, at Bhilai in Madhya Pradesh, costing about Rs. 110 crores, is expected to produce 770,000 tons of salable steel. To build this plant, a credit of Rs. 63 crores (gross) has been arranged from the Soviet Union.

The third plant, at Durgapur in West Bengal, will cost about Rs. 115 crores, of which Rs. 35 crores (gross) in long-term loans is promised by the British Government and British bankers. It is to be equipped to produce light and medium sections of steel and billets amounting to 790,000 tons a year.

All the layouts of the three steel plants are designed for future expansion.

Heavy Foundries, Forges, etc.: These are the basic capital goods industries urgently needed to give India a solid foundation for indus-trial growth.

[1] Oxygen blowing in steel production.

The Chittaranjan Locomotive Factory, which will be expanded so that its output of locomotives can go up from 120 locomotives to 300 per year, will include a heavy steel foundry to provide all railway requirements of heavy castings from within the country. The Government will start manufacture of heavy electrical equipment; of industrial machinery and machine tools under the National Industrial Development Corporation (NIDC);[1] and expand the Hindustan Machine Tools plant (Bangalore). The NIDC will especially foster the development of heavy industrial machinery, and establish heavy foundries, the forge shops and heavy structural shops, essential for its production.

South Arcot Lignite Project: Since South India lacks adequate coal deposits to support industrial expansion, high priority has been given to the development of the newly proved lignite resources in South Arcot (Madras) through a multi-purpose project at Neiveli, where production possibilities have been explored with foreign technical assistance.

The project proposes mining of 3.5 million tons of lignite per year for: (*a*) generation of power in a station of 211,000 kw. capacity; (*b*) production of carbonized briquettes at the rate of 380,000 tons per year; and (*c*) production of 70,000 tons of fixed nitrogen in the form of urea and sulphate nitrate. The Second Plan makes an initial provision of Rs. 52 crores for this project, to be supplemented as progress is achieved.

Fertilizer Production: The Government-owned fertilizer plant at Sindri, which opened in 1951, was India's chief source of supply during the First Plan, producing over 84 per cent of all fertilizer manufactured in India.

The demand for nitrogenous fertilizer is expected to be nearly 3 times as high in 1960–1961 as at the end of the First Plan. To meet the urgent needs of agriculture, Government must assure adequate

---

[1] A private limited company with Government sponsorship set up with the co-operation of leaders of private enterprise. See p. 275.

supplies. Although some demand will be met by private manufacturers, most of the additional production needed will come from new factories set up by Government.

Steps have already been taken to increase fertilizer production by 47,000 tons of fixed nitrogen, through the expansion of the Sindri Fertilizer Factory by using its coke-oven gas.

Three new fertilizer plants are proposed: one at South Arcot, mentioned above, one at Nangal (at the Bakhra-Nangal multipurpose irrigation and power project) with an annual capacity of 70,000 tons of fixed nitrogen, and another at Rourkela with a capacity of 80,000 tons of fixed nitrogen. Plans to launch a fourth are under review.

The Nangal factory will cost Rs. 22 crores, the Rourkela plant tentatively Rs. 15 crores, the Sindri expansion Rs. 7 crores. Combined production at the three new plants (plus Sindri) will be 247,000 tons of fixed nitrogen per year—in the last year of the Second Plan— or roughly two-thirds of total requirements for that year.

Heavy Engineering Industries: Besides heavy machinery, these include manufacturing of railway rolling stock and shipbuilding. The Hindustan shipyard at Visakhapatnam (Andhra) will be expanded so that the rate of ship construction can be speeded up. Upward revision of the original Second Plan shipping targets is under review (see p. 312). A drydock will be constructed at Visakhapatnam; and preparatory work will be done on setting up a second shipyard.

Manufacture of heavy marine Diesel engines is now being considered.

For railway rolling stock, apart from the expansion of Chittaranjan Locomotives, the Government will, under the Railway Plan and at a total cost of Rs. 17 crores: (1) complete the Integral Coach Factory at Perambur (Madras), which opened in 1955, so that it can very soon produce at a rate of 350 railway coaches a year; (2) build a new meter-gauge coach factory; and (3) construct two engineering shops to manufacture spare parts. The two coach factories, together with Hindustan Aircraft, are expected to turn out 1,800 coaches a year, by 1960–1961.

Other Essential Industries: Other projects of the Central Government are: (1) doubling production in the existing DDT factory at Delhi, which was set up in 1955 (with assistance from UNICEF and the UN Technical Assistance Board), and which by mid-1956 was producing 1½ tons daily; (2) establishment of a second DDT plant in Travancore-Cochin; (3) expanding the penicillin factory at Pimpri, opened in 1955 (with aid from WHO and UNICEF), to produce 60 per cent more, and other antibiotics as well; (4) expansion of Hindustan Cables, Limited, the National Instruments Factory and Indian Telephone Industries; and (5) setting up a security paper mill for the manufacture of security and bond paper.

Among industrial projects planned by State Governments, there is expansion of the Mysore Iron and Steel Works, of the U.P. Cement Factory, of the Bihar Superphosphate Factory; establishment of a coke-oven plant at Durgapur; manufacture of electric porcelain insulators in Mysore and Bihar States; re-organization of Praga Tool Factory, Hyderabad.

Through the operation of the coke-oven plants attached to the steel plants, of the Durgapur coke-oven project of West Bengal and the South Arcot lignite project, recovery of substantial quantities of organic chemicals will ensure domestic supplies to the pharmaceutical, plastic and dyestuff industries.

Atomic Energy: [1] India has a substantial program—considering her limited resources—for public development of atomic energy for peaceful uses. The Government's chief aims are to produce electric power, and make possible applied nuclear science in agriculture, health and industry. The research and development program is administered by a Central Department of Atomic Energy.

In five years India expects to have its own separation plants to produce atomic materials. The program is now chiefly one of re-

[1] See also chapter on Scientific and Technical Research.

search, but to ensure later balanced development India will continue over the Second Plan, moving toward self-sufficiency in needed materials and processing techniques.

Extensive geological and geophysical surveys and prospecting are in progress on the basic materials, in many of which India is well endowed, notably monazite, pegmatites, beryl, zirconium, and so on. Among the important industrial projects already developed are a monazite processing plant set up in 1952 (at Alwaye, Kerala), and a thorium-uranium plant (at Trombay, Bombay). Production in both will be greatly expanded over the Second Plan.

New plants already in the advanced planning or investigation stage, and probably to be completed by 1961, are: a pilot plant for extracting uranium ore from copper tailings (at Ghatsila, Bihar); a uranium plant (at Trombay, Bombay); a production purification plant; joint production of heavy water and nitrogenous fertilizer (Nangal, Punjab); plants for processing or producing atomically pure graphite, beryl, titanium sponge metal, zirconium metal.

India's Atomic Energy Establishment, started at Trombay (Bombay) chiefly for research, and India's other atomic research activities are discussed later as part of India's over-all scientific research program.

2. THE ROLE OF PRIVATE INDUSTRY

At the same time that the Government itself launches new essential industries, Indian policy is, as we have seen, to encourage in every way conducive to national growth the vitality and productive capacity of private enterprise.

At the end of the First Plan, almost all medium and large industry was owned and managed by private firms and individuals. Private enterprise will continue to be dominant over the Second Plan in spite of the Government's larger part in industry. It will be remembered that 90 per cent of all production and a very considerable part of all new full-time employment expected over the Second Plan will come from private enterprise—industry, agriculture, and all other.

The role, past and future, of Indian private industry, and what must be done to stimulate it to take a larger role, are of particular interest, as well as importance, within and outside India.

It was mentioned earlier that, although by the end of World War II India ranked among the first ten industrial nations of the world, Indian industry had not developed to the degree warranted by the nation's immediate needs or its potential markets.

For one thing, as we have seen, the traditional pattern of Indian industry as a whole was, with the exception of steel, weighted on the side of consumer goods. Measured by the value of their products, India's major industries are, in order of importance: cotton textiles, tea, jute, sugar, general and electrical engineering, iron and steel.

Moreover, even India's leading industries were relatively small compared to similar industries in developed countries. For example, the Indian steel industry turned out only 1.3 million tons in 1956, or less than a single United States producer, United States Steel, turned out in a month at the same period.

There are ample historical reasons for the relative weakness of Indian capitalism. Without much increase in rural prosperity or the growth of internal and foreign trade, or the development of a modern financial system, Indian businessmen did not have any appreciable amount of capital on which they could draw to finance new enterprises. Moreover, it was only after the First World War that the British Government was prepared to give protection to new Indian industries. Modern industry was a new field for the vast majority of Indian businessmen, whose own associations had been mainly with traditional forms of trade. Nor, at this stage, were there many technically trained Indian men, such as engineers, available. As a whole, then, the essential conditions for the growth of modern industry had not yet arisen.

In these circumstances, the efforts of Indian industrialists between the two world wars to build up new industries, whether for the production of consumer or other goods, had wide support from the Indian public. In a real sense they became part of India's struggle for political freedom and for economic growth. Once freedom was gained, however, Indian industry faced a bigger challenge, and Indian businessmen, no less than others, had to face the problem of how they could contribute their maximum to the building up of the new nation.

The period immediately following the Second World War was, moreover, a critical one for India's industries. Much of the country's industrial equipment, heavily overworked during the war, had become obsolete. The capital market was slack, in view of an expected recession and of the disruption accompanying the Partition of India. Production fell, and the output in many industries was below capacity. Raw materials were in short supply, and there was a steady rise in production costs.

It is not surprising, therefore, that Indian industry, with a few outstanding exceptions, had not developed to the point where, like the more recent forms of capitalism of the West, it brought to workers advances in working conditions and better wages and maintained a high level of social responsibility.

A feature of industrial organization unique to India is the "managing agency" system under which a single firm, sometimes dominated by a single family, controls a number of legally separate and ostensibly independent companies. This system was originally evolved in India to meet problems of shortage of capital and managerial talent. In the hands of responsible businessmen it has been a powerful instrument of economic progress and has fathered India's leading industries. But in the hands of the less responsible it has failed to provide for the best use of a short supply of experienced managers and has encouraged favoritism and impeded development of proper managerial training. India's Companies Act has recently been strengthened to check irregularities and prevent some of the most flagrant abuses of the managing agency system.

Happily, there is now considerable evidence that Indian Independence and national planning have strengthened the business community's desire to take their full share in their country's long-range industrial development, and brought fresh confidence in the future development and needs of the Indian economy.

Indian industry now has assurance that India will expand, not stagnate as before; and the most enterprising businessmen have been quick to see their opportunities. An increasing proportion of the new industries and expansions now being considered by private enterprises are of the "nation-building" character long so urgently needed.

Today India must rapidly speed up its pace of expansion. Businessmen of foresight, who have experience with India's problems, with its long-stagnant economy and the social and political pressures for development, acknowledge that India's only course during these vital years is for Government to use public capital to set up the basic industries that can lift India across the crucial "threshold" of development.

These private industrialists admit freely that on the one hand enough private capital is not available, and that, on the other, fast progress is a social and political necessity. They realize, as well, that the swift growth of private industry itself depends greatly on the speed with which basic materials and transport are made available through Second Plan stimulus.

The new Industrial Policy Resolution, which outlined an important place for private enterprise, was generally well received by industrialists, as it assured fresh opportunities over a wide range of industries.

This is not to say that a portion of private industrialists do not have misgivings over the Government's position vis-à-vis private industry. Some feel that over-all planning may give them insufficient room in which to advance. Some also express the concern that there is insufficient managerial talent on which Government can draw to carry through the program. The Government has welcomed constructive criticism from industrialists and has tried to remove such genuine fears as may have been expressed by representative organizations of commerce and industry.

Both business leaders and Government realize that in this period when India is evolving its unique pattern of a mixed economy, there will inevitably be healthy differences and useful clashes of opinion on procedures and policies which will yield the best results and smoothest functioning from each sector. There must be continuous objective review of policies and methods, continuous adjustment and flexibility.

In working out the best procedures, in making adjustments, it will continue to be the Government's first consideration to encourage rapid development by every possible way of growth consistent with the purposes of the Plan. As the Industrial Policy Resolution reaffirms, private enterprise must be given opportunity and facilities to function effectively; it must be given scope and freedom to develop. At the same time the Government expects that private enterprise will live up to its own responsibility of serving the high objectives of the nation— the strength and democratic vitality of the Indian economy and the advancement of the Indian people.

Nationalization

The traditional doctrine of socialism, in favor of the ownership of all means of production by the State, had gained a measure of influence before Independence. It was reflected in the plea for extension of Government ownership, especially during the Second Plan. The Indian Government, as we have seen, believed that while in certain fields it must take all the initiative necessary, over a wide area the best results could be gained through and in cooperation with private initiative.

Whenever the national interest requires, India, like any other Government, has of course the right to take over an industry. It was for such reasons that the Imperial Bank of India was nationalized in 1955; and in early 1956 life insurance, whose credit resources are vital to national development and which is an important means of stimulating small savings, was put under a new public body, the Life Insurance Corporation. It is significant that the Government has generally refrained from nationalization of existing industries.

Facing India's great needs for development and the scarcity of its funds and trained manpower, the Government feels that its resources, which are necessarily limited, could be employed to the greatest advantage in creating *new* industries, in building *new* and *future* capacity, and in encouraging the fullest contribution of private enterprise to the needs of India's development. The new Industrial Policy Resolution does not, therefore, go into the question of nationalization, but specifically says that "where there exist in the same industry both privately and publicly owned units, it would continue to be the policy of the State to give fair and non-discriminatory treatment to both of them."

India's Prime Minister expressed this view in laying the Second Plan before Parliament.

Calling the idea of seizing private industry "primitive and infantile," the Prime Minister said:

We talk about nationalization as if it were some kind of remedy for every ill. I just do not see why I should do something today which fixes my progress, my increasing production simply to satisfy some theoretical urge. We would much rather build up national industries, new ones, than pay compensation to old and sometimes rather decrepit industries in order to take charge of them.

I have no shadow of doubt, that if we say "Lop off the private sector" we cannot replace it adequately. We have not got the resources to replace it and the result would be that our productive apparatus will suffer.

And why should we do it? We have our industries, there is a vast sector and we have to work it. Let the State go on building up its plants and industries as far as its resources permit.

Why should we fritter away our energy in pushing out somebody who is doing [it] in the private sector? . . . When there is such a vast field to cover, it is foolish to take charge of the whole field, when you are totally incapable of using that huge area yourself.

Therefore, you must not only permit the private sector, but, I say, encourage it in its own field.[1]

With such assurances and with the clear recognition in the Industrial Policy Resolution of the significant role of private enterprise, leading and well informed industrialists are not apprehensive of the possibility of nationalization and understand that, as the economy expands, there will be increasing scope for private industry.

[1] Prime Minister to Parliament, May 24, 1956.

First Plan Achievements by Private Enterprise

When drawing up the First Plan, all that the Planning Commission attempted in regard to private industry was to make an estimate of what each industry was likely to do or could be expected to do. The Government took no responsibility beyond providing such facilities and "amenities" as were in its power. A large part of all production increases were expected to result from using to the full existing plant capacity that was then idle, rather than new investment.

In production, over the First Plan private industry delivered very sizable increases, in many instances well above the targets set. The encouraging and substantial rise in all industrial production over the First Plan (a total rise of 22 per cent, it will be remembered, over 1951) was due in very large part to the performance of private industry.

The most important lags in private production were significantly in those industries where there was also the greatest lag in investment.

While in textiles and power generation investment exceeded Plan targets, broadly speaking the lag occurred in industries which required heavy capital investment and offered a relatively small profit margin.

Over the First Plan private enterprise (medium and large industry only) was expected to invest Rs. 233 crores in new industries and expansion, and another Rs. 230 crores in plant modernization and replacement, or a total of Rs. 463 crores. The goal for investment in new industries was reached, but that for modernization was not. Total private investment in medium and large industry was about Rs. 340 crores.[1]

In the early years (1951–1953) of the First Plan, investment was going so slowly that it was clear that private capital was still, as it had been for decades, sluggish and inert.

[1] Cotton textiles, 80 crores; petroleum refining, 45 crores; iron and steel, 49 crores; heavy and light engineering industries, 25 crores; chemicals, fertilizers, pharmaceuticals, dyestuffs and plastics, 15 crores; cement and refractories, 18 crores; paper and paper board, 11 crores; sugar, 15 crores; electric power generation, 32 crores; jute textiles, 15 crores; rayon and staple fiber, 8 crores; and others, 27 crores.

Because rapid development was so urgent, the Indian Government began to think of planning for private industrial expansion on the basis of what *should* happen, not merely what was *likely* to happen, or what it hoped would happen. It therefore began to take a large number of measures to stimulate expansion of private industry.

One of the first moves of the Government was to help provide credit and capital. The Industrial Finance Corporation, set up in 1948, and the thirteen State Finance Corporations were encouraged to grant more ready and liberal credit to private industry. These agencies, together with ICIC (see below), provided Rs. 18 crores of capital to stimulate industry over the First Plan.

Two new major lending agencies were created in 1954–1955 to stimulate private expansion. During the Second Plan, both of these new agencies, like those begun earlier, will continue to provide capital to private industry.

One of these new agencies is the National Industrial Development Corporation (NIDC), a private limited company with Government-sponsorship set up with cooperation and leadership from private industry. It expects to contribute a total of about Rs. 55 crores to start new industries in fields where high risks have so far made private enterprise hesitant, but which have a vital importance to the Indian economy.

Rs. 35 crores will go to industries which the NIDC will pioneer on its own, or to help Government set up key industries. Typical industries are dyestuff intermediates, aluminum, chemical pulp and newsprint, foundries and forges. The remaining Rs. 20 crores will be made available to modernize the cotton and jute textile industries.

The second major agency is the Industrial Credit and Investment Corporation (ICIC), to which an international group has contributed a total of Rs. 17.5 crores.[1] The value of this organization lies less in its total resources than in its expected underwriting activities and

[1] Indian Government, Rs. 7.5 crores; the International Bank, Rs. 5 crores; the United Kingdom, Rs. 1 crore; the United States, Rs. 5 million; and the remaining Rs. 3.5 crores by private Indian investors.

other measures designed to draw out more capital for private investment.

In order, among other things, to assist private steel companies in accumulating capital for expansion, the Government in 1955 raised the retention price for steel. A rebate allowance of 25 per cent was granted early in 1955 on the cost of all new plants and machinery installed after March 31, 1954, to encourage new plant expansion.

In addition the Government has eased procedures for the granting of loans by institutional agencies to private industries. The new Industrial Policy Resolution reaffirms that the Government will continue to encourage institutions providing credit and that it will make financial help available when desirable to private industry.

In early 1957 the Government announced that it would set up a new institutional agency to give financial assistance to selected industries. The agency will draw its funds from share capital of Rs. 12.5 crores subscribed initially by the Reserve Bank, the State Bank, the Life Insurance Corporation and certain commercial banks. In addition, the Government would place at the disposal of the new agency, as a thirty-year interest-bearing loan, Rs. 26 crores earned from the sale within India of United States wheat, cotton and other agricultural commodities, which were supplied by the United States in 1956, under a grant-loan agreement.[1] The total capital of the new agency, Rs. 38.5 crores, is to be used to underwrite loans given by the participating banks for increasing production in specified industries. Loans can be given to industries for a period of three to seven years, but no single borrower will be advanced more than Rs.5 million.

As already mentioned in the chapter on financing the Plan, all Government lending agencies together will contribute Rs. 115 crores in credit and loans to private enterprise over the Second Plan.[2]

Encouragement of Foreign Capital

The special and serious effort which the Indian Government is making to invite and welcome foreign firms and foreign capital

[1] P. 154.
[2] P. 144.

investment in essential nation-building industries, and to assist private Indian industry to get foreign capital and loans, has already been discussed.

The level of foreign investment which the Indian Government hopes and expects is, as we have seen, more than double for the Second Plan period what it was for the First. This means a rise from the Rs. 42 to Rs. 45 crores of the First Plan to Rs. 100 crores.

Private Investment in the Second Plan

By the very nature of private investment only very rough estimates can actually be given of the total amount expected and of how much will be spent in each kind of industry over the Second Plan period.

It is generally expected, however, that private investment in large and medium industry will be about Rs. 535 crores plus Rs. 150 crores for modernization and replacements, that is, a total of Rs. 665 crores. Another Rs. 55 crores is expected to be available from the National Industrial Development Corporation, bringing the total to Rs. 720 crores. It is important to recall that Rs. 100 crores of this total is expected to be foreign capital and suppliers' credit.

Rs. 665 crores is about twice the actual amount invested by private industry during the First Plan.

The way private enterprise will make its investments over the Second Plan is summarized and described in the next few pages, in so far as it can now be forecast. The estimates are necessarily provisional; as yet, of course, they total less than the full amount of private industrial investment expected over the entire Plan period.

The estimates are based upon detailed discussions in over twenty-two industries between the Planning Commission and representatives of different industries, upon recommendations of the Ministry of Commerce and Industry, and through consultation with industry representatives in Development Councils and panels of industrialists called together from time to time. Private investment, like Government investment in industry, clearly reflects the new order of priorities the Government has set for India's rapid industrial development. It is interesting to note how, in addition to the industrial activity of

SECOND PLAN INVESTMENT BY PRIVATE INDUSTRIES
(Large and medium industry only)

		Rs. Crores
I. METALS		
(a) Iron and steel		115.0
(b) Aluminum and ferromanganese		31.5
II. HEAVY AND LIGHT ENGINEERING		92.5
(a) Cotton textile machinery	4.5	
(b) Jute textile machinery	1.3	
(c) Sugar machinery	2.0	
(d) Paper machinery	1.3	
(e) Light engineering industries	15.0	
(f) Structural fabrication	20.0	
(g) Automobiles	13.0	
(h) Railway rolling stock	5.0	
(i) Others, including cement machinery		
III. CHEMICAL (heavy chemicals, fertilizers, dyestuffs, plastics, oil refining, etc.)		56.2
IV. CEMENT AND REFRACTORIES		89.0
V. CONSUMER GOODS		162.0 [1]
VI. MISCELLANEOUS		24.0
		570.2
VII. MODERNIZATION AND REHABILITATION OF EXISTING INDUSTRIES		150.0 [2]
	TOTAL	720.2 [3]

[1] Rs. 5.0 crores additional for consumer goods are included under light engineering above (sewing machines, etc.).

[2] Includes NIDC investment of Rs. 20 crores for cotton and jute textile industries.

[3] Deducting the total NIDC investment of Rs. 55.0 crores, over-all investment in private industry is placed at Rs. 665.2 crores.

Government, private industry has a continued large role in the heavy basic industries.

As mentioned earlier, the Government expects, as does private enterprise, that the stimulus of the Second Plan, and especially of Government-aided expansion of basic raw materials, producer goods, power and transport will give strong encouragement to private enterprise to expand and invest more and more in long-term "nation-building" industries. In the first year of the Second Plan, a beginning was being made in this direction. There is also considerable invest-

FAMOUS FABRICS: India's hand-woven textiles designed by skilled craftsmen, today as in centuries past are reaching a quality export as well as a domestic market. Above, gold stenciling on the celebrated Mysore silks.

CHITTARANJAN LOCOMOTIVE WORKS: This Government-owned works, at Chittaranjan, West Bengal, was completed during the First Plan period. It will be turning out one locomotive every working day by 1961. Government and privately owned works are expected to more than double production of locomotives over the Second Plan period, to supplement heavy purchases abroad of railroad rolling stock.

EXPANDING PLANE SERVICE: The Government-owned airlines now service most major cities within India. An international service reaches many important foreign countries, West and East. Above, the Willingdon Airport, Delhi.

SMALL INDUSTRIES AID EMPLOYMENT: Over a fourth of all Indians now employed work in small and hand industries, such as this small lock factory at Delhi.

ment in other industries, which, while not directly keyed to Plan targets, are stimulating to the economy as a whole.

The following brief summary indicates some of private industries' most important programs over the Second Plan:

HEAVY INDUSTRIES

Iron and steel hold a dominant place in the private as in Government development programs, and will take more than one-fifth of all private industrial investment under the Second Plan. The large foreign and Indian financing for expansion plans for the two largest producers, Tata Iron and Steel Company and Indian Iron and Steel Company, have already been discussed. Both plants are expected to come into production by 1958. Private steel production will reach 2.3 million tons in 1960–1961 as against 1.25 million tons at the beginning of the Plan.

Aluminum and Ferromanganese: Private capital, plus some funds from the National Industrial Development Corporation, will develop capacity for 30,000 tons of aluminum, and 172,000 tons for ferromanganese.

HEAVY ENGINEERING

Locomotives: Tata Engineering and Locomotive Company, the only private producer, will double its output to a hundred locomotives a year.

Automobiles and Trucks: India has a small but growing automobile industry based on collaboration between Indian private enterprise and leading foreign firms, United States, Italian, German and British. During the First Plan, production merely by assembly of imported parts was discouraged, and steps were taken to promote the manufacture of components and parts in India, so that over a period of years more and more of the parts can be made within the country. The industry was producing 25,000 vehicles in 1955–1956.

Over the Second Plan, it expects to expand production to 57,000 vehicles, 40,000 of them trucks (lorries). India has made some progress in manufacturing more and more of the necessary automobile parts even for foreign cars assembled in India. Over the Second Plan, it hopes to bring the Indian content of automobile manufacturing up to 80 per cent.

CEMENT AND REFRACTORIES

Cement: Demand for cement grows sharply in an expanding economy which is rapidly building schools, factories, roads, and the like. Virtually all India's cement is expected to be privately produced. Total production will more than triple—going to 12.5 million tons from the 1955–1956 level of 4.1 million tons.

Refractories (silica, fire clay, magnesite and chromite refractories): Development in these industries is linked with the rise in iron and steel production. A target of 800,000 tons by 1960–1961 has been set, an increase of 186 per cent.

INDUSTRIAL MACHINERY

Private industry will very significantly expand its capacity to make machines for industrial use. Output [1] of cotton textile machinery will be four times higher than in 1955–1956; of jute textiles machinery nearly forty times higher; of sugar-manufacturing machinery nearly ten times; of cement nearly four times; of electric transformers and motors (200 HP and below) about 2½ times.

Production of this machinery in India will make private expansion possible later in textile, jute, sugar manufacturing and so on, without too much drain on foreign exchange. In these industries, arrangements are being made to get the foreign technical assistance urgently needed.

CHEMICALS

In development of the chemical industry (soda ash, caustic soda, phosphatic fertilizers, industrial explosives, dyestuffs and intermediates) private industry will play the leading part under the Second Plan. The industries must expand both as to quantity and as to grade of product. Production of soda ash is to increase nearly threefold, of

[1] As measured in Rs. crores value.

caustic soda fourfold, of calcium carbide eight times, of dyestuffs 5½ times.

CONSUMER GOODS

Cotton Textiles: As noted earlier, the cotton textile industry is the biggest industry in India. In 1955–1956 it produced 5,100 million yards of cloth.

To protect the important hand-loom industry, with its vast employment potential, new mill looms were not licensed in 1955, although increased spindleage for making yarn was. The industry increased its output over the First Plan substantially (37 per cent), by using its capacity more fully.

Over the Second Plan, it will have to expand somewhat to meet raised targets, but its biggest problem is modernization to help it compete in the export market. A significant part of the Rs. 20 to Rs. 25 crores of NIDC funds for industry modernization are to go to replacement and modernization of the cotton textile industry.

Paper and Paperboard: In India paper products are produced largely from bamboo and sabai grass. A major source of bamboo had traditionally been East Bengal, an area now in Pakistan. India has had to develop alternative sources for materials. With adequate materials, private industry is expected nearly to double production of paper products over the Second Plan.

Vegetable Oils: India is one of the largest producers of oilseeds in the world, and consequently a large producer and exporter of vegetable oils. The Second Plan expects production to increase from 1.8 to 2.1 million tons. The emphasis in new investment is on production of cotton seed oil, and oil from cakes by the solvent extraction process.

Sugar: The sugar industry is the fourth largest industry in India, and demand for sugar is rapidly increasing. Over the Second Plan an increase of 35 per cent (to a total of 2.3 million tons) is proposed. About one-sixth of total production is to come from cooperative mills.

Plastics: The plastics industry was chiefly developed in India in the Second World War, and use of plastics has increased at least fivefold since 1938. In general, finished products have been made from imported raw materials. Over the Second Plan, private industry is expected to increase tenfold its capacity to produce various molding powders in India.

Pharmaceuticals: India has increased sharply both its production and use of drugs since Independence. The industry, in which foreign firms are important collaborators, is now a predominantly processing operation, using imported components and formulae.

Over the Second Plan emphasis is on converting it to genuine manufacturing. Increased domestic production of dyestuff intermediates, some of which are also raw materials for drug manufactures, will assist this development. Production of Vitamin A from domestic lemon grass oil, for example, is being examined.

Private industry, as well as Government, is expected to develop manufacturing of antibiotics. Total private investment in drug manufacturing will be about Rs. 3 crores ($6 million).

FIRST PLAN	Rs. 49.9 crores
SECOND PLAN	Rs. 200 crores [1]

HIGH LIGHTS
of programs for
VILLAGE AND SMALL INDUSTRY

The Second Plan will spend Rs. 200 crores,[1] or four times as much as the First Plan, to develop and strengthen India's village and small-scale industries, with these main targets:

A 30 per cent increase in production—sufficient to meet most of the *increase* in demand for consumer goods expected over the Second Plan.

Half a million new full-time jobs and employment opportunities.

Training for village craftsmen and small manufacturers in use of improved equipment and more productive techniques.

Better facilities for supply of raw materials and of credit, and for marketing research and service, electric power, and so on.

An industrial extension service in every State for small manufacturers.

---

[1] Government expenditures only. Over the Second Plan private enterprise is expected to invest Rs. 100 crores in small industrial and other enterprises.

CHAPTER III

Village and Small-Scale Industries

Village and small-scale industry is, as we have seen, today an important part of India's economy, and of India's way of life. Eleven and a half million people, or 29 per cent [1] of all the people working outside agriculture, are employed in small enterprises. Together these produce about one-twelfth (8 per cent) of all India's goods and services, to a value of as much as the total production of all large- and medium-sized industries.

The decision to strengthen and develop these industries is, as already made clear, one of the key decisions of the Second Plan. Through these village and small industries India hopes to produce more goods and jobs with a small capital investment, help rural people get better incomes and employment, and mobilize and improve the skills of rural craftsmen, which might otherwise be unused in this transition period while large industries are growing up.

[1] 1950–51 figures.

285

The Second Plan has put on small industry, in fact, two big responsibilities: (1) producing a substantial share of the consumer
goods needed to meet the *increase* in demand expected over the Second Plan; and (2) providing an important part of all the new full-time
and part-time jobs proposed outside agriculture.

By the end of the Second Plan, village and small-scale industries
are expected to produce about 30 per cent more goods, or nearly half
again as much as before India began its First Plan. The bulk of the
goods will be consumer goods.

To help village and small-scale industries produce such an increase,
the Government has proposed an intensive program of development
backed by Rs. 200 crores, or about four times the amount spent in
the First Plan.

India's small industries are of two distinct types, and the development programs for each vary accordingly.

The first group are the *small-scale industries*. These industries generally use some power machines and make some effort toward improved techniques. By the working definition adopted by the Small
Scale Industries Board, they include all industries employing less than
fifty persons when using power, and having a capital investment of
less than Rs. 500,000 ($100,000). Some of the principal small-scale
industries are: footwear, bicycles, locks, surgical implements, sewing
machines, builders' hardware, agricultural instruments, hand tools,
electrical appliances, knitted textiles.

Like the "small business" of the West, they are important potential
growing points of the economy. Modern, or potentially modern,
largely urban or semi-urban, they are readily adaptable to modern
machines and techniques, can help supply large industry and cater to
an expanding market. As such, they are also a training ground for the
business and management talent which is needed to revitalize Indian
private enterprise.

If small industrialists can be helped to grow and to become larger
producers, or even to become more efficient small producers, an important influence for dynamism and self-regulation through competition will have been introduced into the Indian economic system,

making for more constructive performance in the public interest by the whole private sector.

The second group are the *traditional hand and "cottage" industries*. These still form an intimate part of Indian village life and economy and of the towns as well, in spite of the keen competition from mechanized Indian industries and imported manufactured goods.

Among these traditional industries are: *hand-loom* (cloth hand woven from mill-made yarn); *khadi* (hand-spun yarn, and cloth hand woven from homespun yarn); *coir making*; *silk* and *sericulture*; *handicrafts*, such as art metalwork, toys, ivory carving, Bidri ware, decorative ceramics; other *"village" industries*, such as hand pounding of rice, pressing of vegetable oils, manufacturing of raw sugar and khandsari, matches, tanning and leather footwear.

In drawing up its development programs for both village and small-scale industries, India has adopted certain guiding policies and aims. While some of these have been generally discussed earlier, it is helpful to give them here precisely. They are:

1. To increase employment as much as possible, and avoid as far as possible further technological unemployment, which occurs especially in the traditional village industries;

2. To foster energetically more productive techniques and equipment;

3. To develop new products and production methods which will serve new demands and markets more effectively;

4. To protect village and small-scale industries from destructive competition of factory industry while they improve their competitive strength;

5. To encourage, as much as possible, the development of production, marketing and credit cooperatives;

6. To work toward a decentralized economy, a pattern of industry in which a group of villagers converging on their natural industrial or urban center form a unit, "a pyramid of industry broad-based on a progressive rural economy."

India put in motion programs to realize these aims during the First Plan, particularly during the last year of the Plan. Under strong leadership in the Central Government, special development programs for small-scale and for village industries were begun, and in the last year of the Plan alone expenditures on their development were as much as in the preceding four years. While the major aims set out in the First Plan were not fulfilled, the role of the small industries in India's growth was more clearly understood, and the organization and way prepared for carrying out larger and more ambitious programs over the Second Plan.

A network of All-India Boards was established for each of the separate groups of industries to give them coordinated stimulus and direction. The Government accepted in principle that certain types of Government purchases would be reserved for village and small-scale industries and that certain price preferences would be given them. Some parts of a so-called "common production program," already discussed, were adopted to protect small industries.

Twenty-six pilot projects were begun to stimulate industries in rural development areas, under a joint program of the Ministries of Community Development and of Commerce and Industries. These were valuable in pointing out some of the problems involved in fostering small and village industries in a way that will go deeper into the life of the rural people.

During the First Plan, production by all small industries rose by 14 per cent.

The Second Plan will intensify the programs already put under way in the First Plan and start important new ones. Rs. 200 crores (as against Rs. 49.9 crores in the First Plan) has been allocated; most of it (Rs. 175 crores) will be spent by the States. Total private investment in all small enterprises is expected to be about Rs. 100 crores.

Small-Scale Industries

The imaginative, extensive program already begun for the development of small-scale industries will be greatly expanded over the Second Plan. The Indian Government feels that this program represents a progressive approach to small manufacturing and that it has already shown the great possibilities of these industries for development.

The program, which has strong support from the Central Government, includes setting up a nation-wide network of Small Industries Service Institutes, with an industrial extension service and outlying extension centers, intensive technical assistance and training for small manufacturers and workmen, market research and credit facilities, and a hire-purchase (installment plan) scheme for aiding small manufacturers to buy machinery.

It also includes plans for encouraging cooperation between the large- and small-scale industries, so that small industry may have an assured share in supplying standard quality parts for large industries.

A Small-Scale Industries Board was set up in 1954 within the Ministry of Commerce and Industry, and a Development Commissioner for Small-Scale Industries was appointed. The Commissioner gives coordinated direction to the following intensified nation-wide program:

1. *Small Industries Service Institutes:* Four regional Institutes were set up in 1954–1955 to provide marketing service, industrial extension work, technical assistance and training to small manufacturers, and to State authorities concerned with small industrial development. The Institutes, by 1956, had begun to establish branches and to launch pilot projects for intensive industrial extension work.

Over the Second Plan, a nation-wide network will be established of at least one service Institute in each State; sixty branch industrial extension and training centers will be set up by 1957–1958. These smaller centers will specialize generally in one or more products particularly manufactured in each area.

Each Institute will have a model workshop. Some of these workshops have already been set up in concentrated production centers (for example, the footwear workshops at Agra and Madras). To reach small manufacturers in outlying small cities and towns, there are workshops mounted on mobile vans demonstrating improved techniques and machinery. Forty-five of these vans were scheduled to be in operation early in the Plan period.

The Institutes are training industrial extension officers for each of the community projects and NES Blocks to provide field service on small industries. Evening courses in business management are being made available to small industrialists.

2. A *National Small Industries Corporation* was established in early 1956. In the first year of the Second Plan, it began its program of helping small industries to procure raw materials and market their products, of channeling Government purchase orders to small producers; arranging hire-purchase of machinery (through the Service Institutes); and of providing a marketing service and wholesale depots for small manufacturers. Under the Second Plan, branches will be set up in Bombay, Calcutta, Madras and Delhi.

3. *Industrial Field Surveys:* Industrial economic investigation teams were set up in 1955, in the office of the Development Commissioner for Small-Scale Industries. These teams carry out field studies in various industry areas and prepare "industry outlook reports" and "area development studies" on opportunities for small industrial development. These reports, the first systematic studies of the facts and problems of each small industry covered, are valuable practical guides both to the small manufacturers and to the Government on the possibilities of expansion.

Over the Second Plan, the teams will be increased so that they may include more areas and more industries.

4. *Technical Assistance:* The Government in the last year of the First Plan brought twelve technical experts, largely from Europe, to give technical guidance on key industries—shoes, glassware, bicycles, surgical instruments, furniture and some others. Over the Second Plan, the Government will continue to provide such experts for important special industries. They work through the Service Institutes and the model workshops.

Hand and Cottage Industries

Hand Loom: The shortage of cloth and India's acute shortage of foreign exchange with which to buy new textile machinery abroad, as well as problems of unemployment, put a new view on India's effort to stimulate handweaving.

During the First Plan period of protection and encouragement, hand looms increased production by 75 per cent to contribute 1,450 million yards of cloth, or over one-fifth of all cotton cloth manufactured in India. The looms also gave employment to about 2 million weavers. (This compares, it will be remembered, with 760,000 textile mill employees producing a little over 5 million yards.)

India hopes Second Plan production of cloth to be 1,700 million yards more than in the First Plan. Only a part of this increase is to be produced by textile mills. The major part, 1,000 million yards, is to come from village looms. If village weavers reach this target, this would bring up the total Second Plan hand-loom production to 2,450 million [1] yards, or almost a third of all cotton cloth produced.

Intense effort will be needed to yield any such increase. It will involve use of idle looms, working all looms more days in the year and raising output per loom. It is known that with improved looms and techniques, production per loom can be raised from four to six yards per day. Loans will be advanced to weavers to assure working capital and to enable them to join cooperatives. The number of hand looms joined in cooperatives is expected to increase from 1 million to about 1½ million.

It is also hoped to install 35,000 power looms, largely in cooperative societies of hand weavers, to help them, as a group, switch over to the more efficient methods which can step up production. Power looms are expected to produce some 200 million yards of cloth over the Plan years, aside from the amount produced by hand looms.

Since many of India's hand-loom fabrics are of exceptionally fine artistic design and color, they are particularly valuable for export. A special United States team in 1956–1957 made a survey at the request of the Government to recommend ways for developing hand-loom exports for Western markets.

Khadi and Hand Spinning: Hand-woven cloth made from home-

---

[1] This figure includes cloth hand woven of mill-made yarn, and of handspun yarn.

spun yarn—the famous "khadi" worn by Mahatma Gandhi and all leaders in the Independence struggle, and widely worn today as a symbolic link with the Gandhian tradition—is expected to supply 300 million yards of all the hand-loomed cloth produced in the Second Plan. During 1955–1956 experimentation was done on a new type of four-spindle spinning wheel, the "Ambar Charkha," which increased production of yarn. A program for promoting the wider use of this new wheel is being undertaken.

"Village" Industries: Considerable effort and money were devoted to developing these industries over the First Plan.

Over the Second Plan, there will be expanded programs to improve cottage methods of processing rice, vegetable oils, raw sugar (gur and khandsari), by promoting use of improved equipment and methods. Proposals now under discussion but not yet confirmed may prohibit setting up or expanding power mills producing rice and vegetable oil.

Village tanning and manufacturing of leather footwear will, it is hoped, meet a substantial part of the increased local demand as rural incomes go up.

The Government hopes to improve technical efficiency and production, and provide loans as working capital. New mechanized large-scale units may be prohibited. For all village industries (except rice), production-and-training centers, started during the First Plan, will be increased in number and made more effective in teaching the advanced trades; cooperatives will be actively promoted, and intensive marketing systems, by integrated areas, set up.

Coir Industry: Promotion will take the form mainly of encouraging production cooperatives and bringing in some new techniques and simple machinery.

Handicrafts: Second Plan proposals to stimulate improved production and design and the marketing of India's fine traditional crafts include: regional design and training centers, craft museums and art schools (with scholarships), research and promotion of new techniques, as well as the development of marketing systems and improved sales depots and purchasing systems to stimulate internal and export sales.

Silk and Sericulture: Sericulture is a valuable means of supplementing village income. It now supports about 5 million persons, and over the Second Plan should employ 60,000 more. The Second Plan program will include expansion, research and training schemes begun earlier, and improvement of techniques and use of by-products.

Facilities for Village and Small-Scale Industry

Industrial Estates: Improving the workshops and working conditions of Indian small industry can, in the opinion of many experts, do as much as any other single factor to increase efficiency, improve quality, assure the more economical use of materials and equipment. Many, indeed the majority, of the village and small industries operate under conditions lacking not only essential facilities of water and power, but light and ventilation, air and space, and freedom of movement.

The First Plan began, and the Second Plan will continue, setting up industrial "estates" to help small industry have the advantage of common services—facilities such as a good site, power, water, gas, steam, compressed air, railway sidings.

As far as possible, estates are being located in or near towns of relatively small size to discourage more congestion in the cities. Regions which offer especially favorable conditions and which need special assistance are being selected.

Power: During the Second Plan the number of towns with a population under 10,000 which will have electricity will increase from 6,500 to 16,500, so that power will be available to many small industries. Rates have already been reduced to all small-scale industries.

Credit: Through the All-India Boards and the States' Departments of Industries and of Cooperatives, credit on more liberal terms is being made available. Coordination of facilities and speed-up of credit-granting procedures are essential. The State Bank of India is engaged in a pilot program in three areas to determine more satisfactory methods of coordinating and supplying credit services to small industries.

Market Research and Service: The various All-India Boards for village and small-scale industries have initiated considerable market research, and more will be done under the Second Plan. State purchase of the products of cooperatives is under consideration.

Administration and Organization

It is certainly true that organizing village and small-scale industries, scattered in over half a million villages and thousands of towns and cities, so that they can step up production by some 30 per cent during the Second Plan period, will require the highest administrative skill and effort.

While the Central Government sets general policies and gives strong over-all direction to the program, the actual administration of the program, like the bulk of its expenditures, is almost wholly in the hands of the States.

The Central Government's program will be carried largely through the Service Institutes and the industrial extension centers.

State Directors of Industries have been appointed, and a high priority in the Second Plan is given to strengthening their departments with appointment of two deputies, one for village industries and one for small-scale industries; of an industries officer in each district, and of State technical experts.

The States will concentrate broadly on four types of activity in closest correlation with Central Government schemes: (1) technical service and research, such as training-and-production centers and polytechnics; (2) pilot production schemes to be turned over later to industrial cooperatives or private enterprise; (3) production projects of a commercial character and loans to private concerns under the State Aid to Industries Acts; and (4) schemes for supply of power.

The Community Development Ministry has a program for an Industries Extension Service to be set up over the Second Plan. It will provide a village industries officer for each "block" of one hundred villages in the rural development program. Together with the extension activities of the Small Industries Service Institutes, this program is expected to constitute a nation-wide small-industry field service for both small-scale and the traditional hand industries. Training of all these officers will be done jointly by the Ministry of Commerce and Industry through the Small Industries Service Institutes and Training Centers of the All-India Khadi and Village Industries Board.

In May 1957 a Coordination Committee on Small Industries was set up by the Ministry of Commerce and Industry to assure coordination between the Ministry and the various Boards and organizations functioning under it, of all programs for developing village and small-scale industries. The Committee will also help to coordinate the efforts of the Ministries of Commerce and Industry and of Community Development, and to build up and strengthen the methods and organization which can bring effective help directly to India's small industries in city, town and village.

FIRST PLAN   Rs. 1 crore [1]

SECOND PLAN   Rs. 73 crores [2]

HIGH LIGHTS
of programs for
MINERAL DEVELOPMENT

The Second Plan will spend Rs. 73 crores,[2] or over eighteen times as much as the First Plan, to explore and develop India's mineral resources for its own industrial growth, and also for export. These are the main targets:

A 58 per cent increase in total mineral production.

A nearly 200 per cent increase (8.2 million tons more) in iron ore production.

22 million more tons of coal (or 58 per cent more than in 1955–1956) produced by both public and private enterprise.

Development of extensive lignite deposits in Madras.

Intensified exploration for new mineral resources, especially of coal and oil.

---

[1] This amount was raised to Rs. 4 crores during the course of the First Plan.
[2] Government expenditures only.

CHAPTER IV

Mineral Development

In mineral wealth, India is believed to rank fairly high among the nations of the world; and its reserves have not yet been fully surveyed.

Coal, iron, bauxite, ilmenite, manganese ore, mica, titanium and thorium ores are plentiful both for India's internal needs and for export. Reserves of aluminum ore, refractories and abrasives and limestones are adequate. What India chiefly lacks, among the vital minerals, are copper, tin, lead, zinc, cobalt, sulphur and—very importantly —petroleum. India now imports over 90 per cent of its petroleum needs.

Distribution of all minerals is geographically capricious, however. Some regions, such as the Bihar-Bengal-Orissa triangle, have an abundance, while others, such as South India, are comparatively poor.

Over the First Plan, mineral development consisted largely of surveys and investigation, although production of all minerals went up substantially, about 24 per cent.

Emphasis on industry in the Second Plan has made the development of minerals especially urgent, and also the obtaining of more detailed information on the extent and quality of possible new deposits. Over the Second Plan India hopes, by exploiting present sources to the full and opening up new deposits, to increase total production by 58 per cent.

COAL

Coal has first place in the Second Plan program of mineral development. Because of its basic importance as a fuel, and as raw material for industries like iron and steel, for coal carbonization, and so on, demand for coal at the end of the Second Plan is expected to be very heavy—60 million tons, or 22 million tons more than was produced in 1955.

In keeping with the new Industrial Policy Resolution, the Government will take the major responsibility in producing this additional coal, and 12 million out of the 22 million tons will be mined by Government-owned collieries. This means considerable expansion by Government, since Government-owned collieries in 1955 produced only an eighth of total production. More than half the total funds for minerals development over the Second Plan (Rs. 40 crores out of a total of Rs. 73 crores) will go to stepping up of coal production.

The control and management of Government-owned collieries has been made the responsibility of a newly set-up (October 1, 1956) National Coal Development Corporation. The Corporation is responsible for increasing coal production, and will secure the foreign technical assistance urgently needed in this field.

Conservation, particularly of metallurgical coal, and control of quality are essential. The new steel mills, plus other essential consumers, will need a total of 11.41 million tons of clean washed coal, or about 19 million tons in terms of raw metallurgical coal against the present production of about 13.5 million tons of this quality.

In order to meet the expanded requirements of essential consumers, the production of this quality has to be raised progressively. To conserve the limited reserves, steps have to be taken to substitute, gradually, for the coking coal now consumed by non-essential consumers like railways, suitable non-coking coal. The railways are planning a phased program for such substitution.

Government has accepted the recommendation of the Coal Washeries Committee that generally all coking coal down to grade II should be washed. There are already three washeries which supply washed coal to the Tata Iron and Steel Company and to the Indian Iron and Steel Company. It is proposed to set up a coal-washing plant at Bokaro-Kargali which will supply washed coal to the Rourkela and Bhilai steel plants. Another washery will be set up in conjunction with the Durgapur steel plant.

For meeting the requirements of the steel plants it has been found necessary for the Government of India to set up three more washeries, since the establishment of additional washeries by private enterprise was not found possible. These three new washeries will be at Dugda, Pathardih and Bojudih.

OTHER MINERALS

Extensive deposits of lignite, estimated at 200 million tons, have been discovered in South Arcot, Madras. Since South India has little to no known coal deposits, exploitation of this valuable lignite resource is essential to the area's industrial development. It is proposed to mine 3.5 million tons of lignite annually by the end of the Second Plan.

Under the revised Industrial Policy Resolution a number of important minerals have been added to the list of those to be exploited by the Government. Atomic energy materials, of which India has good supply, will be extensively developed. Proposals for a diamond and a copper mine, under Government operation, are being worked out. In addition, some States have schemes of their own for mineral development, among them the development of the Hutti Gold Mines in Hyderabad (now Mysore).

Mineral and Oil Investigations

MINERALS

The Geological Survey of India and the India Bureau of Mines will undertake intensive investigation programs, over the Second Plan, on coal, copper, manganese, chromite, gypsum, lead, zinc, tin and other minerals. Prospecting of new coal fields—from which most of the new production must come—is particularly urgent. It is planned to expand both the Bureau of Mines and the Geological Survey substantially; and the resources needed, Rs. 6 crores, have been provided in the Second Plan.

OIL

The exploration and development of the country's oil resources has a high priority under the Second Plan. The Government will continue to work with the Standard Vacuum Oil Company in the exploration of the West Bengal Basin. Negotiations are in progress on the Government of India's participation with the Assam Oil Company in the development of oil fields at Nahorkatiya and Moran (Assam), where oil was struck in 1953 in commercial quantities, and in the establishment of a refinery. These fields when fully developed will meet a considerable share of the country's needs. The Assam Oil Company has also been granted prospecting licenses over certain areas adjacent to Nahorkatiya under agreement that the Government will participate. To what extent the Government will participate financially with these companies in exploration and development has not yet been fully worked out. The required resources will be provided as needed.

In addition, the Government has its own independent program of oil exploration, for which a provision of Rs. 11.5 crores has been made. Technical assistance by Canada and by the Soviet Union is being used, and the services of some technical experts from the United States and France have also been obtained. Exploration begun earlier in the Jaisalmer (Rajasthan) area will be continued and will include ground geological surveys and geophysical investigations and exploratory drilling. An aero-magnetic survey of the Jaisalmer area has been completed with technical assistance from Canada. Reference drilling will be undertaken in Cambay (Bombay) and deep test drilling in Jwalamukhi (Punjab) on the basis of preliminary data which show these areas to be promising. New proposals for oil exploration are being discussed, and further resources will be provided as needed.

To assure that there are enough technically trained men to staff expanded exploration programs, more men will be given specialized training both in India and abroad, in cooperation with foreign governments.

FIRST PLAN	Rs. 497 crores [1]

SECOND PLAN	Rs. 1,309 crores [1]

HIGH LIGHTS
of programs for
TRANSPORT DEVELOPMENT

The Second Plan will spend Rs. 1,309 crores,[1] or over 2 1/2 times as much as the First Plan, to improve India's transportation system—its railways, roads, shipping, ports and harbors. The main targets are:

RAILWAYS

Increasing railroad capacity to carry 35 per cent (42 million tons) more freight traffic.

An increase of 15 per cent in passenger traffic, or 191 million more passengers.

A systematic program for stepping up efficiency of operation.

Increased purchase abroad of new equipment.

Increasing Indian manufacture of locomotives by 129 per cent, of railway coaches by 43 per cent, of freight wagons by nearly 85 per cent.

Modernization of railways, especially by Dieselation and automatic signaling.

ROADS AND ROAD TRANSPORT

About 1,000 new miles—a 7 per cent increase—of national highways.

18,000 new miles—a 17 per cent increase—of other hard-surfaced roads.

A road within five miles of every village in well developed agricultural areas.

Stimulation of private and government-owned road transport.

SHIPPING, PORTS AND INLAND WATERWAYS

Increased Indian shipping tonnage, through purchase of ships abroad and expansion of Indian shipbuilding.

Modernization and expansion of dock and port facilities.

Some expansion of inland waterway traffic.

CIVIL AIR TRANSPORT

Modernizing and expanding airline facilities.

Regular service to all State capitals and important cities.

---

[1] Government expenditures only.

CHAPTER V

Transport

Very nearly one-fourth the entire budget of the Second Plan will go to expanding India's railways, roads, shipping, ports and harbors.

Fast improvement and expansion of transport is, for India, a matter of the utmost urgency. In 1955–1956, the last year of the First Plan, India's transport system, especially railways, was seriously overloaded; there were long delays and difficulties in moving the raw materials and finished goods produced as industry and the whole economy became more active. In the Second Plan, unless transportation is quickly expanded, lack of adequate transport may be a bottleneck in the country's entire economic development.

Over the Second Plan, not only railways, but roads and road transport, shipping and ports facilities and inland waterways must be developed. Transport expansion is seen by the Government and by many Indian and foreign observers as a key problem of India's rapid economic growth.

RAILWAYS

FIRST PLAN	Rs. 268 crores
SECOND PLAN	Rs. 900 crores

The railroads carry nearly all freight and a great part of passenger traffic in India, since other means of transport are by and large undeveloped.

Fortunately, the railroad system which Independent India inherited is, as we have seen, the most extensive in Asia. Government-owned, and the largest national undertaking, it has a capital of Rs. 974 crores and 35,000 miles of track. Over the depression and war years, the railways were, however, starved for capital and improvement; they were also overstrained and undermaintained throughout the war.

During the First Plan, therefore, the urgent need was to make up for the lack of maintenance of the war years. One-fifth to nearly one-third of India's rolling stock (that is, locomotives, coaches and freight wagons) was over-aged, and replacement was a top priority.

Most of the new equipment [1] was purchased abroad, principally from the United States under the United States Technical Cooperation Mission program, but also from the United Kingdom and West Germany. But India takes some pride that roughly over a third was produced in India by the newly completed Government-owned Chittaranjan Locomotive Works, the Tata Engineering and Locomotive Company, and the Government's Integral Coach Factory which went into production October 1955. Indian freight-car production increased four times over the First Plan period.

Over the First Plan, a modest amount of new line was constructed and some formerly dismantled line was restored.

[1] Total Indian and foreign purchases by the end of the First Plan, March 1956, were estimated at 1,589 new locomotives, 4,837 coaches, and 61,713 (4-wheeler) freight cars.

Even with these many efforts to rehabilitate, five years was too short a time to make up the lack of replacements over the war years; and the proportion of over-age locomotives and wagons was higher at the end than at the beginning of the Plan. Carrying capacity fell below demand by 5 million tons,[1] as India's growing industries and trade brought more traffic to the railroads than they could carry. In the last year of the First Plan more freight moved [2] than at any time in thirty years, except during the strain of the war and Partition.

With the Second Plan's heavy emphasis on expanding industry, both capacity and efficiency have to be rapidly stepped up over the next five years. By the end of the Second Plan, freight traffic is expected to be 50 per cent higher than in 1955–1956, passenger traffic, 15 per cent higher.

To get about the urgent business of expanding railway facilities, the Second Plan provides for more than double (Rs. 900 crores) the First Plan actual expenditures for railway development, with an additional sum (Rs. 225 crores) to be used from the Railway Depreciation Fund.

Altogether, this amount (Rs. 1,125 crores, or $2.25 billion) to be spent on railways is so substantial that it has attracted considerable attention and discussion both within India and among interested groups abroad. It is just under a fifth of all Government expenditures of the entire Plan.

Large as it is, it represents a sizable reduction from the initial estimates of railway authorities, and is believed to be still inadequate to satisfy Second Plan needs. Even with the heavy expenditures, it is believed that, with the economy rapidly expanding, railway facilities may fall short of requirements by 10 per cent in rolling stock and by 5 per cent in line capacity.

The key to the difficulty is, of course, that railway expansion and rehabilitation, the buying of locomotives and coaches, the laying of track, are always costly, in any country, at any time. In India the

---

[1] Total tons carried: 115 millions against demand of 120.
[2] As measured in millions of net ton-miles.

problem is further complicated by the shortage of foreign exchange. New locomotives and steel rails must still come to a considerable extent from abroad, and be paid for in dollars or pounds sterling, of which India is so seriously short. Even if India tries—as it is trying— to produce more equipment within the country, the steel with which to build it must be imported.

Foreign exchange needed for the railway imports proposed in the Second Plan amounts to Rs. 425 crores according to the original estimates, a sizable part of the total foreign exchange requirements for all purposes of the Second Plan. About one-third of the railway total is for steel alone.

To save foreign exchange, India's alternative has been to cut down railway expenditures (both in rupees and in foreign exchange) as much as possible and still meet the needs of the Second Plan and future Plans, by the following means:

1. Stepping up Indian manufacture of locomotives, coaches and wagons;
2. Intensifying efforts to increase operational efficiency, for which there is believed to be considerable scope;
3. Undertaking detailed study and planning for the kind of efficient long-term and also short-term development which can be done at least cost.

Under the Second Plan program to expand Indian manufacture, India can produce a substantial share of its total needs for coaches, and wagons. However, in spite of increasing output of locomotives, India must buy abroad, over the Second Plan, about one-fourth of all its locomotives.

The Second Plan provides for remodeling and expansion of several of the existing workshops and running sheds, and establishment of six new workshops, a new meter-gauge coach-building factory and a furnishing unit for the Integral Coach Factory. As noted earlier, the Government will put Rs. 22 crores of direct investment on expanding these railway engineering industries.

The Integral Coach Factory is expected to reach a rate of production of 200 coaches a year early in the Second Plan period, and 350 coaches a year on the Factory's completion. The capacity of the Chittaranjan Locomotive Works is to be stepped up to 300 locomotives a year from 129 in 1955–1956. Expansion of the Tata Engineering and Locomotive Company (TELCO) will increase production of locomotives from 50 to 100 a year. Annual production of 1,800 coaches and 25,000 wagons is expected.

In a further effort to save foreign exchange, some over-age (forty to forty-five-year-old) locomotives and wagons, and even a certain proportion older than these, will be kept in service.

Although there was improvement in operating efficiency in the last years of the First Plan, detailed study is now being undertaken, with the assistance of an American group of railway consultants, to step up efficiency substantially and begin systematic and effective expansion. The study will recommend ways of rapidly increasing railway capacity and efficiency, at as low a cost as possible in domestic and foreign exchange.

Tentatively, pending final results of the study, the Second Plan provides, among other programs, for: doubling of 1,607 miles of track and the conversion of 265 miles of meter-gauge lines into broad gauge; renewal of 8,000 miles of track; the electrification of 826 miles of railway lines; and Diesel motive power for 1,293 miles of track. Provision has also been made for improved signaling, including automatic signaling on busy sections.

The programs for doubling of track and electrification are particular objects of the development study, since they are costly methods of increasing carrying capacity. Final decision on the best methods over the Second Plan depends on further study and the availability of domestic and foreign exchange. Pilot and demonstration projects may be undertaken.

Meanwhile, the Government expects to proceed on procurement of the considerable amount of basic rolling stock which will be necessary regardless of what over-all plan of long-range railway development is ultimately chosen.

ROADS

FIRST PLAN Rs. **135 crores**	
SECOND PLAN	Rs. **246 crores**

Roads are an intimate part of India's urgent transport problem. While India's road system improved over the First Plan, good roads link only the major cities and towns. Few roads exist in rural India and fewer still from villages to marketing centers. Most of the few are unsurfaced *kutcha* roads, which have been justly described as "unusably bad in the rains, unspeakably bad all the year round."

While the motorized United States is hardly a fair comparison, it is an illuminating one: in 1951 there were 11 miles of United States road per square mile of area, and 2,143.7 miles of road per 100,000 population. For India, at the end of the First Plan, the figures were 0.24 and 87.5 respectively. This is roughly the amount of road in United States desert areas. The Indian figure, moreover, includes roads of all kinds, although over two-thirds are the *kutcha* roads impassable during the monsoon.

In building roads for new India, there have been special problems to solve. Some of the former princely States, each almost a world unto itself, had built roads which ended abruptly at their borders. The new larger States of independent India, in which princely States were incorporated, have had to build road links and bridges to tie these old roads into a connected road system within each of the new States. In some cases it has even been necessary to see that the new State capitals had road links to their newly included Districts and that there were road connections between the Districts themselves. Moreover, since roads were to be built by many agencies—the Central Government, the States, the Districts and local communities —it is also necessary to plan carefully to assure a coordinated program that can produce a network of roads for rural and other areas over the future.

Development of the road system proposed over the First Plan—and the Second Plan—followed in general what is known as the Nagpur Plan of 1943. Its main objective is that by 1963 no village in a well developed agricultural area should remain more than five miles from a main road; and in a non-agricultural area, none more than twenty miles.

By the end of the First Plan, the broad target of total road mileage under the Nagpur Plan was nearly achieved; some States even exceeded their targets. Some 24,000 miles of surfaced road were built, which included many missing links and many missing bridges. In the rural areas 44,000 miles of *kutcha* roads were constructed, a good part of them under the rural development program. Many of these were built by the people themselves, who contributed in labor, cash and kind from one-third to one-half the cost.

Considerable work was done during the First Plan to improve the natural highways system. The target for completing missing links was almost fully achieved, and nearly twice as much work was done on improvements as originally expected.

As part of the national highway program, work was begun on the Bannihal tunnel into Kashmir. Work was also begun on many inter-State roads, roads of economic importance and others including the Assam-Agartala Road, the Passi-Badarpur Road, and the West Coast Road.

The Second Plan will continue these major projects, and continue to concentrate on inter-State roads and roads of economic importance. For the national highway program, the main emphasis, as in the First Plan, will be on construction of major bridges, missing links and improvement of existing roads. Road building in India, as in the United States, is largely in the hands of the States, and the major portion of the Second Plan's funds for roads will be spent by the States.[1]

By the end of the Second Plan, all missing road links of present surfaced road systems will be completed, and all major bridges in the

---

[1] Out of the Rs. 246 crores total for roads over the Second Plan, Rs. 164 crores will be spent by the States. An additional Rs. 25 crores will come from the Central Road Fund, making a complete total of Rs. 271 crores.

national highway system. The targets for further mileage set by the Nagpur Plan will be practically reached. And it is expected in general that every village in a developed agricultural area will have a road within five miles. Many village links to these roads will be built by the villagers under the rural development program.

A Central Road Research Institute near Delhi is studying road construction and, in particular, attempting to develop types of low-cost road surfaces that can withstand heat and heavy rains and can be maintained easily and inexpensively.

ROAD TRANSPORT

FIRST PLAN	Rs. 12 crores
SECOND PLAN	Rs. 17 crores

No reliable figures exist on the amount of freight and passenger traffic carried by road as against railways. It is known to be considerable, though far less than it could and should be.

The total number of motor vehicles on the road is about 415,000 as against 306,000 in 1951. It is being urged more and more that short-haul freight should be carried by road, to relieve strain upon the railways for whom short hauls are costly and inefficient. For long hauls, however, considering the high cost of constructing transcontinental highways, the railways can move goods more economically.

Although over the First Plan, carriers on the road increased by about a fourth, the Government is concerned that motorized road transport has not developed as much as should be expected in view of India's available roads, the country's population, the shortage of railway facilities, and the general needs of the economy.

Lack of capital to buy trucks and lorries is probably an important reason, although it has been increasingly realized that restrictive tax and regulatory measures by the various States have played a large part.

Because of the urgent need to expand transport facilities, the Plan-

SCHOOL LESSON: This young villager is busy with a lesson in Kannada, the language of her area in Mysore. While only half as many Indian girls as boys go to grade school, the number is now rising rapidly.

ENGINEERS IN TRAINING: Students at the engineering college of Aligarh University. Nation-wide training facilities for engineers, greatly expanded over the First Plan period, are being enlarged still further to turn out about 11,000 men a year by 1961.

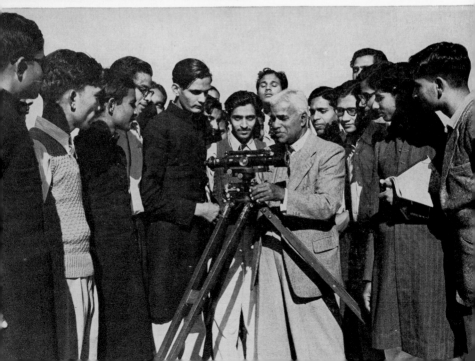

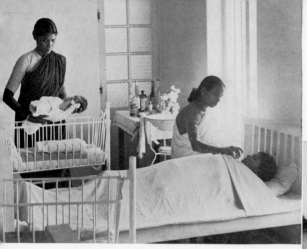

BETTER MATERNAL AND CHILD HEALTH: A maternity center in Salem, Madras. India's nation-wide rural health, maternity and child care program is bringing clinics and hospital facilities to rural as well as city areas. Three thousand new health centers for villagers will be built over the Second Plan period.

YOUNG SCIENTIST: Woman botany student at Muslim University Women's College, Aligarh. She is one of many young Indian men and women entering science under expanded science education programs of the Second Plan.

A HARIJAN'S NEW HOME: At Mysore a Harijan shows off his new home, built by his own family labor with the help of a Government loan. The national and State governments, and the rural development program, provide special housing, education and welfare assistance for the Harijans (a group formerly called the "untouchables"), for tribal peoples and other backward and especially underprivileged groups.

ning Commission, in consultation with the Ministry of Transport, has had the problems of road-transport development reviewed by a special study group.

Earlier in the First Plan, many of the States were in favor of putting road transport under State ownership. On the basis of the special study, the Planning Commission has recommended that private transport operators should be assisted in setting up effective service and that the States should liberalize the terms on which licenses are granted to private operators. Many have already begun to do so, and there is increasing emphasis on assisting private transport to develop. The Planning Commission recommends that freight (goods) transport services should not be nationalized during the Second Plan period, and that State Governments wishing to nationalize passenger service should proceed with caution, in a gradual manner over the Second Plan period.

Other proposals for development of road transport are being actively looked into, including a scheme for encouraging the educated unemployed to enter into road transport.

The amount of goods carried by bullock cart in India is very substantial. There are over 9½ million carts in India.[1] Methods of improving the efficiency of the carts, with improved wheels, self-aligning hubs, and rubber tires, are being studied by the Central Road Research Institute.

Tourism

Tourism, while not well developed in India, is important as an earner of foreign exchange. In 1956, 75,000 foreign tourists brought over Rs. 15 crores in foreign exchange into the country, as against 20,000 tourists in 1951 bringing Rs. 7.7 crores for the year as a whole. The Second Plan proposes development of tourism by providing accommodation, transport and recreational facilities at important tourist centers, especially those situated in out-of-the-way places.

[1] *All-Indian Rural Credit Survey*, 1954, II, 96.

SHIPPING, PORTS AND HARBORS, INLAND WATERWAYS

FIRST PLAN	Rs. 67 crores
SECOND PLAN	Rs. 100 crores

Shipping

India was fortunate to have, on Independence, a fairly well developed series of ports and harbors, a legacy of the active trade of its colonial rulers. Also, unlike many Asian countries, such as India's near neighbor Burma, its ports were not destroyed or damaged in World War II.

Indian shipping, however, was far behind the needs of an independent country. A Shipping Policy Committee in 1947 recommended a target of 2 million tons of Indian shipping in the next five to seven years. By subsidies to private shipping companies, and by purchase and development of the shipyard at Visakhapatnam, India hoped to come near to this goal.

Progress in shipbuilding and purchase, however, in the years since Independence has been slower than was hoped for. At the end of the First Plan, India had only 500,000 GRT, about one-fifth of that of Japan, and only 0.5 per cent of the world's total. Of this, moreover, one-half is used only in coastal shipping, which, under present policy, is reserved for Indian tonnage.

What the Second Plan hopes to do is to develop coastal trade more fully and thus relieve the overburdened railways; to secure an increasing share of India's overseas trade for Indian ships; and to build up the nucleus of a tanker fleet.

The Second Plan provides Rs. 48 crores for shipping as against Rs. 26.3 crores [1] in the First Plan. Of the total amount provided in

---

[1] Actual First Plan expenditures for shipping were Rs. 19 crores. The balance unspent, about Rs. 8 crores, was carried over and is included in the Rs. 48 crore allotment of the Second Plan.

the Second Plan, about Rs. 20 crores are earmarked for direct investment in the Eastern Shipping Corporation and a new shipping corporation which will be set up. The balance will go to assist expansion programs of private shipping companies. An additional Rs. 10 crores will be spent by private shipping companies from their own resources.

In the Second Plan, it was originally proposed to bring India's total tonnage to 900,000 GRT. This would enable Indian tonnage to carry 12 to 15 per cent of the country's overseas trade and 50 per cent of its trade with adjacent countries against the present proportions of 5 per cent and 40 per cent. The funds originally provided in the Second Plan (Rs. 48 crores) were barely enough to reach this target. With the rise in prices of both new and second-hand ships, the amount has become even more inadequate and is expected to buy less than half as much tonnage as was set in the target. It is now estimated that an additional Rs. 45 to 50 crores (almost all of it in foreign exchange) may be needed to reach the target of 900,000 GRT hoped for in the Plan period.

The question of acquiring additional tonnage is under constant review. As already noted, expansion of the Visakhapatnam shipyard has been proposed. Preparatory work on a second shipyard, probably on the West Coast is under way. India is also negotiating for purchase of ships from Yugoslavia, the United Kingdom, Germany, and the United States.

Because of the heavy burden of traffic on the railways, a Rail-Sea Coordination Committee was appointed by the Government to study the present flow of freight shipments within India, to suggest how rail and coastwise shipping could be coordinated. As a result of the Committee's recommendations, some of the traffic now being moved by rail may be diverted to coastwise shipping.

Ports and Harbors

The seaports of India are of two kinds: "major ports" administered by the Central Government, and "minor ports" administered by the

State Governments. After Partition, India was left with five major ports: Calcutta, Bombay, Madras, Cochin and Visakhapatnam.

At the beginning of the First Plan period, these ports together handled about 20 million tons of traffic a year, which was about equal to their capacity.

The programs for development, for which Rs. 37 crores was allotted in the First Plan, provided for improving and modernizing the existing major ports, constructing a marine oil terminal at Bombay, and developing a new major port at Kandla. Kandla was built to give India a substitute port on the upper northwest coast after the port of Karachi had been taken into Pakistan when India was partitioned.

As a result of work done in the First Plan, India's major ports are now able to handle about 25 million tons of traffic. This made it possible to meet some of the increased load which has developed in the past three years.

The broad aim in the Second Plan is to complete work started earlier and modernize and equip the docks for new needs arising from the economic and industrial development of the country. Rs. 40 crores have been provided in the Second Plan for all development of the major ports, which include Calcutta, Bombay, Madras, Cochin, Visakhapatnam and Kandla. Work which will be started, together with what is continued from the First Plan, is expected to cost in all about Rs. 76 crores.

Development at the various ports is expected to step up port capacity by 1961 to about 33 million tons a year. Among the important plans for Bombay port is to develop Prince's and Victoria docks to permit ships to enter at any time of the day regardless of tide, to dredge the main harbor channel, and to electrify cranes at Alexandra docks. At Calcutta, in addition to improving existing docks and berths, the Second Plan includes the construction of a general cargo berth and river training works to improve navigation in the Hooghly River.

At Madras six additional berths are to be constructed under the wet-dock scheme. Cochin will get a new coal berth, a berth at Fort

Cochin, and a berth for a second tug. At Kandla, besides completion of work started in the First Plan, two new jetties will be built for handling ore traffic, and the township at Gandhidham near the port will be developed. At Visakhapatnam, it was originally expected to build two new berths. This target may now be raised to four berths, to help handle two million tons of ore a year.

The Second Plan also provides for developing minor ports, as well, in seaboard States; for investigations on development of all-weather harbors (at Paradip, Mangalore and Malpe, and Tuticorin); and for constructing a number of lighthouses and modernizing existing ones with new standard equipment.

Inland Water Transport

India has over 5,000 miles of navigable inland waterways. The most important are those of the Lower Ganges and the Brahmaputra and its tributaries in the West Bengal basin; and, in the South, the Godavari and Krishna rivers, the backwaters and canals of the Malabar Coast (now in Kerala State) and canal systems in Madras, Andhra and Orissa.

The new multi-purpose river valley projects are producing some new inland navigation also, as, for example, the eighty-five-mile channel now connecting the Hooghly River and Calcutta with the Raniganj coal fields.

While these inland waterways were for a long time considered of only local importance, the part they can play in the whole country's transportation system—especially to help relieve pressure upon the overburdened railways—is now becoming much more clearly realized. For the first time India has, under the Second Plan, set aside some funds (Rs. 3 crores), however small, for their development. This includes development of the Buckingham Canal and the West Coast Canals. The Rs. 3 crores will be supplemented by contributions from State Governments to the Ganga Brahmaputra Board, for the Board's development projects. The Board, set up during the First Plan, has already taken up experimental projects, one on the Upper Ganges, one on the feeder rivers of Assam and the third on the Brahmaputra in Assam.

CIVIL AIR TRANSPORT

First Plan	**Rs. 23 crores**
Second Plan	**Rs. 43 crores**

India's civil aviation has grown fast since Independence, whether measured by number of cities served, passengers, freight and mail carried, or air miles flown. Today, most important cities are served by regular flights, and eighty-one aerodromes are maintained and operated by the Civil Aviation Department, compared to forty-four in 1947.

As in France or Sweden, India's air services are Government-owned. Two air corporations, the Air India International and the Indian Airlines Corporations (internal flights only), were bought from private owners, and set up as Government services in August 1953.

During the First Plan, eleven new aerodromes were constructed, and over the Second Plan eight new aerodromes and gliderdromes will be built to provide airports in all State capitals and in other important towns throughout the country.

Funds have been allotted in the Second Plan for purchase of additional aircraft and improving facilities for both the international and the domestic airlines.

FIRST PLAN   Rs. 60 crores

SECOND PLAN   Rs. 76 crores

HIGH LIGHTS
of program for
COMMUNICATIONS DEVELOPMENT

The Second Plan allocates Rs. 70 crores, a fourth again as much as the First Plan, to bringing telephone, postal, telegraph and radio facilities to more of the Indian people. The main targets are:

Expanding telephone and telegraph service, toward a future goal of service within five miles of any place in the nation.

A post office within a four-mile radius of each group of villages having a total population of 2,000.

Community radio sets for all villages of over 1,000 population.

Direct radio-telegraph, radio-telephone and radio-photo circuits between India and twenty-five additional countries.

FIRST PLAN	Rs. 60 crores

SECOND PLAN	Rs. 76 crores

HIGH LIGHTS
of programs for
COMMUNICATIONS DEVELOPMENT

The Second Plan allocates Rs. 76 crores, a fourth again as much as the First Plan, to bringing telephone, postal, telegraph and radio facilities to more of the Indian people. The main targets are:

Expanding telephone and telegraph service, toward a future goal of service within five miles of any place in the nation.

A post office within a four-mile radius of each group of villages having a total population of 2,000.

Community radio sets for all villages of over 1,000 population.

Direct radio-telegraph, radio-telephone and radio-photo circuits between India and twenty-five additional countries.

CHAPTER VI

Communications and Broadcasting

Better postal, telephone, telegraph and radio services are, of course, essential to India's expanding commerce and industry. But they are also essential to help the people emerge from the isolation of the past and keep in ready touch with the new ideas, the new programs, the new advances of their nation and the world.

All these services are, and traditionally have been, in India as in Britain, Sweden and many European countries, Government-owned and operated. During the First Plan years India progressed remarkably in their expansion and improvement.

Telephone Services: In the five years of the First Plan, 60 per cent more telephones were installed than in all previous years of Indian history. There was demand for twice the number if the instruments and equipment had been available.

The Second Plan will step up the number still more sharply until, at the end of the Plan, India will have nearly half a million, or about three times as many phones as in 1950–1951.

The long-range objective is to have trunk (long-distance) telephone service available not merely in all towns and administrative headquarters (such as block development headquarters in rural areas) but within about five miles of any place in the nation. This means very considerable expansion of exchange lines, of public call offices and of long-distance underground cables, and increasing use of automatic devices.

India makes a very large proportion of its own telephone equipment in the Indian Telephone Industries Factory (Bangalore), begun in 1948. The factory started by assembling imported parts but now has tooled itself to make 520 out of the 539 parts needed for a telephone instrument. All but two of the remaining parts are also made in India, by private firms. During the Second Plan, India expects to be able to produce 85 per cent of all the components needed for line equipment, and to turn out 40,000 exchange lines and 60,000 telephone instruments a year.

Postal Service: India inherited on Independence a well developed postal service that reached from remote Himalayan areas to the backwater villages in Malabar.

Far too few villages, however, had local post offices. Over the First Plan and Second Plan, the Indian Government will have far more than doubled the number of post offices in existence in 1950–1951, and hopes to put a post office within a four-mile reach of every group of villages with a total population of 2,000 people.

The Second Plan also expects to improve the efficiency of postal service by extending air mail routes, adding more railway mail vans, and trucks, and using more mechanical devices at major post offices.

Telegraph Service: The Second Plan will also step up the efficiency and extent of telegraph service, using more modern devices such as teleprinters, and adding a substantial number of new telegraph offices.

By the end of the Plan, the number of telegraph offices will have nearly doubled over the number in 1950–1951, and the goal for the future is an office within five miles of every place in the country.

The Second Plan allots Rs. 63 crores for expanding telephone, telegraph and postal facilities.

Overseas Communications: For extending and strengthening contacts with other countries, India needs a well developed system of overseas communication services, and the Second Plan provides for considerable expansion.

Before the First Plan India had direct radio services with six countries, but by the beginning of the Second Plan it had developed radio-telegraph circuits with fourteen countries, radio-telephone circuits with sixteen countries and radio-photo service with five countries.

During the Second Plan, it is hoped that direct radio-telegraph, telephone and photo circuits will be established with twenty-five additional countries.

Progress in COMMUNICATIONS

Local Telephones   📞 = 40,000 telephones
1950-51 📞📞📞📞 168,000
1955-56 📞📞📞📞📞 📞📞 277,600
1960-61 📞📞📞📞📞 📞📞📞📞📞 📞 457,600

Telegraph Offices   🏢 = 1,000 offices
1950-51 🏢🏢🏢🏢 3,592
1955-56 🏢🏢🏢🏢🏢 🏢 5,057
1960-61 🏢🏢🏢🏢🏢 🏢🏢 6,457

Post Offices   🏢 = 10,000 post offices
1950-51 🏢🏢🏢🏢 36,000
1955-56 🏢🏢🏢🏢🏢 🏢 54,900
1960-61 🏢🏢🏢🏢🏢 🏢🏢🏢 74,900

Community Radio Sets   📻 = 7,000 radio sets
1950-51 Negligible
1955-56 📻📻 14,000
1960-61 📻📻📻📻📻 📻📻📻📻📻 📻 74,000

Broadcasting: Shortly after India became Independent, the Government-owned All-India Radio, established in 1935, merged with the broadcasting stations of the princely states to form a nation-wide network.

By the end of the First Plan, there were twenty-six stations. Each language area had been provided with at least one transmitting station, and fairly effective coverage was given to almost all the regions in the country.

The aim during the Second Plan is to extend the services now available for all languages, and to as wide an area as possible. In some parts of the country, because of the nature of the terrain and the needs of the region, short-wave transmitters are to be installed.

For meeting the growing demands for national programs and for ensuring a country-wide hookup of national broadcasts, one 100-kw. short-wave transmitter and one 100-kw. medium-wave transmitter will be installed at Delhi. Services from Calcutta, Bombay and Madras will be made available to the entire country by the installation of 50-kw. or 100-kw. short-wave transmitters in these cities. A limited beginning will be made in the field of television.

Additional facilities for the services beamed to countries outside India will also be provided by the installation of two 100-kw. short-wave transmitters at Delhi. India now has external broadcasting services in sixteen different languages.

To promote rural listening, community receivers are to be provided in the villages with a population of 1,000 and above, to a total of 60,000 sets, and new emphasis will be put on developing programs for farmers and other rural people.

FIRST PLAN	Rs. 5 crores [1]
SECOND PLAN	Rs. 30 crores

HIGH LIGHTS
of programs for
SCIENTIFIC RESEARCH

The Second Plan allocates Rs. 30 crores to advance scientific research fostering India's industrial and technological progress, in addition to substantial amount spent on research by the universities and some ministries.[2] The main targets are:

Expanding research training and facilities in universities.

Enlarging the facilities of India's network of national laboratories.

Strengthening the atomic energy research program.

Establishing one hundred scientific research and information centers for rural people.

[1] Expenditures.
[2] Ministries of Railways, Communications, and Irrigation and Power.

CHAPTER VII

Scientific and Technical Research

In every field of India's development, pressing problems call for scientific study, investigation and applied research. Fortunately, in the last fifteen years India has developed a fairly extensive research system which can be strengthened and expanded over the Second Plan period.

Scientific research first became organized during World War II, when the stress of wartime needs gave it urgency. The then Government of India constituted the Board of Scientific and Industrial Research in 1940, and followed with the creation of the Council of Scientific and Industrial Research in 1942.

After Independence, scientific and technological research was given high priority in view of its importance for national development.

The Council of Scientific and Industrial Research was made responsible for the financing of research laboratories and for the promotion, guidance and coordination of scientific and industrial research in the country.

In the first phase of its work, the Council has set up a chain of fourteen national laboratories. They are:

The National Physical Laboratory, New Delhi.

The National Chemical Laboratory, Poona.

The National Metallurgical Laboratory, Jamshedpur.

The Central Fuel Research Institute, Dhanbad.

The Central Glass and Ceramics Research Institute, Calcutta.

The Central Drug Research Institute, Lucknow.

The Central Food Technological Research Institute, Mysore.

The Central Electro-Chemical Research Institute, Karaikudi.

The Central Leather Research Institute, Madras.

The Central Building Research Institute, Roorkee.

The Central Salt Research Institute, Bhavnagar.

The Central Electronics Engineering Research Institute, Pilani (being completed).

The National Botanical Gardens, Lucknow.

The Central Road Research Institute, New Delhi.

The national laboratories conduct fundamental and applied research, with special reference to the industries in their fields. These laboratories are actively associated with the problems of industrial development and standardization, each having its own detailed program of work drawn up by expert committees.

The Government has established a National Research Development Corporation which sets up plants to test the utility of new inventions and discoveries.

Besides the national laboratories, there are research departments in thirty-three universities, eighty-eight research institutions and research centers, and fifty-four associations for scientific and technological research. The work of the regional and State institutions is linked up with that of the national laboratories.

The First Plan provided assistance to a number of important research institutions such as the Indian Institute of Science, Bangalore; the Tata Institute of Fundamental Research, Bombay; the Indian Institute of Nuclear Physics, Calcutta; the Bose Research Institute,

Calcutta; the Indian Association for the Cultivation of Science, Calcutta; the Birbal Sahni Institute of Palaeobotany, Lucknow; and the Sri Ram Institute for Industrial Research, Delhi. In addition to these, science departments and research institutes at the universities were given aid by the Ministry of Education and the Universities Grants Commission.

The Indian National Scientific Documentation Center is now providing documentation services to the national laboratories, scientific institutions, universities and industrial concerns. In 1952 the Government of India entered into an agreement with UNESCO, under which UNESCO agreed to provide technical assistance for the organization of the Center.

The Council of Scientific and Industrial Research brings out reports, monographs and bulletins which discuss the activities of the research committees and the national laboratories, and publishes two monthly journals, the *Journal of Scientific and Industrial Research*, in English, and *Vigyan Pragati*, in Hindi. An important publication of the Council is the *Dictionary of Indian Raw Materials and Industrial Products*, popularly known as the Wealth of India, to be completed in ten volumes.

The Second Five Year Plan has earmarked Rs. 20 crores, in addition to Rs. 10 crores for current expenses, for the development programs of the Council of Scientific and Industrial Research. The purpose is to enlarge present laboratory facilities and bring the results of scientific research to bear more closely upon vital problems of industrial development. As under the First Plan, the University Grants Commission will spend a substantial amount of scientific and technological research in the universities, totaling Rs. 16 crores over the Second Plan period.

The new research institutions to be established over the Second Plan include a Mining Research station at Dhanbad, a Central Mechanical Engineering Institute near Calcutta, a National Biological Laboratory, a Science and Industry Museum, and a regional laboratory in Assam. A salt research station is to be set up in Sambar in Rajasthan for the exploitation of the valuable Sambar salt bitterns.

Centers or units are also to be started for research work in the fields of gas turbines, rain and cloud physics, essential oils, wind power and medicinal plants. Investigations on the replacing of coking coals by non-coking coals in the smelting of iron ore are also to be carried out on a pilot-plant basis. The research committees of the Council have drawn up a comprehensive program of work for the various units. Under programs of many of the Ministries, such as Agriculture, Health, Irrigation and Power, Railways, and Communications, considerable research will be done. Counting these with all other research programs, India will be spending about Rs. 50 crores on research.

ATOMIC DEVELOPMENT

In the field of atomic research, India has made an excellent start. India created an Atomic Commission as early as 1948 to lay the foundation of the country's atomic development.

Its immediate aims were the promotion of nuclear research, the survey, prospecting and processing of raw materials, and the setting up of an experimental reactor.

India's long-term objective is the generation of power from atomic energy to light the countryside, to give power to industries, and supply tools to science to improve agriculture and to fight disease.

Some phases of India's atomic energy work have already been discussed. As far as basic research is concerned, the work is largely concentrated in the Tata Institute of Fundamental Research, Bombay. India has done good work in the field of primary cosmic-ray radiations, nuclear collisions and research into the life of mesons at high altitudes. Important work has also been done at the Bose Institute and the Institute of Nuclear Physics in Calcutta and other research centers.

The Department of Atomic Energy was opened in 1954, and the work of setting up the Atomic Energy Establishment was started at Trombay (near Bombay) in the following year. The Establishment consists of three main groups, for physical, chemical and engineering research. It has a staff of two hundred (it is to have eight hundred by 1959), and has facilities for pilot-plant experiments. A "swimming pool" reactor went into operation in mid-1956 to produce isotopes for biological, medical and industrial research. A high-power, high-flux reactor received under the Colombo Plan will start operating in 1958.

DISSEMINATING SCIENTIFIC KNOWLEDGE

Among the associations which disseminate scientific knowledge are the Indian Science Congress Association, the National Institute of Science, New Delhi, and the Indian Academy of Sciences, Bangalore. These associations publish academic journals and provide forums for scientific thought and discussion. Similar work is undertaken by associations representing different branches of modern science, such as the Indian Physical Society and the Indian Chemical Society.

One of India's interesting and special problems is how to bring some knowledge of science to rural areas. The Second Plan includes a program to establish about one hundred rural Vigyan Mandirs ("Temples of Knowledge"). Their function is to help and advise villagers on how to use the benefits of science and research in agriculture, health, sanitation, and so on.

METRIC SYSTEM AND STANDARDIZATION

The Government made the important decision in early 1956 to adopt the metric system, in order to standardize weights and measures all over the country. The Government felt that a reform of this kind is best introduced in the early stages of industrialization, and introduced gradually, so that it will involve only a minimum of problems. As a prelude to the reform, decimal coinage was introduced on April 1, 1957.

An Indian Standards Institution was established in 1946, to improve quality and uniformity of grades of industrial products and processes.

SECTION III

THE SOCIAL SERVICES

FIRST PLAN	Rs. 170 crores
SECOND PLAN	Rs. 307 crores

HIGH LIGHTS
of programs for
EDUCATION

The Second Plan will spend nearly twice as much on the advancement of education as did the First Plan, to achieve these main targets:

8 million more children in primary school.

800,000 more young people in secondary school.

27 per cent more teachers in training.

Rural higher education for village young people.

Intensive emphasis on technical training.

Reforms in quality and character of secondary and higher education.

275,000 scholarships for primary, secondary and higher education for all groups.

CHAPTER I

Education

When India won Independence its education system had to be adapted, both in quality and in quantity, to the needs of a developing nation.

The new Government's first need was to make schooling available to more of its young people so that education was no longer the privilege of the few. Here the first task was to increase rapidly the number of schools, and very particularly of elementary and secondary schools. The new Constitution committed India to provide compulsory education for all Indian children through the age of fourteen.

The second need was to change the character of education from primary school upward so that Indian youth of all classes might be trained in the independence of thought and action, in the sense of social responsibility, in the skills and knowledge demanded of citizens

333

of a free and developing India. For this purpose, the Government [1] appointed a series of eminent commissions to diagnose the problems of the education system, and prescribed sweeping principles of reform.

Elementary Education

The cost of free primary education for all of India is of Himalayan proportions. A recent estimate indicates it would cost over a fifth as much as the entire Second Plan. India's swiftly rising population compounds the problem. By the end of the Second Plan nearly 3 million more children will be added to the already vast total of 48 millions of primary school age.

At the opening of the First Plan, fewer than half of all children eligible were in school. The First Five Year Plan set a goal of 60 per cent. It did not reach this high target, although over 6 million more children went to school—a very sizable number by any standard. In areas under community development where particular stress is placed on schools, doubled and even quadrupled school attendance was not uncommon.

The Second Plan hopes to raise the total number in elementary school by nearly 8 million more, so that by the end of 1961, about two-thirds of all children of primary age may have at least a chance to start the climb up the education ladder to opportunity. So-called "middle schools," which take children from eleven to fourteen years, will also be expanded—by over a million pupils.

The State Governments also worked on improving the quality of elementary education. Chiefly, they urged adoption of the craft-centered "basic" education first evolved by Mahatma Gandhi—a learn-by-doing system. While by the end of the Plan the number of (new or converted) basic schools and their pupils had multiplied six fold, India feels that, in general, progress has been too slow.

[1] In India, as under the federal system of the United States, education is the financial and administrative concern of the States, and two-thirds of both the First and the Second Plan budgets consist of State, not Center, funds. The Union Government, however, plays a very substantial role in formulating education policy at all levels through conferences and consultations with State education authorities.

Under the Second Plan, elementary education gets somewhat less funds than under the First Plan. But the amount will be supplemented by Rs. 12 crores for general education provided under the rural development program, almost all of which will go to elementary schools.

The cost of universal primary schooling is so great that the Second Plan frankly admits that the chief hope for making it possible lies in local communities bearing some of the cost of both schools and teachers. This practice, long familiar in village India, is now becoming more widespread.

The rural development program has shown, moreover, that education stands high on the villagers' scale of values; villagers have contributed in labor and materials up to half of the cost of their new schools. With these means, and with some help, such as authority to levy a local school tax (recommended in the Second Plan), India's villagers may yet win what they, like the people of other

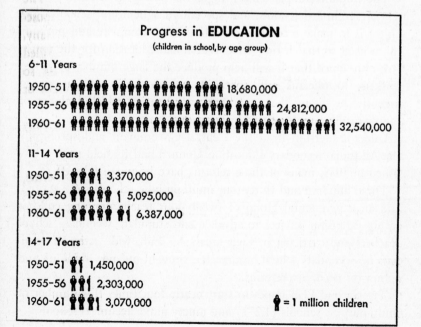

Progress in EDUCATION
(children in school, by age group)

6-11 Years

1950-51 18,680,000
1955-56 24,812,000
1960-61 32,540,000

11-14 Years

1950-51 3,370,000
1955-56 5,095,000
1960-61 6,387,000

14-17 Years

1950-51 1,450,000
1955-56 2,303,000
1960-61 3,070,000

= 1 million children

nations, so cherish—the privilege of universal primary education for their children.

Secondary Education

In secondary education the significant advances under the First Plan have been in the direction of quality, and the Second Plan's main effort will be to go ahead with the reforms already started.

In general, these have followed the recommendations of the Secondary Education Commission which laid down these major principles of reform: diversification of the study programs to prepare students for vocations other than Government service and university entrance; reform in both teaching and examinations to encourage active learning rather than rote memorizing; relating studies to the community and to good citizenship; raising the economic and professional status of teachers and headmasters.

The Commission particularly urged the setting up of multi-purpose schools, technical schools, and specialized agricultural schools. The object is to make secondary education more complete and purposeful in itself so that it may serve as terminal education for the many. It is also hoped that it will help produce the large number of skilled workers, technicians and specialists whom India now needs so urgently, by giving them a secondary education which includes or can be readily supplemented by vocational training.

Under leadership from the Central Government and specifically the All-India Secondary Education Council and its field staff, established in 1955, many of these reforms have begun to take effect.

Three hundred and thirty-four multi-purpose schools were started, and an experimental group of twenty-four teacher-training colleges set up extension services to advance and stimulate secondary school teachers and curricula in their areas. An India-wide series of seminars for secondary school headmasters brought out new thinking and action on necessary reforms.

The Second Plan hopes to start nearly four times this number of multi-purpose schools (1,271) and ninety junior technical schools.

Reforms in secondary education are the more urgent since attendance is rising rapidly. Over the First Plan, the number of secondary students increased by more than half; by the end of the Second it is expected to be double what it was in 1950–51.

Higher Education

The Second Plan allocates to university education nearly four times as much as did the First Plan (Rs. 57 crores against Rs. 15 crores). Most of it will go to improve and expand technical and scientific education in the universities, to fill the pressing demands for skilled and trained personnel for a developing nation.

At the same time, very real efforts will be made to improve the liberal arts colleges, stressing quality more than expansion. College enrollment has been rising very rapidly; even in the last five years alone, it has gone up almost 80 per cent. In some colleges and universities, where staff and facilities could not expand fast enough to keep pace, this has brought about serious overcrowding and a lowering of standards.

Reform measures being undertaken through the newly established University Grants Commission include: instituting three-year degree courses, organization of tutorials, emphasis on the social and natural sciences and the humanities with special relation to Indian life and needs.

It is hoped that by adopting higher standards and strengthening secondary schools, the flood tide of students seeking higher degrees can at least be prevented from rising higher. It is also being considered whether a university degree should continue to be a requirement for Government service—which is, of course, among the chief reasons for the rush to the colleges.

Some expansion of college facilities is, however, being planned. Seven new universities will be added; and many existing colleges will get new buildings, hostels and laboratories and libraries. Research scholarships and an urgently needed increase in faculty salaries are also proposed.

A special problem for India is rural higher education. Almost wholly urban and academic in character, Indian college training has long tended to widen the gulf between city and village, between the "educated" few and the millions of peasants.

During the First Plan the Government took two steps to provide higher education that is meaningful to and can serve India's rural people.

One is the development of Janata (people's) Colleges or "Folk Schools" taking some inspiration from the Danish Folk Schools which played such an important part in Denmark's rural development. For a number of years, in Mysore and elsewhere, India has been experimenting with various types of folk schools. With reinforced stimulus from study of the Danish and other efforts, the Second Plan proposes a number of such colleges, beginning with about one to every State.

An equally important proposal is to initiate some type of rural university which can train village young people for service and citizenship in rural areas, conduct research on rural problems and do extension work in neighboring villages. Over the Second Plan, ten Rural Higher Institutes will be developed.

At the same time, India's agricultural colleges and the special training centers for rural development work are, as we have seen, expanding considerably.

GIRLS' EDUCATION

Education of girls lags far behind that of boys, as was true during the development of the West. In primary grades (6–11), only a third of all girls go to school, against two-thirds of all boys. Only 3 per cent of girls get to secondary school at all. While the number of girls going to college has gone up considerably, they still constitute only 15 per cent of all college students. Future Five Year Plans will put their greatest stress on girls' education, and India is making a special effort during the Second Plan to train the women teachers who will be needed. In 1956 four teachers out of five were men.

TECHNICAL EDUCATION

Intense emphasis and funds will be placed on technical education over the Second Plan. The problem, so intimately part of India's problems of skilled manpower resources, has been discussed in the chapter on manpower and employment.

TEACHERS AND TEACHER TRAINING

Basic to any effort to improve Indian education is the raising of teachers' salaries at least to reasonable levels of living, and the expansion and improvement of teacher training.

Average salaries are currently Rs. 35 ($7) a month for primary teachers; Rs. 75 ($15) for secondary. To raise them to levels which would draw and hold adequate teachers would dip heavily into India's resources. One estimate puts it at $32 million a year for elementary teachers alone.

The need is so urgent, however, that under the Second Plan the Central Government has agreed to assist the States up to 50 per cent of the cost of additional expenditures needed to raise salaries of primary teachers.

But the Government feels that basically the responsibility is up to the States, and again urges putting more financial responsibility on local communities. In rural development areas the villagers are being encouraged to accept partial support of schoolteachers, by giving them grants of land or part of the harvest, and by providing living quarters. This points to an important new solution.

Teacher training is a sizable problem in India. Over a third of all India's primary teachers and nearly half of all secondary teachers are untrained. While the number of trained teachers increased over the First Plan period, there is still a long way to go. The means by which it is hoped to increase training facilities and the proportion of trained teachers have been discussed in the chapter on manpower.

LITERACY AND ADULT EDUCATION

No new census was available at the end of the First Plan period to show how successfully India progressed against illiteracy. Some progress certainly was made in the areas under the rural development program, where literacy classes reached nearly one million adults.

Very rough estimates assume that literacy may have risen from 20 per cent in 1950–1951 to about 25 per cent in 1956.[1] Efforts so far, however, have made clear that literacy teaching is most successful when part of a general program of community development. The Second Plan allots a total of Rs. 15 crores to literacy teaching and social education, Rs. 10 crores to be spent under the rural development program where motivation for literacy is highest.

SCHOLARSHIPS

To prevent education from continuing to be, as in India it historically has been, the privilege of the élite, the Indian Government has for some time had an extensive system of special scholarships, principally for backward and so-called "scheduled" castes.

Under the Second Plan, the Government has so extended and diversified its scholarships that a fair proportion of all students with ability and aptitude, who wish to do higher studies or research, should be able to get financial help. There are also special scholarships for artists and musicians. A total of Rs. 12 crores is allotted for new scholarship programs. These, with Central and State programs already in effect, will provide 275,000 scholarships. This is in addition to a large number of fellowships and scholarships, totaling well over 3 million, which have been provided for scheduled castes, tribals and other underprivileged groups.

OTHER PROGRAMS

The Indian Ministry of Education has other important functions of cultural integration and development for which the Second Plan has provided. These include: promotion of Hindi and of the

[1] Omitting children up to ten years of age.

regional languages; a National Book Trust to promote publication of good literature in the regional languages; establishing a Sanskrit University and Sanskrit studies; support of the newly formed Academies of Letters, of Dance, Drama, and Music, and of the Fine Arts; development of India's museums; of the National Library (Calcutta); of the Departments of Archives and Anthropology; and the opening of a Central Institute of Indology.

FIRST PLAN	Rs. 140 crores
SECOND PLAN	Rs. 274 crores

HIGH LIGHTS
of programs for
HEALTH

The Second Plan will spend almost double as much as the First Plan to raise health standards and services, with these main targets:

MORE HOSPITALS AND HEALTH CENTERS

30,000 (24 per cent) more hospital beds.

3,000 more health centers in rural areas.

MORE AND BETTER TRAINED MEDICAL PERSONNEL

12,500 more doctors.

15,000 more nurses and midwives.

WIDER CONTROL OF COMMUNICABLE DISEASES

Malaria: The control program will be extended to cover the entire population now exposed to malaria.

Tuberculosis: The mass BCG inoculation campaign will be extended to entire susceptible population below twenty-five years of age.

AN ACTIVE CAMPAIGN ON ENVIRONMENTAL SANITATION

Funds doubled for rural and urban pure drinking water systems and sanitation.

New emphasis on health education.

FAMILY PLANNING

A high-level Central Board to direct research, training and a national family planning service.

500 Family Planning Clinics in cities and towns; 2,000 clinics for rural areas.

CHAPTER II

Health

To provide even minimum medical care on a nation-wide basis is at present beyond India's resources in money or trained personnel. Both the First and Second Plans have, therefore, focused on disease prevention and on building the framework of adequate health services.

The gains made over the First Plan were real, if modest in relation to need. An extensive and effective malaria control program, a mass BCG inoculation campaign (believed to be the largest in the world), a start on providing primary health centers and centers for maternity and child care, improved medical education and training —these were some of the First Plan's accomplishments. The eagerness of the people for medical help, even in the most backward villages, was established beyond question; as was the overwhelming need for a new approach to rural people in teaching sanitation and disease prevention.

343

While figures for the last First Plan Year are not yet available, and health statistics in India are not comprehensive, there is clearly a trend to health improvement. For example, infant mortality dropped from 127 per 1,000 live births in 1950 to 113 in 1954.

The Second Plan, with double the funds [1] of the First Plan, will intensify the programs already started, preventive services being given, as before, the high priority. Among the recent programs, nation-wide family planning is one of outstanding importance.

More Hospital and Health Centers

While the First Plan increased the total number of hospitals, dispensaries and health centers by about 16 per cent over all, and doubled the number of rural clinics, there are still far too few. Hospitals continue to be mostly in large towns and cities. Many hospitals, urban or rural, are poorly equipped, understaffed and do not come up to acceptable standards.

Under the Second Plan Rs. 43 crores will go to increase the number of hospital facilities, and to improve equipment, services and staff in present institutions. What is aimed at is a four-part integrated regional system of hospitals which would include the teaching hospital, the District hospital, the tehsil hospital, and the rural medical center associated with a health unit.

The Government considers bringing more adequate health service to the villages by far the most urgent program of the Second Plan period. The object is to set up about one primary or central health unit in as many of the rural development blocks as possible. While one health unit cannot serve a block of one hundred villages adequately, it will at least be the cornerstone for a future expanded and comprehensive service. About three thousand new centers are proposed over the Second Plan at a cost of Rs. 23 crores.

---

[1] Although under the Indian Constitution, health is largely in the hands of the States, and State expenditures make up two-thirds of the total health budget of the Second Plan, all health plans are carried out as a joint venture of the Central and State Governments.

Training of Health Personnel

The urgent needs are to increase training facilities, and improve the quality of training with special emphasis on preventive medicine and techniques of public health education. The Second Plan's proposals have been discussed in the chapter on India's manpower problems.

Medical Research

Since Independence, India has set up several institutes for medical research, as well as for research on leprosy, on cancer, on drugs, on mental health. Over the Second Plan, an Institute of Biology, and one for Occupational Health, will be started and the present Virus Research Center at Poona expanded into a full-fledged institute.

In general, however, medical research now receives too little attention. To stimulate interest in research work, to train research personnel, and increase research facilities in the colleges and in special institutions, the Indian Council of Medical Research proposes to set up a cadre of trained men.

It also proposes, in addition to the nine specialized research units it has already organized in university departments and institutes, to start new units for study of mycology, parasitology, and pediatrics. Special research projects are planned on nutrition, drugs, industrial health, maternal and child health, tuberculosis and environmental hygiene.

Laboratory facilities for clinical and public health purposes are becoming more and more important to health administration. The Second Plan will set up and expand facilities to help in disease control programs and on food and drug adulteration problems.

The Second Plan allots Rs. 6.5 crores for developing indigenous systems of medicine (such as the Ayurvedic system), principally to bring their teaching institutions up to a standard that will enable them to undertake research. It is of interest that *Rauwolfia serpentina*, the drug now used in the West for treatment of mental illness, high blood pressure and as tranquilizers, was developed from India's indigenous medicines.

Wider Control of Communicable Diseases

Communicable diseases—that is, diseases which are preventable—have traditionally accounted for half of all deaths in India. Their prevention has, therefore, a high priority.

Malaria is India's foremost public health problem. About 200 million people in India live in malarial areas. While exact data are lack-

Progress in HEALTH

Medical Institutions   ⌂ = 1,200 institutions

1950-51   ⌂ ⌂ ⌂ ⌂ ⌂   ⌂ ⌂ ⌂ 8,600
1955-56   ⌂ ⌂ ⌂ ⌂ ⌂   ⌂ ⌂ ⌂ ⌂ 10,000
1960-61   ⌂ ⌂ ⌂ ⌂ ⌂   ⌂ ⌂ ⌂ ⌂ ⌂ ⌂ 12,600

Rural Health Centers   ▥ = 500 health centers

1950-51   Negligible
1955-56   ▥ ▥ 725
1960-61   ▥ ▥ ▥ ▥ ▥   ▥ ▥ ▥ 3,725

People Protected from Malaria   ♟ = 10 million people

1950-51   Negligible
1955-56   ♟ ♟ ♟ ♟ ♟ ♟ ♟ ♟ ♟ ♟ ♟ 112,000,000
1960-61   ♟ ♟ ♟ ♟ ♟ ♟ ♟ ♟ ♟ ♟ ♟ ♟ ♟ ♟ ♟ ♟ ♟ ♟ ♟ ♟ 200,000,000

B.C.G. Vaccination Program (number of persons vaccinated)   ♟ = 10 million people

1950-51   ♟ 3,250,000
1955-56   ♟ ♟ ♟ ♟ ♟ ♟ ♟ 71,170,000
1960-61   ♟ ♟ ♟ ♟ ♟ ♟ ♟ ♟ ♟ ♟ ♟ ♟ ♟ ♟ ♟ ♟ ♟ ♟ ♟ ♟ 200,000,000
                                                                 (approx.)

Doctors Available   ♟ = 5,000 doctors

1950-51   ♟ ♟ ♟ ♟ ♟ ♟ ♟ ♟ ♟ ♟ ♟ ♟ 59,000
1955-56   ♟ ♟ ♟ ♟ ♟ ♟ ♟ ♟ ♟ ♟ ♟ ♟ ♟ ♟ 70,000
1960-61   ♟ ♟ ♟ ♟ ♟ ♟ ♟ ♟ ♟ ♟ ♟ ♟ ♟ ♟ ♟ ♟ ♟ 82,500

ing, it is estimated that until recently some 57 million persons a year suffered from malaria; and possibly 800,000 a year died from it.

The First Plan's nation-wide control program which cut incidence of malaria in half in the first year alone, covered, by the end of the Plan, 132 million people. Studies indicate that the program has been important in raising agricultural production; it not only relieved individual farmers of disease, but made it possible to cultivate once malaria-infected lands.

The Second Plan will use Rs. 28 crores to extend the program to give full protection to all the 200 million people living in malarious areas. Eradication of malaria is now a foreseeable possibility, and an eradication campaign may be undertaken in the last years of the Plan.

Filariasis: Filariasis, also a mosquito-borne disease, affects about 25 million people in India. Mosquito control and hetrazen treatment in all affected areas are the Second Plan's proposed methods of prevention. To the thirteen control units set up over the First Plan, sixty-five new units will be added.

Tuberculosis ranks next to malaria as India's greatest killer. In 1951 it was estimated to cause as many as half a million deaths a year. The mass BCG (Bacillus Calmette Guerin) vaccination campaign begun in the First Plan is believed to be the largest of its kind undertaken in any country. Over seventy million people were tuberculin-tested, 24.5 million were vaccinated. The campaign will be expanded under the Second Plan to cover the entire susceptible population under twenty-five years old.

At least one TB clinic will be provided for each district, and clinics already operating will be brought up to a higher standard. Fifteen new demonstration and training centers will be established and four thousand new beds provided, with facilities for isolation of advanced cases and for aftercare.

Leprosy: Not less than a million and a half people in India suffer from leprosy. The incidence varies from the average rate of 2 to 4 per cent, to as high as 15 to 20 per cent in some villages, particularly in the east coast and the South.

Leprosy colonies are not feasible in India, and sulphone therapy fortunately makes a new approach possible. The First Plan set up a teaching and research institute in Madras, four treatment and study centers and thirty-six subsidiary centers for treatment. The Second Plan will add eighty-eight more subsidiary centers and provide for isolation care and rehabilitation.

Venereal Diseases: Shortly before the First Plan began, extensive field surveys in venereal diseases, assisted by the World Health Organization and UNICEF, were undertaken in Himachal Pradesh; four clinics were established and medical personnel from various parts of the country were given training in control methods and in the use of recent laboratory techniques. During the Plan period fifty VD clinics were set up, and seventeen received equipment from UNICEF. A plant for producing antigen, which is used in the diagnosis of venereal diseases, began production in 1954. Training centers were established in Delhi and at the Madras General Hospital. An expert committee for venereal diseases has been established under the Indian Council of Medical Research for advising on research problems, and cooperative research arrangements have been made between various laboratories.

Over the Second Plan, the general objective is to begin the attack on three fronts—educational, epidemiological and therapeutic, with special stress on prevention of parental syphilis.

An Active Campaign on Environmental Sanitation

Most communicable diseases are due directly or indirectly to India's extremely low standards of public health and sanitation in both city and village—to contaminated water supplies, improper disposal of human feces, poor housing, diseases carried by flies or rats, and the like.

Water supply and sanitation programs were begun over the First Plan, and in community development areas alone, nearly 100,000 sanitary drinking water wells were built or renovated and thousands of yards of drains constructed.

Yet on the whole there was far too little progress. Partly to blame were shortage of materials (especially iron pipe), of trained public health education and engineering staff, and of adequate organization.

The Second Plan provides Rs. 91 crores (nearly double the funds of the First Plan) for drinking-water supply and sanitation programs. Two-thirds of the amount will go to city areas, one-third to rural areas.

A Bureau of Health Education was set up in November 1956 in the Central Health Ministry; some of the States have added public health engineering and health education departments. India's first Public Health Association, formed in October 1956, represents the mounting interest in this critical field.

For the villages, a special research-cum-action program has been started to determine for the first time on a scientific basis how environmental hygiene, and particularly the use of latrines, can be taught to and understood by rural people, and how their old customs can be changed to conform to new knowledge of disease prevention.

Maternal and Child Health

While infant and maternal mortality rates have gone down over recent years, they are still appallingly high, especially in rural areas. The Government's objective is to provide maternal and child care centers attached to rural health units, and greatly to increase the number of trained midwives available in the villages.

In the Community Development areas, a good number (578) of maternity and child health centers were built during the First Plan with the help of funds and labor of the villagers themselves. Nearly four times as many more (2,100) will be built over the Second Plan. Over 36,000 local midwives will be given training. As a start on reducing child mortality, five pediatrics training institutions, training specifically for work in rural maternity centers, are to be set up.

Nutrition: India's low nutrition standards are partly due to poverty, partly to lack of education on use of protective foods, especially for children and expectant mothers. Nutrition teaching is an important part of the women's extension work programs planned for rural areas. The Indian Council of Medical Research proposes nutrition research; national nutrition surveys are planned, and establishment of nutrition laboratories and diet kitchens.

Family Planning

Control of population is, as we have seen, one of the decisive factors in India's efforts to raise standards of living.

During the First Plan period, a small beginning was made in experimental family planning centers, in demographic research, and in testing of various methods for use with a largely illiterate and poor population lacking sanitary facilities. The studies indicated the great acceptability of family planning and readiness to seek help. In 1955–1956 the Government took the major decision to make family planning an intensive nation-wide program during the Second Plan period.

The Government considers family planning, not narrowly as a way to control population, but as a priority health service. Its objectives are to improve maternal and child health through child spacing and through family limitation where indicated for medical and economic reasons; to help raise family living standards; to stabilize population at a level consistent with the national economy; and, through sterility and fertility clinics, to help childless couples to parenthood.

General direction of the program is vested in a Family Planning Board, established within the Ministry of Health in October 1956 as an advisory body, to determine policy and specific programs and review and evaluate progress. Over the Second Plan, the chief programs proposed are:

Family Planning Advice and Service: There will be family planning units in each of the two thousand primary health centers in rural areas, and some five hundred centers in the cities.

Setting Up Adequate Training Centers: Two centers have already been set up, one of which, the All-India Institute of Family Planning (training and research) in Bombay, emphasizes training for urban work. The other, in Mysore State, will devote itself largely to training for family planning work in rural areas.

Biological and Medical Field Research: Two studies already begun, in the Punjab and in West Bengal, are experimenting with contraceptive methods, and the best ways to provide family planning service. The Bengal field survey is being assisted by the Rockefeller Foundation. Preliminary study in the Punjab indicates the foam tablet as the most acceptable method. At the Indian Cancer Research Institute, a center for testing contraceptives has been set up.

Demographic research is essential to long-range planning of the program, and a Demographic Center has now been established in Bombay. The Center will be developed into a regional organization in collaboration with the United Nations to serve the needs of other Asian countries as well. It will receive financial assistance from the United Nations and the Population Council of New York.

FIRST PLAN   Rs. 7 crores

SECOND PLAN   Rs. 29 crores

HIGH LIGHTS
of programs for
LABOR

The Second Plan, with over four times the funds of the First Plan, will seek to increase labor's share and participation in India's progress and to strengthen the labor movement. These are the main targets:

The strengthening of trade unions.

A new, extensive program of workers' education.

Labor-management cooperation in production problems.

An expanded and integrated social security system.

Trebling of training facilities for craftsmen and skilled workers.

Expanded vocational and employment services.

Stepped-up program of industrial housing.

Labor

India's emphasis on industrialization over the next five years brings into new focus the role of industrial labor. While the number of industrial workers is small—about 7 million out of a total labor force of 154 million, another 750,000 will be added over the Second Plan alone.

The degree to which the growing labor force shares in the benefits of industrial progress and is made to feel its importance in building the nation will be a measure of India's whole effort to raise incomes and levels of living, to go forward without class conflicts toward a stable productive society. The increasing role of Government in industry high-lights the responsibility of Government to develop and pursue labor policies that will lead to labor's greatest cooperation and advancement.

The coming of Independence itself marked a new day for Indian labor, and the Directive Principles of the Indian Constitution gave recognition of economic rights that had long been neglected.

In general, the Indian Government's policy on labor is based on principles evolved by Mahatma Gandhi, who, as we have seen, had very particular concern for labor's place in society, and for the avoidance of class conflict.

These principles are: (1) non-violence; (2) arbitration and adjudication to settle labor disputes; (3) increasing participation of workers in management; (4) joint "trusteeship" of management and labor and a realization that they have common aims in national progress; (5) emphasis on a reform program which would provide improved education, housing, health, credit and other benefits. In various ways these principles have been incorporated in both First and Second Five Year Plans.

The First Plan brought progress in improved industrial relations, a rise in real earnings, and in the expansion of social security, in the setting up of some labor legislation and machinery for adjudicating disputes.

A Central Labor Institute was established to study problems of productivity, especially in relation to working conditions and health and safety factors. Labor welfare centers, and a considerable program of industrial housing, were begun.

In the Second Plan, the Government took the occasion to restate its policy objectives for the five-year period, as well as to set out specific programs for labor's advancement:

Trade Unions

The Government believes that a strong trade union movement is necessary in a democracy, both for safeguarding the interests of labor and for achieving targets of production.

The trade union movement in India suffers from some major handicaps. There are too many small local unions; many do not have enough funds. As a result, many unions lack bargaining strength and there is disunity among the rank and file. Although some national federations are being formed, the national, regional and industry-wide side to union organization is not generally developed. Each of the major unions is affiliated with a specific political party. This has led to some strengths, and also some obvious weaknesses.

There are many reasons for these various handicaps. Present trade union legislation needs revision, since much of it is based on conditions that no longer hold good. For example, as few as seven employees now may form a union eligible for registration. Many industrial workers, moreover, come from the villages and expect to return, and in the past have not regarded their factory jobs as a permanent way of life; therefore they have not seen the need of union membership. Union dues are very low and payments far behind.

Relatively few union leaders have as yet come from the ranks of labor itself, but are "outsiders." While many of these outside leaders have greatly helped to organize and lead the largely illiterate workers, the stage has now been reached when the number of outsiders in union management can be restricted, so that union leaders can be drawn from the ranks of the workers themselves.

But even with these weaknesses, an impressive number of workers, 2.5 million, or about a third of the industrial labor force, belong to unions, and an increasing number realize that they must organize effectively to share the benefits of, and act as partners in, the nation's progress.

An intensive program of labor education is agreed to be the key to achieve the Government's and labor's objective of a strong, democratic and responsible labor movement. The Second Plan has given Rs. 5 million to labor education, and in early 1957 the Government recruited a combined Indian and foreign (United Kingdom, Sweden, United States) labor team to draw up recommendations for effective national labor education programs.

The team's key recommendations are:

Setting up a nation-wide organization for labor education, composed of representatives of labor, management, education and Government to form policy and education programs, for workers and union leaders at every level;

Preparation of all types of audio-visual and other educational materials;

Creation of a more favorable "climate" for labor education through strengthening the trade union movement, coordination of the various items of labor legislation affecting unions, and the setting by the Government of an example as an ideal employer.

The Government is moving rapidly to carry out these recommendations.

The Second Plan also advocates improvements in State laws in regard to union recognition, in order to reduce the number of unions and allay the chaotic relationships among them.

Industrial Relations

Industrial peace is vital to the nation's progress. The Government believes that this can best be achieved by the parties themselves in mutual negotiation, conciliation and voluntary arbitration, and, only where necessary, through adjudication.

India has since Independence developed an elaborate system of labor legislation and conciliation machinery, and recent efforts have been made to overhaul, consolidate and strengthen it.

The success of collective bargaining in India, as elsewhere, depends, of course, on the character of the relationship between employers and workers. Where Indian unions are too small or weak for effective bargaining, or where, on either side, there is an atmosphere of suspicion and fear, it is inevitable that one or both parties have tended to fall back upon adjudication rather than attempt to work through the alternative processes of settlement. Adjudication is sought from the various industrial tribunals set up in the States, or the higher Government conciliation machinery. To handle adjudication, India has a three-tier system of industrial courts; it has also simplified procedure for the settlement of disputes and speeded up the time taken for decisions.

Collective bargaining has, however, had appreciable success in the major industries. Controversial subjects upon which agreements have been reached include the perennial bonus issue (a form of wage increase), productivity and measures for joint consultation.

Both employers and workers have complained that inadequate enforcement often deprives them of the rights conferred by labor legislation, or arrived at through awards and agreements. The Second Plan recommends that an adequate agency, at the Center and in the States, should be built up to investigate and, where necessary, to deal with the violation of labor laws. A Standing Industrial Tribunal, armed with suitable powers in the case of non-compliance, has been recommended to ensure that awards are carried out.

To help bring about mutual understanding and a common approach to industrial problems, the Government, in the Second Plan, also urges use of the joint consultative machinery available at the Center, in the States and, in individual plants, with works committees.

The non-official Joint Consultative Board of Industry and Labor, reconstituted in April 1954, offers a common forum in which unions and management, with some public members, can get together to frame sound labor policy and iron out differences. The Board has already achieved some success in solving problems through mutual consultation and negotiation. Its activities have been widened and it has undertaken the study and discussion of a number of controversial issues, including wages, profit sharing, productivity and discipline. Similar bipartite negotiating machinery is to be set up in the States and at the plant levels. This will provide a two-way flow of consultation on problems and ways to solve them. At the plant level, a Works Committee will be used with a clear demarcation between its duties and those of the representative union.

In a developing democracy, the burden of responsibility for increased productivity and harmonious labor relations must be shared equally among the management, the technicians and the workers. India feels that the common goal—increased industrial production and greater benefits for workers—requires identity of purpose and a united effort as between labor and management. The Plan recommends that councils of management representing both labor and management should be set up in selected industries.

In the winter of 1956–1957 an official Study Group went to survey the working of the systems of labor cooperation in management in Europe [1] and to suggest how India might use or adapt such systems to its own conditions. The report of the Study Group has emphasized that: (1) a sustained educational program can help in improving attitudes; (2) joint consultation should be "built in"; (3) permissive legislation for setting up such joint councils should provide the framework, but procedures should be developed through joint consultation; and (4) Government should provide an advisory service on personnel management.

WAGES

Wages and wage issues are in India, as elsewhere, one of the major causes of industrial disputes. On the whole, Indian labor, through what are called "dearness allowances" added to basic wages, has managed just to keep abreast of the steep (271 per cent) war and post-war rise in living costs. There was a 50.3 per cent increase in real wages between 1946 and 1954, which served largely to restore real earnings to pre-war levels and even, by 1954,[2] to make some slight advance. But this was not true of all sections even of organized industry.

A wage policy which will assure labor of a fair share in industrial progress must be evolved, and is admittedly difficult. Marginal units with low wage structures are a "drag" on raising wages elsewhere, as is widespread unemployment.

Higher wages must also be related to productivity. While productivity has risen over 38 per cent between 1946 and 1954, recent studies by ILO experts show that Indian industry can go a long way toward greater productivity, even though poorly equipped. Better plant layouts and working conditions alone can lead to large increases in productivity.

[1] France, Germany, Sweden, Belgium, the United Kingdom, Yugoslavia.
[2] 1954 index = 102.7; 1939 = 100.

Few comprehensive wage and cost-of-living data are available, or kept current. To evolve a wage policy, a wage census and a realistic cost-of-living index are essential. Both will be undertaken over the Second Plan.

Until a general wage policy is evolved, peaceful settlement of wage disputes is, of course, necessary. It is recommended that tripartite wage boards—representatives of labor and management under an independent chairman—be set up over the Second Plan for individual industries in different areas.

SOCIAL SECURITY

Social security has made a beginning in India but still has a long way to go. In addition to the provident funds and welfare schemes of various industries, such as the Coal Mines Provident Fund, and funds for Government employees, there are two principal social security schemes for factory workers.

One is the Employees State Insurance Act of 1948, a pioneer measure of social and health insurance for India. Largely because workers' families have not been included in benefits, it has not made the progress hoped. By the end of the First Plan it covered only about half of the 2.2 million persons eligible. Early in the Second Plan it was decided to extend coverage to families.

The Employees Provident Fund Scheme (old-age assurance) covered about 1½ million people by the end of the First Plan in a group of specified industries. Extending the Scheme's coverage and raising employers' and workers' contributions from 6¼ to 8⅓ per cent are being considered over the Second Plan period. A study group has been set up to see how the various present schemes can best be integrated into one unified system.

RATIONALIZATION

Unions now have few protections against technological unemployment. In 1955–1956 some of the major industrial disputes involved introduction of labor-saving machinery. Basic principles were laid down in the First Plan for easing the transition from outmoded to new machinery, and for retraining and re-employment of workers. The Government urges that these principles be adopted in individual contracts. In cases where there is disagreement on details, arbitration can be aided by technical examination of each issue by independent experts. Where inter-State problems arise, a high-power authority should be appointed by the Central Government.

Special labor problems—the study and improvement of conditions of contract labor, equal pay for women workers, the setting up of more industrial welfare centers—are other issues needing attention over the Second Plan.

Specific development programs for labor over the Second Plan, other than these described, include:

1. Trebling the number, to a total of about thirty thousand, of craftsmen in training, with an apprenticeship scheme for skilled craftsmen and a training center for instructors;

2. Improvement of Employment Services (see p. 110);

3. Expanding the work of the Central Labor Institute to deal with industrial psychology and continue productivity studies;

4. A Rs. 45 crores program of industrial housing (see p. 364).

FIRST PLAN	Rs. 49 crores
SECOND PLAN	Rs. 120 crores

HIGH LIGHTS
of programs for
HOUSING AND URBAN DEVELOPMENT

The Second Plan will spend nearly two and a half times as much as the First Plan to improve rural and urban housing, with these main targets:

About 1,075,000 new public housing units, largely for low-income groups in urban areas.

A rural housing program in the community development areas.

A beginning program on slum clearance.

A beginning program on urban development.

CHAPTER IV

Housing and Urban Development

Good housing for India's vast and growing population is a task of enormous dimensions. The already congested cities face an increase of population by one-third by 1961 and a shortage of at least 5 million houses.

Of the city housing already available, nearly half (44 per cent) consists of a single room. Light, ventilation, sanitation average from poor to non-existent. In rural areas 85 per cent of the houses are made chiefly of mud, bamboo or reed, and the large proportion need to be rebuilt or substantially improved. Traditional designs of village housing provide neither light, ventilation nor sanitary facilities.

The chief problems in providing adequate housing are lack of developed sites in rapidly growing towns; concentration by private builders on high-rent housing; lack of an adequate system for financing home building; failure of cooperative housing to expand; need for research in building materials and techniques; lack of organiza-

363

tion within State Governments (with a few exceptions) to carry out a housing program.

The need for town planning and development is equally important. The growth of new industries gives special urgency to avoidance of slums and even more city congestion. The need for environmental sanitation gives new importance to village planning and housing.

The Second Plan is making the following efforts to meet these problems:

PUBLIC HOUSING AND HOME FINANCE PROGRAMS

Over the First Plan, 742,000 new houses were built by various agencies of the Central and State Governments, nearly half of them to house the refugees from Pakistan, the remainder for various low-income and labor groups.

The Second Plan proposes 1,075,000 new houses through the following Government programs:

NEW HOUSING UNDER THE SECOND PLAN

	SECOND PLAN ALLOTMENT Rs. CRORES	No. OF HOUSES EXPECTED
GOVERNMENT FINANCED OR SUBSIDIZED HOUSING		
Subsidized Industrial Housing	45	128,000
Low-Income Group Housing	40	68,000
Rural Housing	10	(to be determined)
Slum Clearance and Sweepers' Housing	20	110,000
Middle-Income Group Housing	3	5,000
Plantation Housing	2	11,000
Coal Mine Labor Board Housing [1]	8	30,000
All other Schemes		723,000
		1,075,000
PRIVATE CONSTRUCTION	625	800,000
TOTAL		1,875,000

[1] Funds come from a tax on coal dispatched from collieries.

The Subsidized Industrial Housing Program will consist of loans and 50 per cent subsidies from the Central Government to State

Governments, and 25 per cent subsidies to employers, and to workers' cooperatives.

Under a similar program during the First Plan, 85 per cent of the housing (68,200 units) was constructed by State Governments, 13 per cent by private employers, 1.6 per cent by cooperatives. Over the Second Plan, steps will be taken to increase home building by the last two groups.

Low Income Group Housing Program consists of a long-term loan program (maximum loan Rs. 8,000 per house constructed), and three-year loans, at 3¼ per cent interest to local bodies, for acquisition and development of land.

Lack of developed sites held back progress under this program over the First Plan. Under the Second Plan, part of the allotted funds will be used to develop sites in rapidly growing areas for sale or lease to home builders.

Rural Housing: A rural housing program must necessarily be in the nature of an aided self-help program in which education and guidance play a large part. For example, in the rural development areas a relatively small expenditure, used largely as low-interest and long-term loans to villagers, was able to get 29,000 houses constructed and another 29,000 improved during the First Plan.

Over the Second Plan, the rural housing proposals include launching of a nation-wide housing program in rural development areas, with a housing authority in each State. The State will give technical assistance and planning guidance, and establish new research-and-training centers (as part of the rural extension training centers) on house construction.

The Central Ministry of Works, Housing and Supply, which will give technical direction to this program, has already set up a unit for study of rural building materials, design and techniques.

Village industry and employment have much to gain by a strong housing program and the Ministry of Commerce and Consumer Industries and the Ministry of Production will cooperate in organizing village artisans to provide building supplies.

The Second Plan allotment of Rs. 10 crores to rural housing will go largely to low-interest building loans to villagers.

Some of the special funds allotted for general aid to Harijans, tribal peoples and other underprivileged groups (see p. 377) will go toward housing loans for these groups. The rural development program will assist villages to provide building sites for these groups, most of whom have no land.

Slum Clearance and Sweepers' Housing: Most slums in Indian cities are those of urban workers' and sweepers' colonies. To provide better housing for these depressed groups, the Second Plan allocates Rs. 20 crores for a slum clearance and re-building program.

Twenty-five per cent of the cost is to be direct subsidy from the Central Government, 50 per cent in long-term loans, and a 25 per cent subsidy from the State Governments participating. The new housing must, as much as possible, be built on the sites cleared so that the groups remain near their employment, and rents must be kept low enough to meet their needs.

The long-term need for slum prevention and clearance is part of the over-all problem of urban development.

Other Building and Finance Programs: Good housing for *plantation workers* (principally on tea and coffee plantations) is required under the Plantation Labor Act. Rs. 2 crores is being made available in building loans to assist small planters to meet this requirement. *Coal miners* will get new housing under a plan of the coal miners' labor welfare boards. Funds are to be drawn from a tax on coal shipments. A similar plan is proposed for mica workers.

For the middle income group, a scheme is proposed to give long-term loans for building five thousand houses. On the over-all problem of financing home building, a special study is under way on providing real-estate credit. State Housing Finance Corporations have been proposed.

Regional and Urban Development

India is on the threshold of rapid industrial growth. Unless there is adequate forethought and planning, industrial progress will be accompanied in congested cities by serious social problems that will be increasingly difficult to manage.

Urban population is already growing rapidly; as we have seen, a 33 per cent gain is expected between 1951–1961. Enlightened efforts are necessary at once to draw up policies to secure planned development, expand urban housing and develop progressive civic administration.

Not only must the development of the city or town itself be considered as to the location of industries, for example, but the city's needs must be viewed in relation to the adjoining rural area, and in relation to the region. This last is especially important for large and growing towns, for river-valley areas under development, and for areas where large new industrial plants are being introduced.

The Second Plan outlines in general terms a program on regional and urban planning and development, presenting for the first time for the States, cities and towns, the need for such development as a matter of national interest and policy. While further details are to be worked out for specific areas, the Plan suggests the following broad policy:

1. Each State should have a phased program for the survey and preparation of master plans for all its important towns.

2. Regional plans should be prepared for new towns which have recently come into existence and are likely to develop rapidly because of industrialization.

3. Development of river-valley areas should be based on careful surveys of their topography, resources, development needs and potential.

4. Town and country planning legislation should be enacted in all States and the necessary machinery for its implementation should be set up.

5. Programs in the Second Plan which have considerable bearing on urban development and re-development, such as industrial projects, industrial estates and townships, irrigation and power projects,

small-town and rural electrification schemes, housing programs, urban water-supply and sanitation schemes, should be carried out in an integrated manner. There must be careful consideration of their impact on urban and regional development and on the present and future needs of different parts of each State or region.

The aim ultimately must be to evolve balanced urban-rural regions which would provide stable and diverse employment and, by providing the necessary economic and social facilities and amenities, achieve development at reasonable social and economic cost.

Early in the Second Plan, a project in urban planning and development was begun in Delhi, the nation's capital, under a joint Indo-American team of architects and town planners. The Delhi project is expected to give leadership and example to urban planning elsewhere. A pilot project for a regional survey of the Damodar Valley area is also now under way.

FIRST PLAN	Rs. 5 crores
SECOND PLAN	Rs. 29 crores

HIGH LIGHTS
of programs for
SOCIAL WELFARE

The Second Plan will spend nearly six times as much as the First Plan to improve its social welfare services. The main targets are:

Stimulating voluntary welfare agencies to expand and improve their services, with help of grants-in-aid.

Four women's welfare extension blocks in every district in India.

Model schools for the deaf and blind.

Increased aid to youth activities.

Reform and rehabilitation homes for women, men and for juvenile delinquents.

CHAPTER V

Social Welfare

India has adopted a broad definition of social welfare. The problems which the Government puts under this category and for which, under both the First and Second Plans, it has allotted specific funds include: the advancement of women, children and youth; rehabilitation of the handicapped; juvenile delinquency; beggary and social vice; family and social legislation.

For dealing with these problems, there has grown up in India over the last thirty years a considerable group of private social welfare agencies, many of them founded on the direct inspiration of Mahatma Gandhi.

During the First Plan the Central Government set up a Central Social Welfare Board especially to assist [1] these voluntary groups to carry on such programs. The Board, in cooperation with the States, established State Welfare Boards. The nation-wide organization thus

[1] Over the First Plan, the Board assisted 2,128 private welfare organizations.

formed will, under the Second Plan, undertake considerably expanded welfare activities, working as before through private agencies. The Board will use Rs. 14 crores for these activities.

Welfare of Women and Children: The Board launched, during
the First Plan, a women's "welfare extension" plan in which groups
of villages (twenty-five villages to an extension area) are given a
general program of women's and children's welfare work.

There is now one of these extension areas in nearly every District
in India. Its work usually includes a day nursery for working mothers,
a nursery school, sewing and similar classes for women. Under the
Second Plan there will be four such areas in each District, reaching a
total of fifty thousand villages.

Shortage of trained women workers of all kinds for rural areas is
a problem throughout India. One of the particularly helpful activities resulting from the welfare extension program has been to increase
training facilities of women for general rural service, principally for
nursery and child care, for women's activities and midwifery. The
agency which has done much of this training, with financial assistance from the Government, is the Kasturba Trust, named for the
wife of Mahatma Gandhi.

For city women, the Central Social Welfare Board's program
concentrates largely on providing some opportunities for women to
earn income at home, in various home crafts.

Another important Second Plan program is providing more homes
and rehabilitation centers. The types of institutions which have
been suggested include those for rehabilitation of unfortunate
women, and for rehabilitation of men and women who have served
in criminal and other correctional institutions. Similar homes and
rehabilitation centers will be set up in the Districts.

Handicapped Persons: Rehabilitation of the handicapped has received relatively little attention in comparison to the great need.
There are, for instance, only nine schools in all India caring for the
crippled. The poverty of people sound of body and limb has meant
that little resources or effort could go to people with special handicaps. The number of handicapped is known to be very large, al-

though no exact figures are available. India has, for instance, one of the world's highest proportions of blind, owing to the prevalence of eye diseases.

A National Advisory Council for the Education of the Handicapped was set up by the Education Ministry in 1955, and the Second Plan proposes to make some advance in services for the handicapped. A study of the size of the problem will be undertaken; some model schools and special scholarships for the blind and deaf are being established by the Central and State Governments.

Youth: The object of the Government-aided programs for youth welfare, under both the First and the Second Plans, is to encourage the participation of young people in national constructive activities.

Three-fourths of the First Plan's budget for youth welfare went to support youth camps. Through these camps, about a hundred thousand young people helped build roads, schools, clear slums, conduct sanitation drives and do similar constructive work.

The groups which have done this sort of work on a national scale are the Bharat (India) Scouts and Guides, the National Cadet Corps and the Auxiliary Cadet Corps. These groups have expanded in strength [1] and activity during the First Plan, and over the Second Plan will continue to do so, with Government support of work-camp programs.

Juvenile Delinquency: Juvenile delinquency is on the increase in Indian cities, as the heavy urban migration has resulted in the break-up of joint families. The most common offense is theft. There is legislation in some States, but it is not often adequately enforced. Juvenile courts and correctional homes are few. The Home Affairs Ministry has allocated Rs. 2 crores to assist States to set up the necessary correctional institutions, both for juvenile and for young delinquents, and urges development of adequate legislation and adoption of a probationary system.

Beggary, a problem in India as throughout the East, arises from mass poverty and the lack of institutional care for the handicapped

---

[1] Scout membership in 1956 was 438,405; Guides, 68,118; National Cadet Corps, 120,000; Auxiliary Cadet Corps, 619,000.

and destitute. Studies are being made under the Research Programmes Committee in the Planning Commission to determine the size and character of the problem and what solutions are possible.

Prohibition: India considers prohibition as a social welfare question. There is a strong sentiment in India in favor of prohibition; the vast majority of Hindus do not drink, and Mahatma Gandhi's strong opposition to drinking has still a dominant influence. The Indian Constitution set prohibition as a national objective.

As in temperance movements elsewhere, the particular concern is that the poorer working classes may be protected. For this group the principal liquor is toddy, a fermented drink made from palm sap. One State [1] now has total prohibition and ten have partial prohibition (such as restrictions as to hours and volume of sale of liquors). About one-third of India's total population is now under some form of prohibition.

Following the report of a Prohibition Enquiry Committee in September 1955, and passage in Parliament of a non-official resolution asking the Planning Commission to develop a program, the Planning Commission in the Second Plan suggests that the States adopt a phased program which would discontinue advertising and public inducement to drink, stop drinking at public places, progressively restrict the sale of liquor and encourage use of soft drinks and healthy forms of recreation.

[1] Bombay.

First Plan	Rs. 32 crores

Second Plan	Rs. 91 crores

HIGH LIGHTS
of programs for
TRIBAL PEOPLES AND HARIJANS [1]

The Second Plan will spend nearly three times as much as the First Plan to help advance Harijans, tribal peoples and similar backward groups. The Second Plan's major targets are:

FOR TRIBAL PEOPLES

One million tribal people to be placed under the rural development program, in over forty development blocks.

A third of a million scholarships for primary school children and over 34,000 scholarships for higher education.

46,000 new homes.

FOR HARIJANS [1]

40,000 trained in crafts and trades.

Over 3 million scholarships for primary and higher education.

About 129,300 new homes.

---

[1] "Harijans," or Children of God, is the name Gandhi gave to those formerly called "untouchables."

CHAPTER VI

Advancement of Tribal Peoples and Harijans

Beyond the vast problem of providing some welfare services for the great mass of India's poor, social welfare in India must attack the particular problems of advancement of its 19 million tribal people, and the lifting up of the 51 million Harijans, now at the bottom of the social and economic ladder. It is hoped that with programs especially designed for their advancement, they can come more rapidly up to the level of other groups, in addition to the general benefits they will share from the planned advances of the country as a whole.

Tribal peoples in India constitute about 8 per cent of the total population. They are generally accepted to be the oldest inhabitants of India, and spread over a wide central belt from Bombay State, Madhya Pradesh, Andhra, Bihar, Orissa, through Assam in the east. In some States they constitute a sizable part of the population

—34 per cent in Assam, 25 per cent in Orissa, 23 per cent in Madhya Pradesh.[1] Some primitive tribes are also found in the South.

Some of them are nomadic; others use a shifting system of cultivation; all live more or less primitively in forest and hilly regions, and have a colorful and characteristic culture.

The Government's policy, in the First Plan and again in the Second, is to help these people to advance, to develop their natural resources, and evolve a productive economic life free from outside exploitation. No effort will be made to impose changes in their religious and social customs, except with their own initiative and consent. Their tribal culture, their dialects and crafts are to be fostered and preserved.

The people themselves are to be brought into decisions affecting their welfare, and educated young people from the tribes are to be used as much as possible as extension workers among them. Over the First Plan years eight states set up tribal institutes to train workers for tribal areas, and a social education organizers' training center was set up under the community development program, to train especially for work among tribal peoples.

The development programs, of both the States and Central Government, over the Second Plan, as over the First, will concentrate on communications, education, development of tribal economy, health, housing and water supply.

Illiteracy is almost universal among tribal peoples. The First Plan made some real progress—four thousand schools of various types were put up and nearly half a million children given scholarships to attend school. Tribals are being trained as teachers; primers and texts have been printed in tribal dialects.

The Second Plan will provide over three thousand more schools, and scholarships for about a third of a million children; 34,425 young people who have finished their schooling will be given scholarships by the Education Ministry for higher education.

Special technical training in agriculture, crafts, mechanical and civil engineering are being made available.

[1] 1951 Census before States Reorganization in Nov. 1956.

The health of the tribal peoples is invariably poor. Malaria, yaws, tuberculosis, smallpox, skin and eye disease and venereal disease are common. The lack of pure drinking water, of a balanced diet, or protection against extremes of climate (such as the intense rainfall in eastern India), and poor housing are largely responsible.

A considerable number of dispensaries and health units (3,144) were set up during the First Plan; a fifth as many more are proposed under the Second Plan, with special training centers for midwives and nurses. Some 41,000 pure water wells will be provided. About 46,000 new homes will be built as another health and welfare measure.

Economic development for tribal peoples presents some challenging problems, the most significant of which is replacing shifting cultivation with settled agriculture.

Small pilot schemes have been carried out over the First Plan period. While no thorough evaluation has been made of their success, it is clear that what is needed are fertile lands, irrigated if possible; provision of bullocks, plows, seeds, and finance; and steps to assure that moneylenders who have traditionally exploited tribal peoples are not permitted to do so in new settlements. There is also legislation to protect the tribes' ownership of its land.

Development of cooperatives which can provide credit, and marketing and supply facilities, may be the solution, since the economic life and customs of the tribal people particularly lend themselves, it is believed, to successful organization and use of cooperatives.

For those tribal peoples who cannot be settled, efforts are being made to see that their methods of shifting cultivation do not lead to still more denuding of forests. For tribes which live in and depend on forests for their living, national and State forestry programs are so planned as to help the tribes and protect the forests.

The Second Plan will spend Rs. 11 crores to build bridle and hill paths and bridges (against Rs. 60 million spent in the First Plan) in forest and hill areas.

Tribesmen have considerable native skills, and a program of assisting them to settle in small industries and develop their skills for commercial use is also planned, with craft training and cottage industry centers and credit facilities, run chiefly on cooperative lines.

To bring about development of the tribes on an organized basis, tribal areas will come under the rural development program over the Second Plan. Some forty multi-purpose blocks will be started in the most backward tribal areas, to work toward all-round development of the people—in health, education, agriculture, crafts, community welfare.

A special group of tribes—in all about 4 million people—belong to what were once, under British rule, called "Criminal Tribes." They are nomadic peoples who could not adjust to a settled life or a law-and-order society. While they are no longer pre-judged as criminal, efforts for their resettlement put special stress on economic rehabilitation and vocational training and education. About Rs. 4 crores will be spent on these programs.

Welfare of Harijans

Fifty-one million people, or roughly 13 per cent of India's total population, belong to the so-called "scheduled castes." Many of them are the so-called "untouchables," whom Gandhi referred to as Harijans, or the Children of God. India's goal is to "exorcise the demon of untouchability" so that these people may have and give their rightful share in India's progress.

The Indian Constitution abolished untouchability and forbids its practice in any form. In 1955 the practice was made an offense punishable by fine and up to six months in prison.

The practice of untouchability is diminishing, but there is still a long distance to go. To exorcise this age-old institution requires laws, but more than laws. As in all cases where deep-seated race or class prejudice must be overcome, education, the practice of democratic behavior, and increasing economic, social and educational opportunity are needed, to help the depressed group raise itself so that economic equality can help pave the way to integration.

The Central and State Governments have undertaken extensive

propaganda and publicity to mobilize public opinion against untouchability, with some success. Over the Second Plan, this effort will be continued, with special aid to the voluntary Harijan-welfare groups, many of which were started by Gandhi or formed under his inspiration, and have worked constantly to alter public opinion toward caste.

The Second Plan proposes a large program for improving economic and educational opportunities for Harijans. Rs. 27.5 crores, four times the funds of the First Plan, will go for housing, for wells for Harijans (in many villages Harijans may not use public wells), for education. Under Central and State Government programs, over 129,000 houses will be built for Harijans, and 24,000 wells.

Education and training in new skills are essential if Harijans are to move up the economic and social ladder. During the Second Plan, over forty thousand of them are to be trained in new trades, and given subsidies for setting up in these trades. Those who get land (most Harijans are landless) under land-distribution schemes will be given subsidies to buy work animals and implements. Well over 3 million Harijan children will get scholarships to help them attend school and college.

While providing additional schools, hostels, housing and wells for the Harijans, both the Center and State Governments take every care to avoid segregation of Harijans and to see that they are helped to live as members of the same community.

FIRST PLAN	**Rs. 136 crores**
SECOND PLAN	**Rs. 90 crores**

HIGH LIGHTS
of programs for
DISPLACED PERSONS

The Second Plan will spend Rs. 90 crores to care for, resettle and rehabilitate the refugees from Pakistan (now principally from East Pakistan), with these main targets:

Loans to 19,000 families to resettle in urban areas.

Loans to 70,000 rural families.

Housing loans to 13,000 families, as well as the building of 12,000 new homes.

Employment for 50,000 refugees in medium- and small-scale industries.

Vocational training for 80,000 refugees.

CHAPTER VII

Rehabilitation of Displaced Persons

Within a few months of the Partition of India in August 1947, 5 million Sikhs and Hindus living in West Pakistan, and 2.6 million persons in East Pakistan, migrated to India in search of permanent homes. For the new Indian Government this flood of displaced people presented a refugee problem of a size and suddenness unequaled in any country of the postwar world.

About half of the refugees from West Pakistan were agricultural people, half were urban. The majority were families who were able to carry with them few, if any, of their possessions; many were widows or children orphaned in the Partition disturbances.

By 1951, the beginning of the First Plan, nearly all the rural refugees from West Pakistan had been resettled. Many were settled on lands evacuated by the Muslim migrants to Pakistan, principally in the Punjab and PEPSU; others were placed on new farms reclaimed from jungle and waste lands.

To resettle and rehabilitate the urban people was far more difficult. The majority of them were traders, businessmen and shopkeepers, who could not easily be absorbed in India in the same work.

Rehabilitation involved retraining for small industry and business and the professions, assistance with schools and scholarships, building of extensive housing to replace refugee camps and shelters. To prevent further congestion of the cities, refugee townships with production-and-training centers, schools and homes sprang up in several parts of India, some of them built by the refugees themselves.

Resettling the remaining West Pakistan refugees was in larger part completed before the end of the First Plan. India has reason to feel satisfied that, in this emergency confronting a newly formed Government, so vast a task could be completed so swiftly and efficiently.

Settling of the East Pakistan refugees has presented even more complex problems. Because of difficulties experienced by them in East Pakistan, including insecurity of life and property and various kinds of harassment, the refugees have continued steadily to migrate into West Bengal. In mid-1956, 170,000 families had still to be resettled and rehabilitated, with new migrants constantly flowing in. The majority are rural people, and the rural areas of West Bengal are already densely populated.

The First Plan allotted Rs. 136 crores, or 7 per cent of India's total Plan budget, to rehabilitate the migrants. About two-thirds of this was used chiefly for housing and loans for urban and rural resettlement and for education and vocational training. The Second Plan has allotted less, Rs. 90 crores to begin with. Over three-fourths of this will go to East Pakistan migrants.

As under the First Plan, the funds will be used chiefly on housing, home loans, loans for persons setting up in industry, for education and vocational training, and loans for farmers. A survey has been made of land available in States outside Bengal which could be reclaimed for settlement, and funds are available to acquire and develop nearly 100,000 acres in various States.

Some idea of the size of the task still remaining over the Second

Plan years is revealed in these figures: 19,000 families will be given urban loans, nearly 70,000 families rural loans, and 13,000 families home-building loans; 12,000 new homes will be built; 61,000 persons will be employed in medium and small industry; 80,000 will be given vocational training.

GOVERNMENT OF INDIA

INDUSTRIAL POLICY RESOLUTION

New Delhi, the 30th April, 1956

No. 91/CF/48.—The Government of India set out in their Resolution dated the 6th April, 1948, the policy which they proposed to pursue in the industrial field. The Resolution emphasised the importance to the economy of securing a continuous increase in production and its equitable distribution, and pointed out that the State must play a progressively active role in the development of industries. It laid down that besides arms and ammunition, atomic energy and railway transport, which would be the monopoly of the Central Government, the State would be exclusively responsible for the establishment of new undertakings in six basic industries—except where, in the national interest, the State itself found it necessary to secure the co-operation of private enterprise. The rest of the industrial field was left open to private enterprise, though it was made clear that the State would also progressively participate in this field.

2. Eight years have passed since this declaration on industrial policy. These eight years have witnessed many important changes and developments in India. The Constitution of India has been enacted, guaranteeing certain Fundamental Rights and enunciating Directive Principles of State Policy. Planning has proceeded on an organised basis, and the first Five Year Plan has recently been completed. Parliament has accepted the socialist pattern of society as the objective of social and economic policy. These important developments necessitate a fresh statement of industrial policy, more particularly as the Second Five Year Plan will soon be placed before the country. This policy must be governed by the principles laid down in the Con-

stitution, the objective of socialism, and the experience gained during these years.

3. The Constitution of India, in its preamble, has declared that it aims at securing for all its citizens—

"JUSTICE, Social, economic and political;
LIBERTY of thought, expression, belief, faith and worship;
EQUALITY of status and of opportunity; and to promote among them all
FRATERNITY assuring the dignity of the individual and the unity of the Nation."

In its Directive Principles of State Policy, it is stated that—
"The State shall strive to promote the welfare of the people by securing and protecting as effectively as it may a social order in which justice, social, economic and political, shall inform all the institutions of the national life."
Further that—
"The State shall, in particular, direct its policy towards securing—

(a) that the citizens, men and women equally, have the right to an adequate means of livelihood;

(b) that the ownership and control of the material resources of the community are so distributed as best to subserve the common good;

(c) that the operation of the economic system does not result in the concentration of wealth and means of production to the common detriment;

(d) that there is equal pay for equal work for both men and women;

(e) that the health and strength of workers, men and women, and the tender age of children are not abused and that citizens are not forced by economic necessity to enter avocations unsuited to their age or strength;

(f) that childhood and youth are protected against exploitation and against moral and material abandonment."

4. These basic and general principles were given a more precise direction when Parliament accepted in December, 1954, the socialist pattern of society as the objective of social and economic policy. Industrial policy, as other policies, must therefore be governed by these principles and directions.

5. In order to realise this objective, it is essential to accelerate the rate of economic growth and to speed up industrialisation and, in particular, to develop heavy industries and machine making industries, to expand the public sector, and to build up a large and growing co-operative sector. These provide the economic foundations for increasing opportunities for gainful employment and improving living standards and working conditions for the mass of the people. Equally, it is urgent, to reduce disparities in income and wealth which exist today, to prevent private monopolies and the concentration of economic power in different fields in the hands of small numbers of individuals. Accordingly, the State will progressively assume a predominant and direct responsibility for setting up new industrial undertakings and for developing transport facilities. It will also undertake State trading on an increasing scale. At the same time, as an agency for planned national development, in the context of the country's expanding economy, the private sector will have the opportunity to develop and expand. The principle of co-operation should be applied wherever possible and a steadily increasing proportion of the activities of the private sector developed along co-operative lines.

6. The adoption of the socialist pattern of society as the national objective, as well as the need for planned and rapid development, requires that all industries of basic and strategic importance, or in the nature of public utility services, should be in the public sector. Other industries which are essential and require investment on a scale which only the State, in present circumstances, could provide, have also to be in the public sector. The State has therefore to assume direct responsibility for the future development of industries over a wider area. Nevertheless, there are limiting factors which make it necessary at this stage for the State to define the field in which it will undertake sole responsibility for further development, and to make a selec-

tion of industries in the development of which it will play a dominant role. After considering all aspects of the problem, in consultation with the Planning Commission, the Government of India have decided to classify industries into three categories, having regard to the part which the State would play in each of them. These categories will inevitably overlap to some extent and too great a rigidity might defeat the purpose in view. But the basic principles and objectives have always to be kept in view and the general directions hereafter referred to followed. It should also be remembered that it is always open to the State to undertake any type of industrial production.

7. In the first category will be industries the future development of which will be the exclusive responsibility of the State. The second category will consist of industries, which will be progressively State-owned and in which the State will therefore generally take the initiative in establishing new undertakings, but in which private enterprise will also be expected to supplement the effort of the State. The third category will include all the remaining industries, and their future development will, in general, be left to the initiative and enterprise of the private sector.

8. Industries in the first category have been listed in Schedule A of this Resolution. All new units in these industries, save where their establishment in the private sector has already been approved, will be set up only by the State. This does not preclude the expansion of the existing privately owned units, or the possibility of the State securing the co-operation of private enterprise in the establishment of new units when the national interests so require. Railways and air transport, arms and ammunition and atomic energy will, however, be developed as Central Government monopolies. Whenever co-operation with private enterprise is necessary, the State will ensure, either through majority participation in the capital or otherwise, that it has the requisite powers to guide the policy and control the operations of the undertaking.

9. Industries in the second category will be those listed in Schedule B. With a view to accelerating their future development, the State will increasingly establish new undertakings in these indus-

tries. At the same time private enterprise will also have the opportunity to develop in this field, either on its own or with State participation.

10. All the remaining industries will fall in the third category, and it is expected that their development will be undertaken ordinarily through the initiative and enterprise of the private sector, though it will be open to the State to start any industry even in this category. It will be the policy of the State to facilitate and encourage the development of these industries in the private sector, in accordance with the programmes formulated in successive Five Year Plans, by ensuring the development of transport, power and other services, and by appropriate fiscal and other measures. The State will continue to foster institutions to provide financial aid to these industries, and special assistance will be given to enterprises organised on co-operative lines for industrial and agricultural purposes. In suitable cases, the State may also grant financial assistance to the private sector. Such assistance, especially when the amount involved is substantial, will preferably be in the form of participation in equity capital, though it may also be in part in the form of debenture capital.

11. Industrial undertakings in the private sector have necessarily to fit into the framework of the social and economic policy of the State and will be subject to control and regulation in terms of the Industries (Development and Regulation) Act and other relevant legislation. The Government of India, however, recognise that it would, in general, be desirable to allow such undertakings to develop with as much freedom as possible, consistent with the targets and objectives of the national plan. When there exist in the same industry both privately and publicly owned units, it would continue to be the policy of the State to give fair and non-discriminatory treatment to both of them.

12. The division of industries into separate categories does not imply that they are being placed in water-tight compartments. Inevitably, there will not only be an area of overlapping but also a great deal of dovetailing between industries in the private and the public sectors. It will be open to the State to start any industry not included

in Schedule A and Schedule B when the needs of planning so require or there are other important reasons for it. In appropriate cases, privately owned units may be permitted to produce an item falling within Schedule A for meeting their own requirements or as by-products. There will be ordinarily no bar to small privately owned units undertaking production, such as the making of launches and other light-craft, generation of power for local needs and small scale mining. Further, heavy industries in the public sector may obtain some of their requirements of lighter components from the private sector, while the private sector in turn would rely for many of its needs on the public sector. The same principle would apply with even greater force to the relationship between large scale and small scale industries.

13. The Government of India would, in this context, stress the role of cottage and village and small scale industries in the development of the national economy. In relation to some of the problems that need urgent solutions, they offer some distinct advantages. They provide immediate large scale employment; they offer a method of ensuring a more equitable distribution of the national income and they facilitate an effective mobilisation of resources of capital and skill which might otherwise remain unutilised. Some of the problems that unplanned urbanisation tends to create will be avoided by the establishment of small centres of industrial production all over the country.

14. The State has been following a policy of supporting cottage and village and small scale industries by restricting the volume of production in the large scale sector, by differential taxation, or by direct subsidies. While such measures will continue to be taken, whenever necessary, the aim of the State policy will be to ensure that the decentralised sector acquires sufficient vitality to be self-supporting and its development is integrated with that of large scale industry. The State will, therefore, concentrate on measures designed to improve the competitive strength of the small scale producer. For this it is essential that the technique of production should be constantly improved and modernised, the pace of transformation being regu-

lated so as to avoid, as far as possible, technological unemployment. Lack of technical and financial assistance, of suitable working accommodation and inadequacy of facilities for repair and maintenance are among the serious handicaps of small scale producers. A start has been made with the establishment of industrial estates and rural community workshops to make good these deficiencies. The extension of rural electrification and the availability of power at prices which the workers can afford will also be of considerable help. Many of the activities relating to small scale production will be greatly helped by the organisation of industrial co-operatives. Such co-operatives should be encouraged in every way and the State should give constant attention to the development of cottage and village and small scale industry.

15. In order that industrialisation may benefit the economy of the country as a whole, it is important that disparities in levels of development between different regions should be progressively reduced. The lack of industries in different parts of the country is very often determined by factors such as the availability of the necessary raw materials or other natural resources. A concentration of industries in certain areas has also been due to the ready availability of power, water supply and transport facilities which have been developed there. It is one of the aims of national planning to ensure that these facilities are steadily made available to areas which are at present lagging behind industrially or where there is greater need for providing opportunities for employment, provided the location is otherwise suitable. Only by securing a balanced and co-ordinated development of the industrial and the agricultural economy in each region, can the entire country attain higher standards of living.

16. This programme of industrial development will make large demands on the country's resources of technical and managerial personnel. To meet these rapidly growing needs for the expansion of the public sector and for the development of village and small scale industries, proper managerial and technical cadres in the public services are being established. Steps are also being taken to meet shortages at supervisory levels, to organise apprenticeship schemes of training

on a large scale both in public and in private enterprises, and to extend training facilities in business management in universities and other institutions.

17. It is necessary that proper amenities and incentives should be provided for all those engaged in industry. The living and working conditions of workers should be improved and their standard of efficiency raised. The maintenance of industrial peace is one of the prime requisites of industrial progress. In a socialist democracy labour is a partner in the common task of development and should participate in it with enthusiasm. Some laws governing industrial relations have been enacted and a broad common approach has developed with the growing recognition of the obligations of both management and labour. There should be joint consultation and workers and technicians should, wherever possible, be associated progressively in management. Enterprises in the public sector have to set an example in this respect.

18. With the growing participation of the State in industry and trade, the manner in which these activities should be conducted and managed assumes considerable importance. Speedy decisions and a willingness to assume responsibility are essential if these enterprises are to succeed. For this, wherever possible, there should be decentralisation of authority and their management should be along business lines. It is to be expected that public enterprises will augment the revenues of the State and provide resources for further development in fresh fields. But such enterprises may sometimes incur losses. Public enterprises have to be judged by their total results and in their working they should have the largest possible measure of freedom.

19. The Industrial Policy Resolution of 1948 dealt with a number of other subjects which have since been covered by suitable legislation or by authoritative statements of policy. The division of responsibility between the Central Government and the State Governments in regard to industries has been set out in the Industries (Development and Regulation) Act. The Prime Minister, in his statement in Parliament on the 6th April 1949, has enunciated the policy of the

State in regard to foreign capital. It is, therefore, not necessary to deal with these subjects in this resolution.

20. The Government of India trust that this restatement of their Industrial Policy will receive the support of all sections of the people and promote the rapid industrialisation of the country.

SCHEDULE A

1. Arms and ammunition and allied items of defence equipment.
2. Atomic energy.
3. Iron and steel.
4. Heavy castings and forgings of iron and steel.
5. Heavy plant and machinery required for iron and steel production, for mining, for machine tool manufacture and for such other basic industries as may be specified by the Central Government.
6. Heavy electrical plant, including large hydraulic and steam turbines.
7. Coal and lignite.
8. Mineral oils.
9. Mining of iron ore, manganese ore, chrome ore, gypsum, sulphur, gold and diamond.
10. Mining and processing of copper, lead, zinc, tin, molybdenum and wolfram.
11. Minerals specified in the Schedule to the Atomic Energy (Control of Production and Use) Order, 1953.
12. Aircraft.
13. Air transport.
14. Railway transport.
15. Shipbuilding.
16. Telephones and telephone cables, telegraph and wireless apparatus (excluding radio receiving sets).
17. Generation and distribution of electricity.

SCHEDULE B

1. All other minerals except "minor minerals" as defined in Section 3 of the Minerals Concession Rules, 1949.
2. Aluminium and other non-ferrous metals not included in Schedule "A."
3. Machine tools.
4. Ferro-alloys and tool steels.
5. Basic and intermediate products required by chemical industries such as the manufacture of drugs, dyestuffs and plastics.
6. Antibiotics and other essential drugs.
7. Fertilizers.
8. Synthetic rubber.
9. Carbonisation of coal.
10. Chemical pulp.
11. Road transport.
12. Sea transport.

Index

397